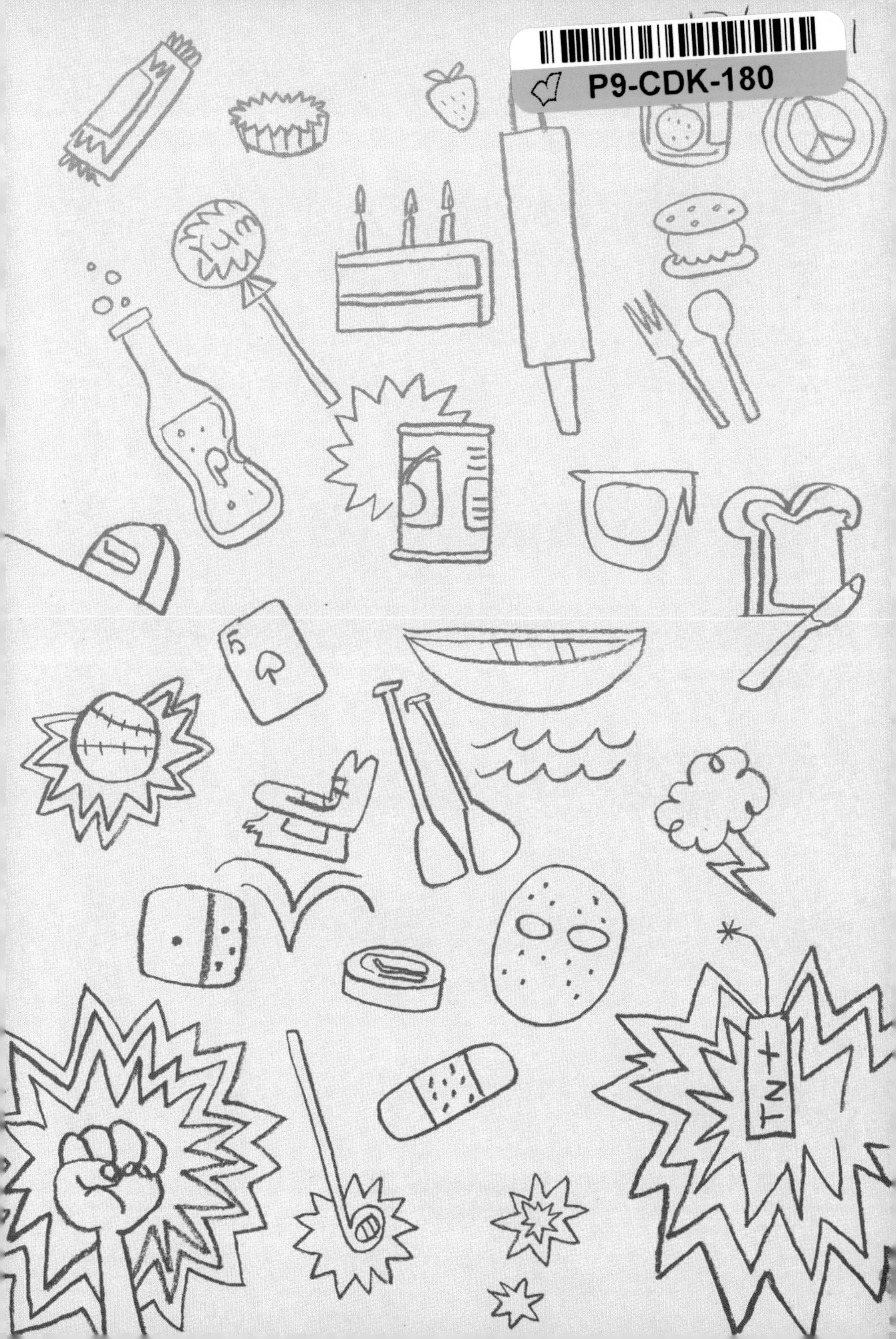
TNT

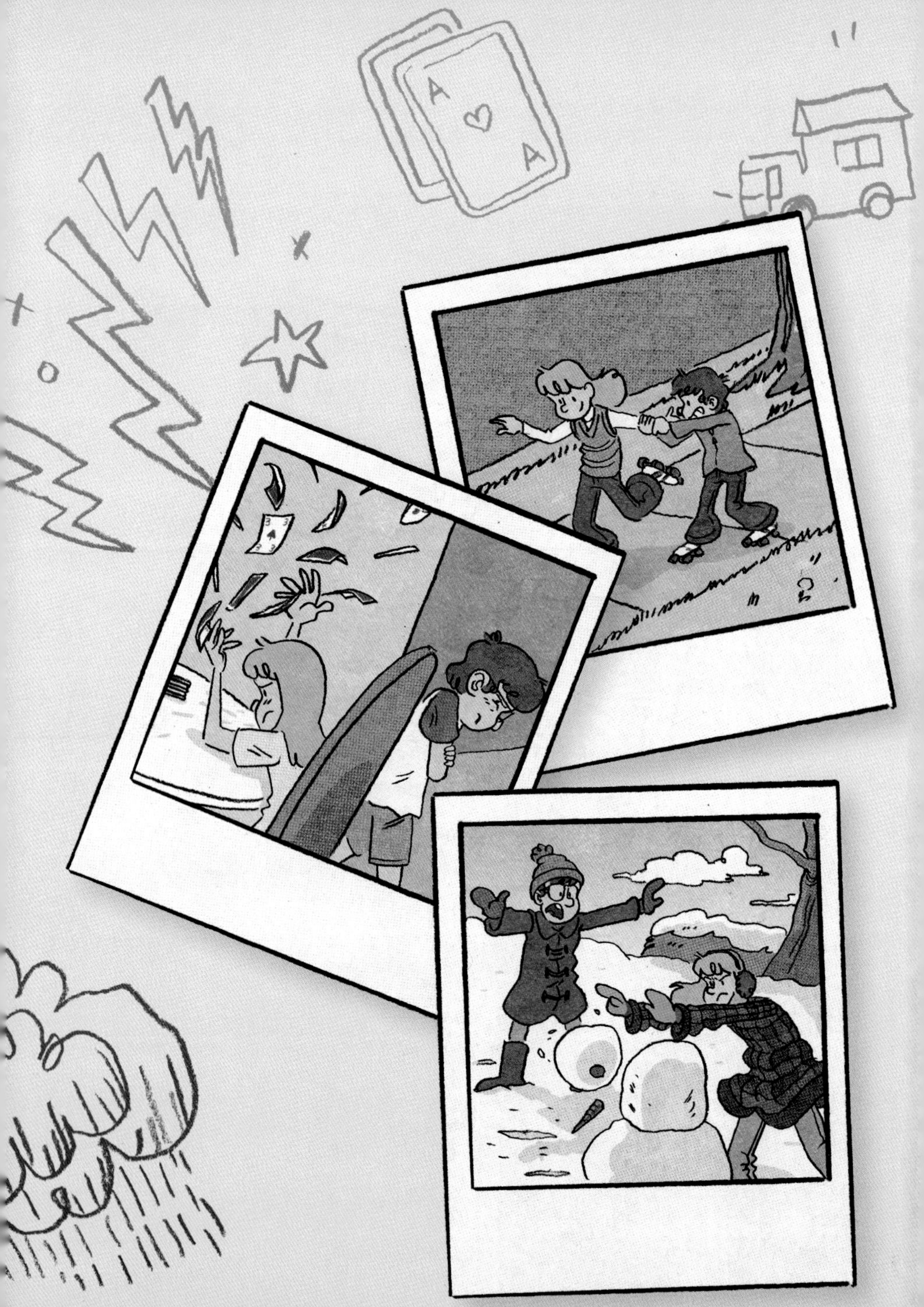

BAD SISTER

Written by
Charise Mericle Harper

Art by
Rory Lucey

:01
First Second
New York

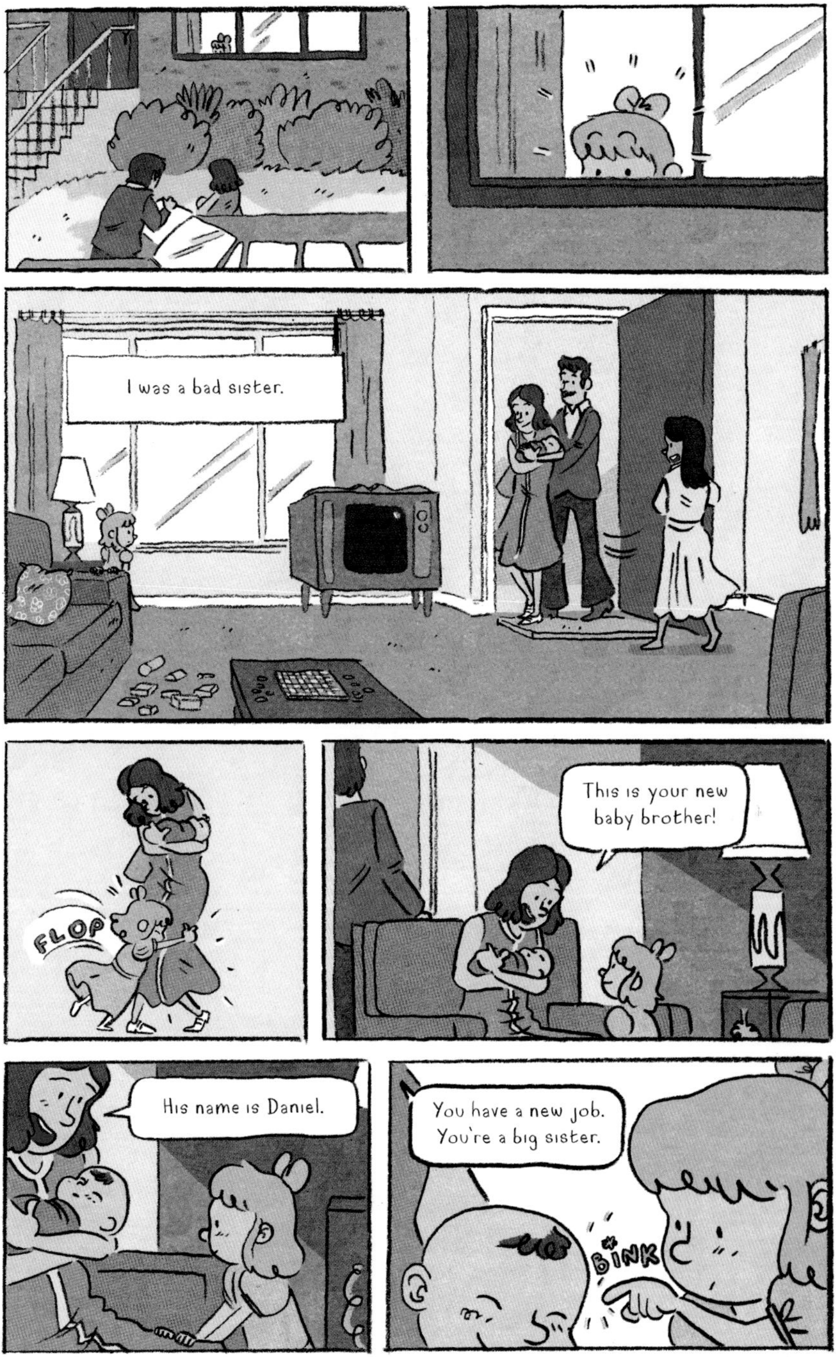
I was a bad sister.
FLOP
This is your new baby brother!
His name is Daniel.
You have a new job. You're a big sister.
BINK

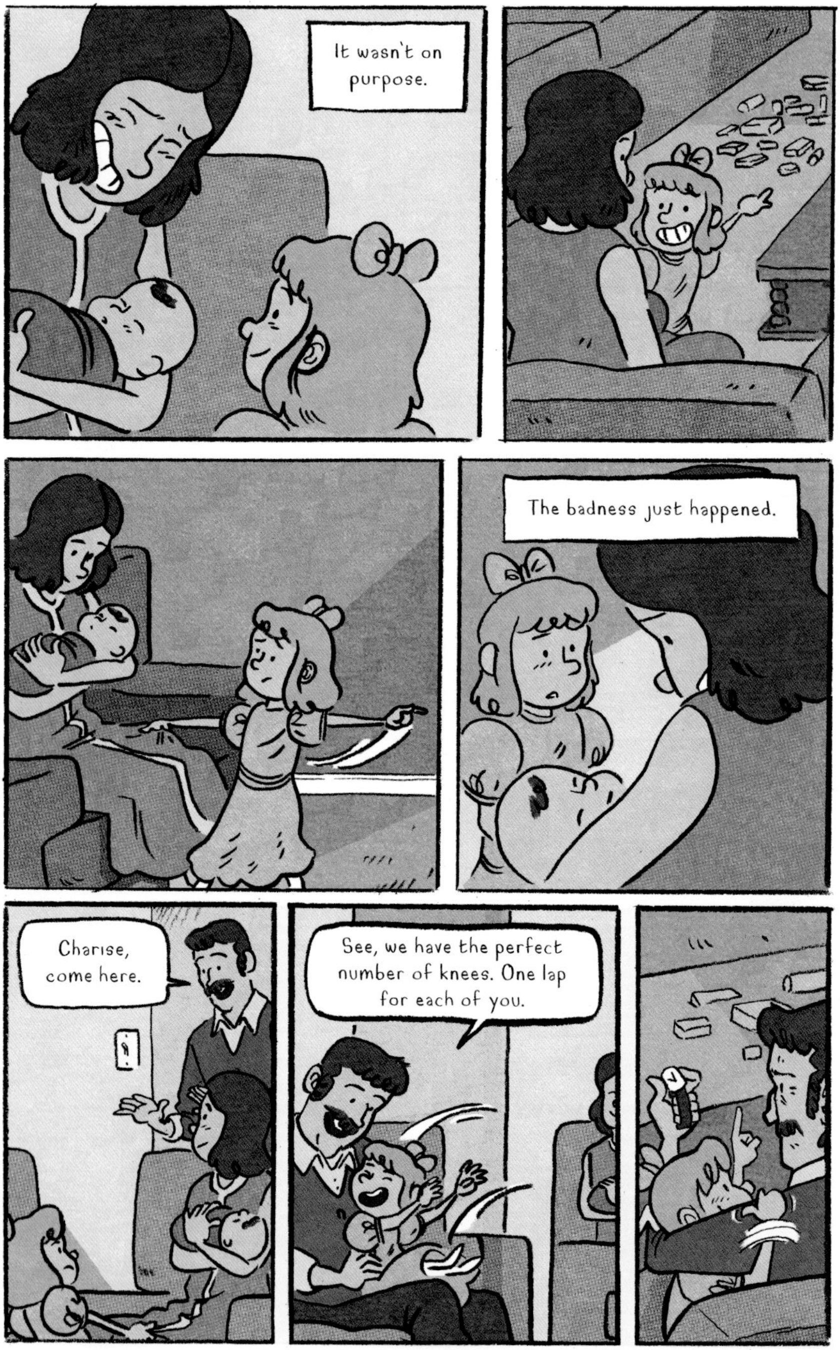
It wasn't on purpose.
The badness just happened.
Charise, come here.
See, we have the perfect number of knees. One lap for each of you.

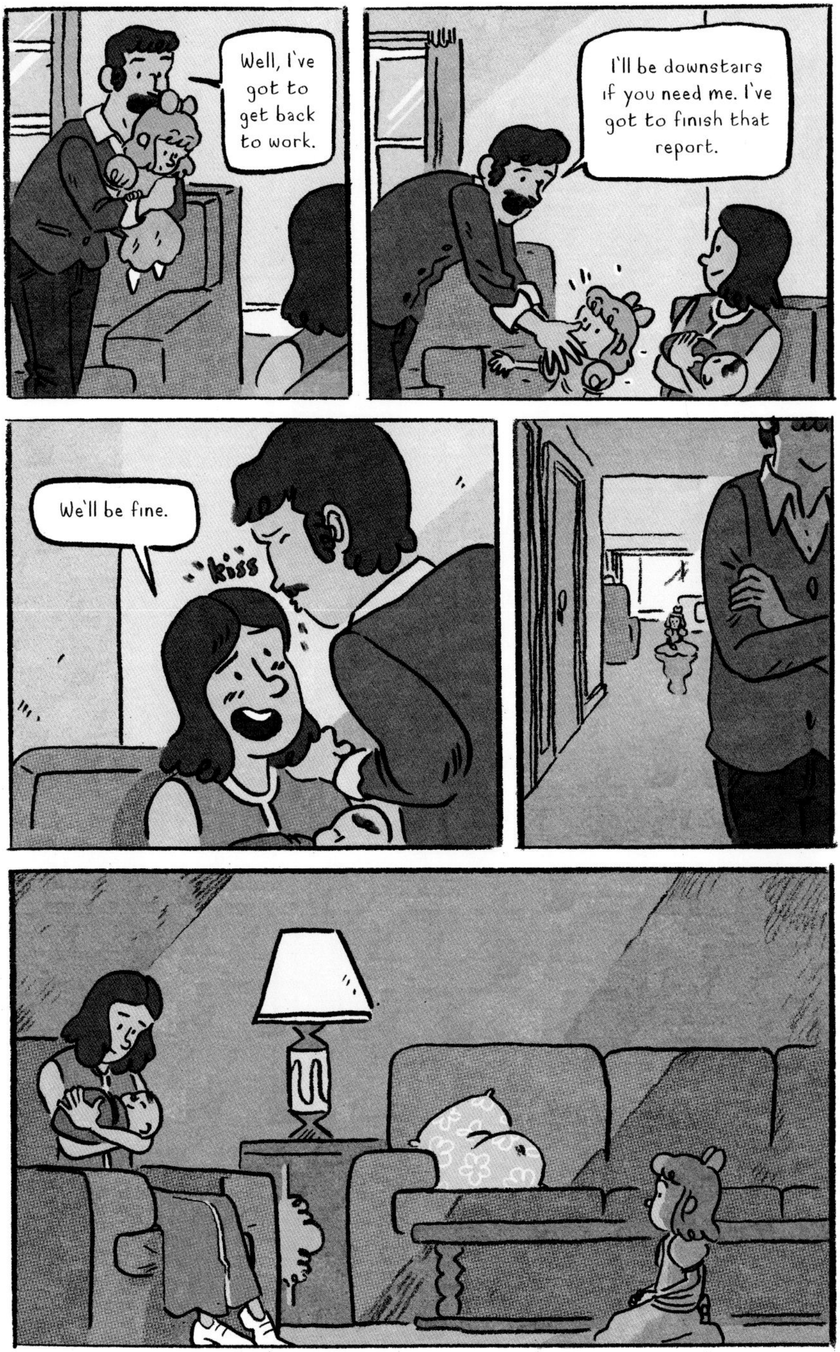
Well, I've got to get back to work.
I'll be downstairs if you need me. I've got to finish that report.
We'll be fine.
KISS

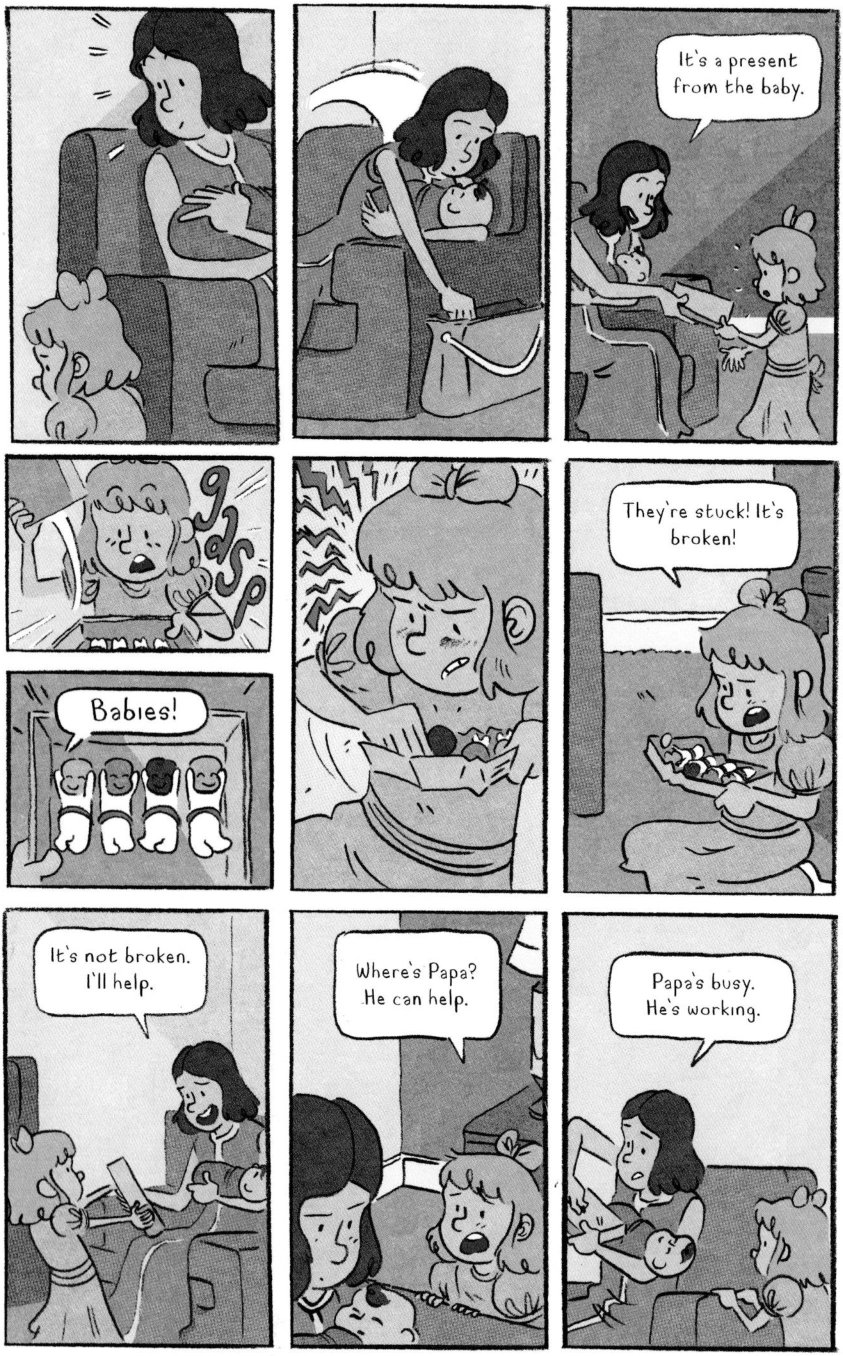
It's a present from the baby.
gasp
Babies!
They're stuck! It's broken!
It's not broken. I'll help.
Where's Papa? He can help.
Papa's busy. He's working.

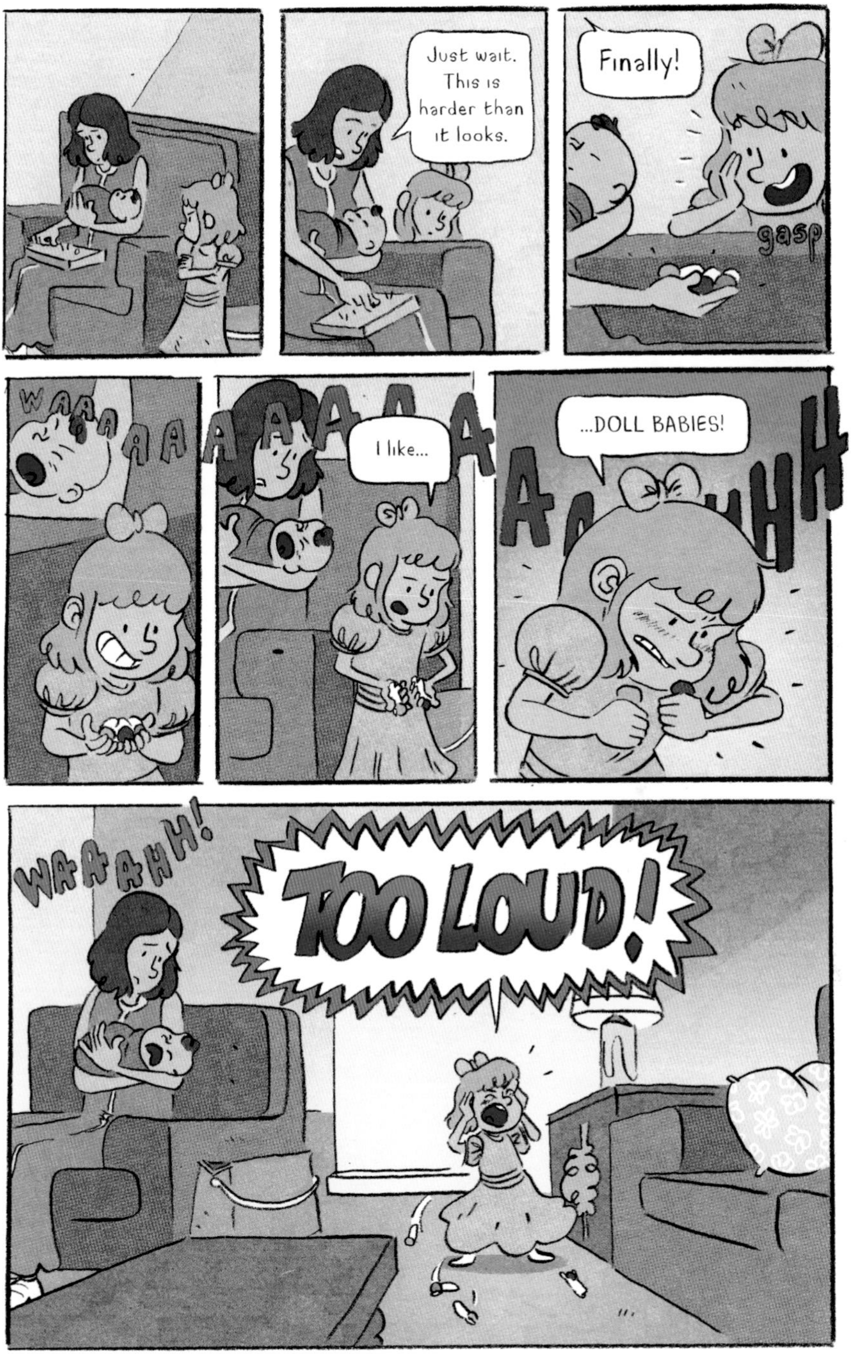

Just wait. This is harder than it looks.
Finally!
gasp
WAAAAAAAAAAAAA
I like...
...DOLL BABIES!
AAAHHH
WAAAHHH!
TOO LOUD!

The Power of the Trick!

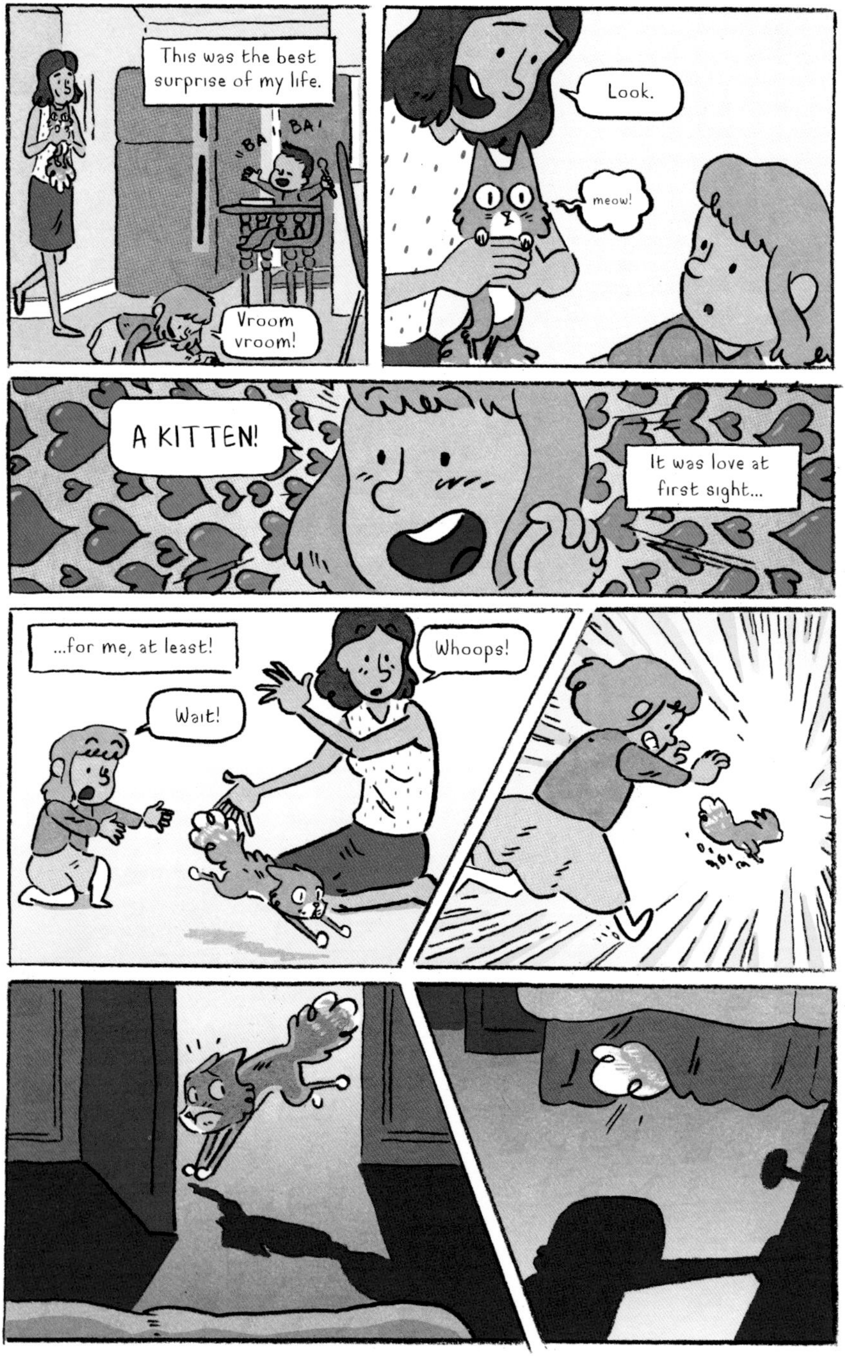
This was the best surprise of my life.
BA
BA
Vroom vroom!
Look.
meow!
A KITTEN!
It was love at first sight...
...for me, at least!
Whoops!
Wait!

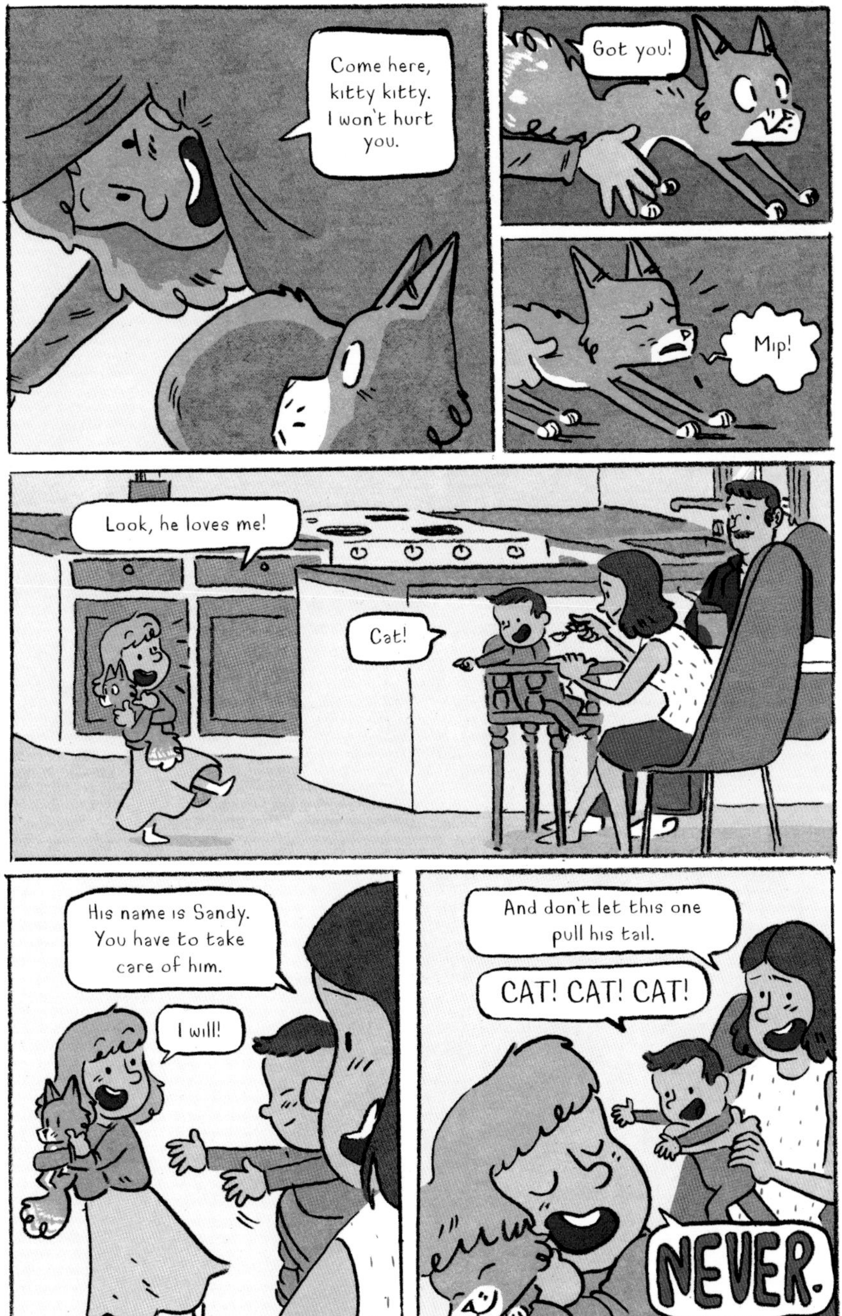
Come here, kitty kitty. I won't hurt you.
Got you!
Mip!
Look, he loves me!
Cat!
His name is Sandy. You have to take care of him.
I will!
And don't let this one pull his tail.
CAT! CAT! CAT!
NEVER.

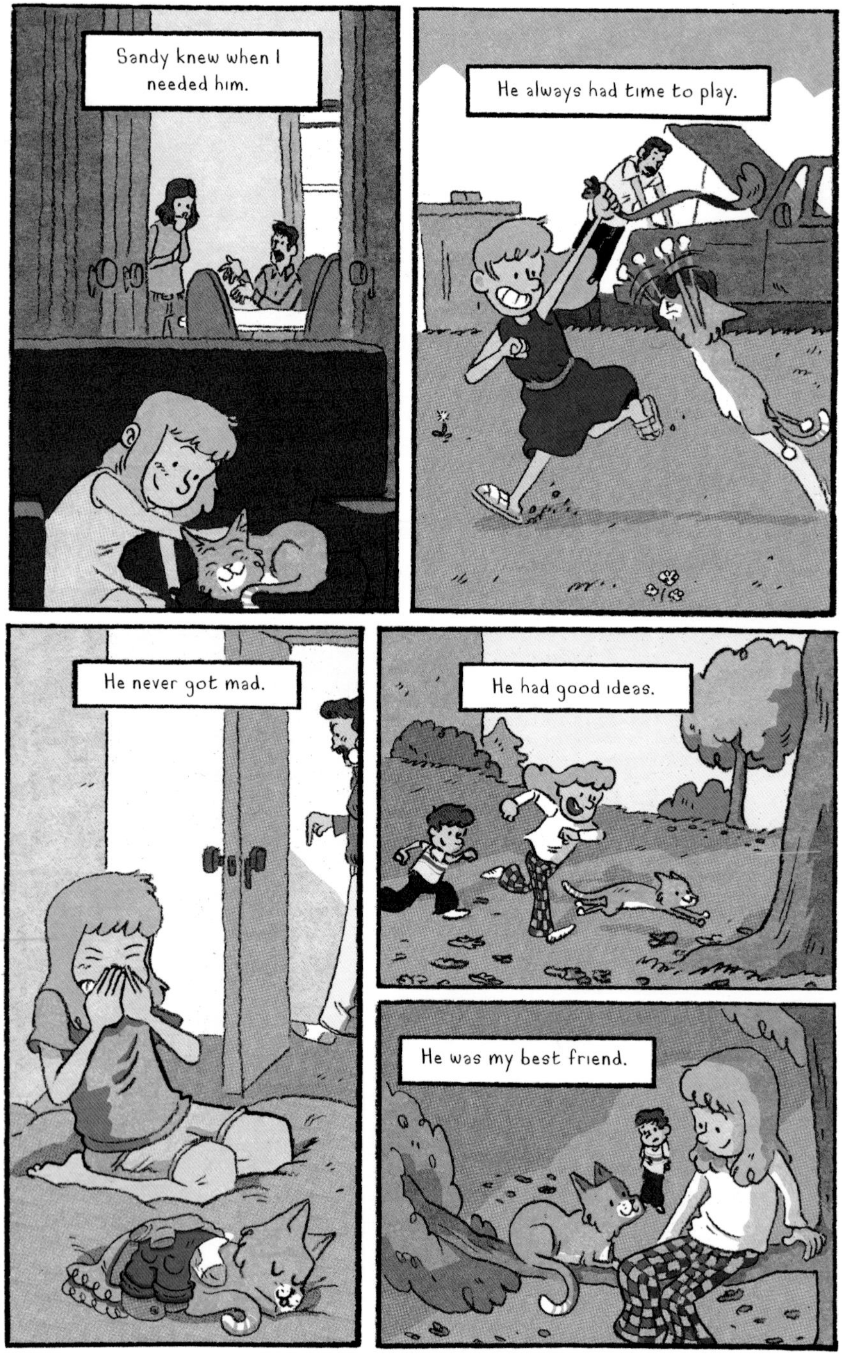
Sandy knew when I needed him.
He always had time to play.
He never got mad.
He had good ideas.
He was my best friend.

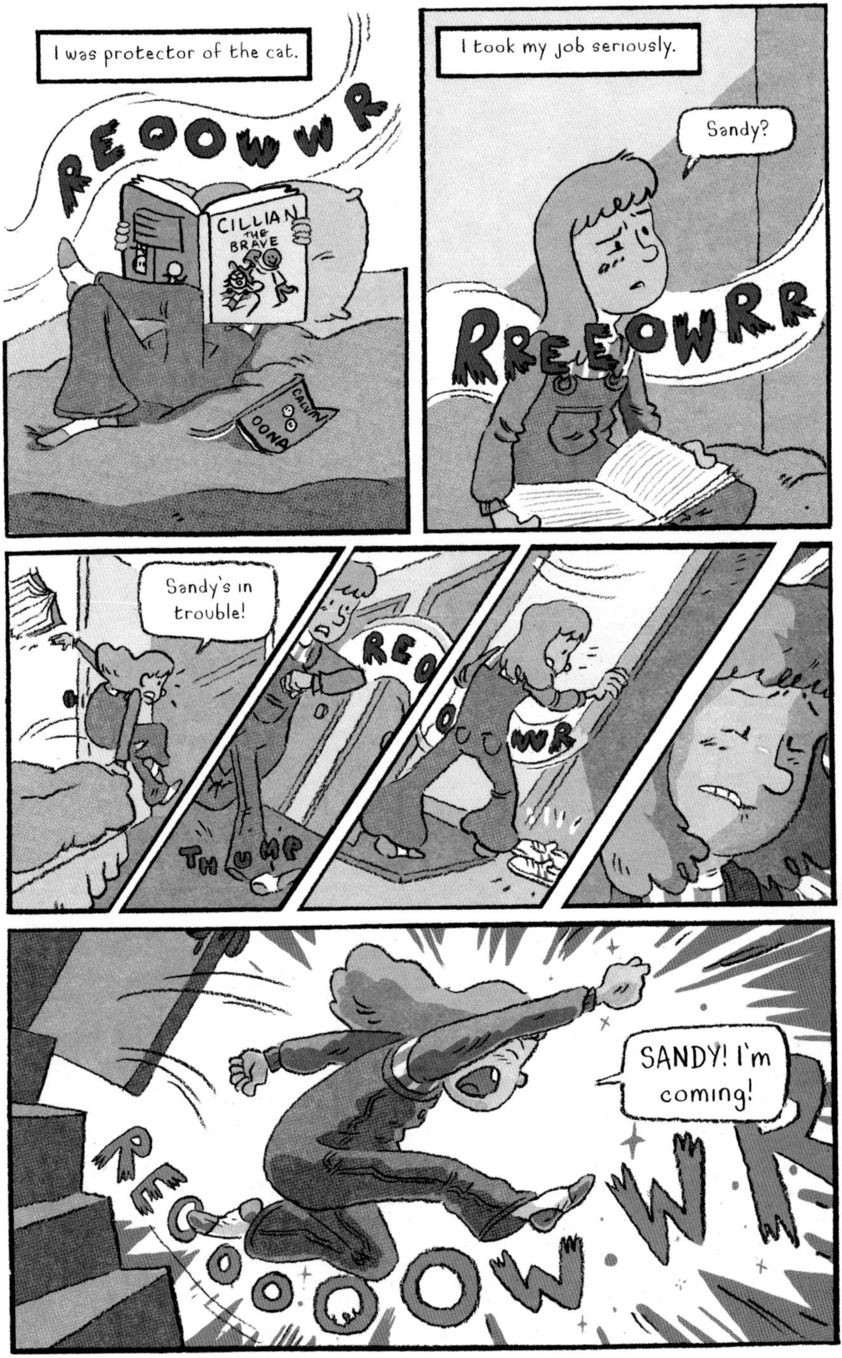
I was protector of the cat.
REOOWWR
CILLIAN THE BRAVE
CALVIN OONA
I took my job seriously.
Sandy?
RREEOWRR
Sandy's in trouble!
REO
O
WR
THUMP
SANDY! I'm coming!
REOOOOOWWR

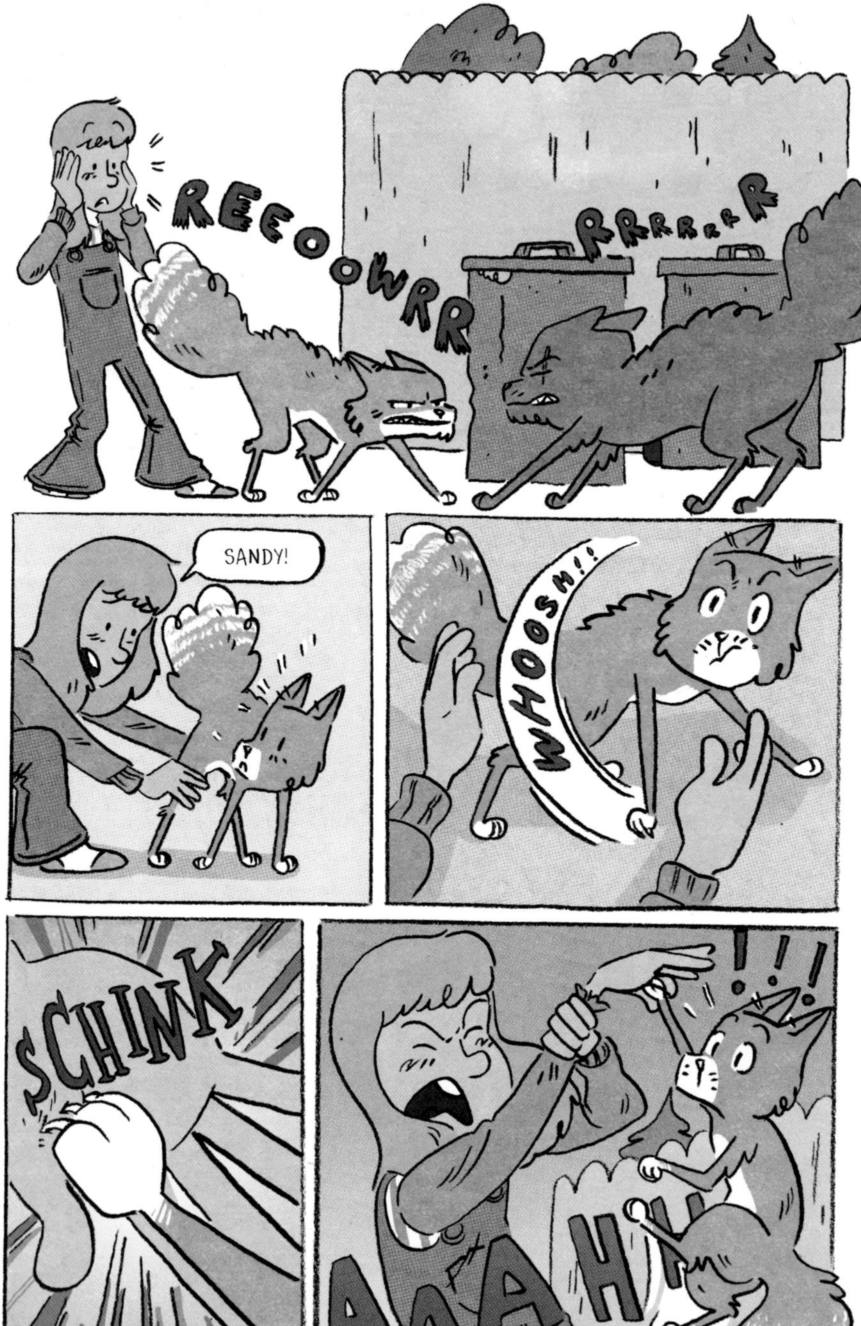
REEEOOOWRR
RRRRRRRR
SANDY!
WHOOSH!!
SCHINK
!!!
AAAHH

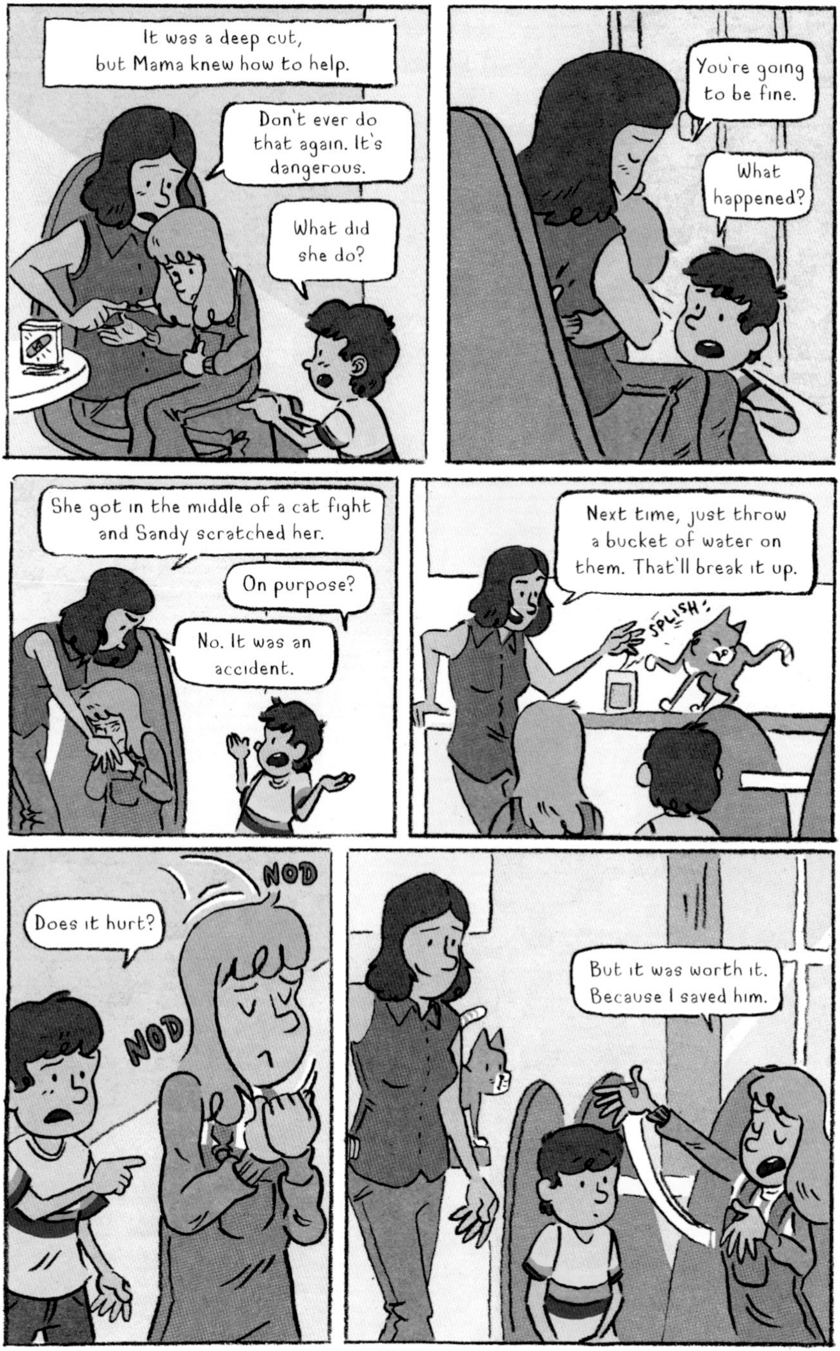
It was a deep cut, but Mama knew how to help.
Don't ever do that again. It's dangerous.
What did she do?
You're going to be fine.
What happened?
She got in the middle of a cat fight and Sandy scratched her.
On purpose?
No. It was an accident.
Next time, just throw a bucket of water on them. That'll break it up.
SPLISH
Does it hurt?
NOD
NOD
But it was worth it. Because I saved him.

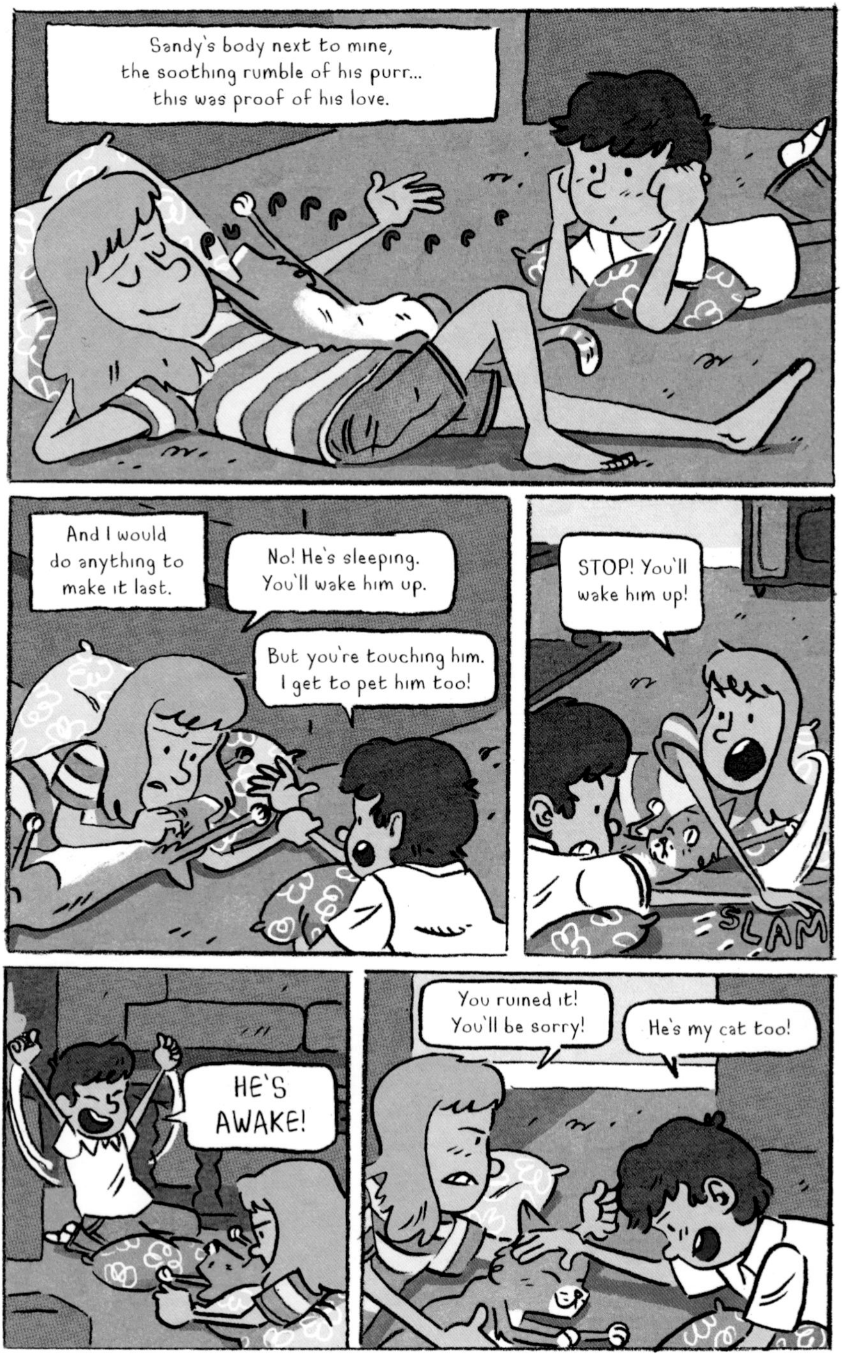
Sandy's body next to mine, the soothing rumble of his purr... this was proof of his love.
PURRRRRRRR
And I would do anything to make it last.
No! He's sleeping. You'll wake him up.
But you're touching him. I get to pet him too!
STOP! You'll wake him up!
SLAM
HE'S AWAKE!
You ruined it! You'll be sorry!
He's my cat too!

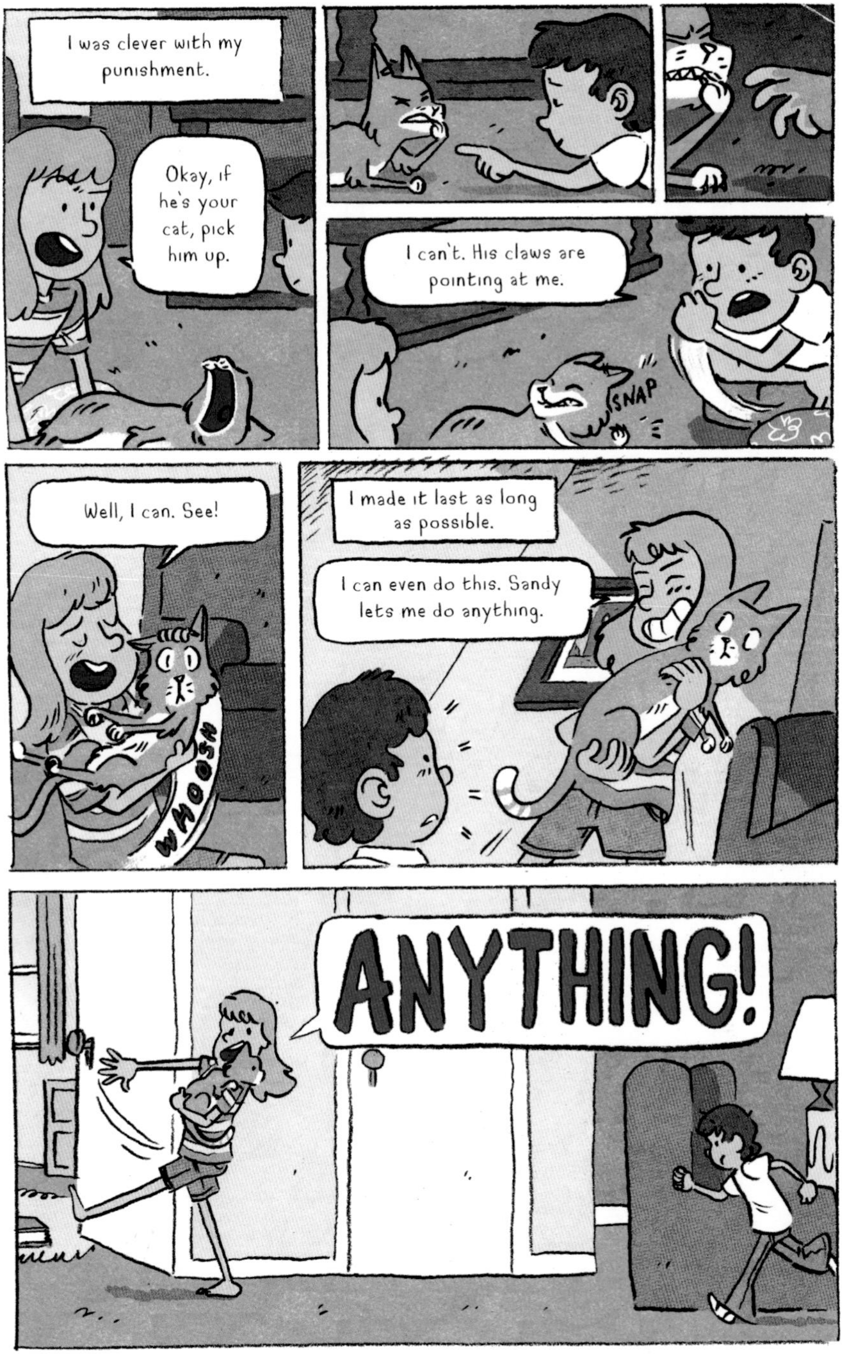
I was clever with my punishment.
Okay, if he's your cat, pick him up.
I can't. His claws are pointing at me.
SNAP
Well, I can. See!
WHOOSH
I made it last as long as possible.
I can even do this. Sandy lets me do anything.
ANYTHING!

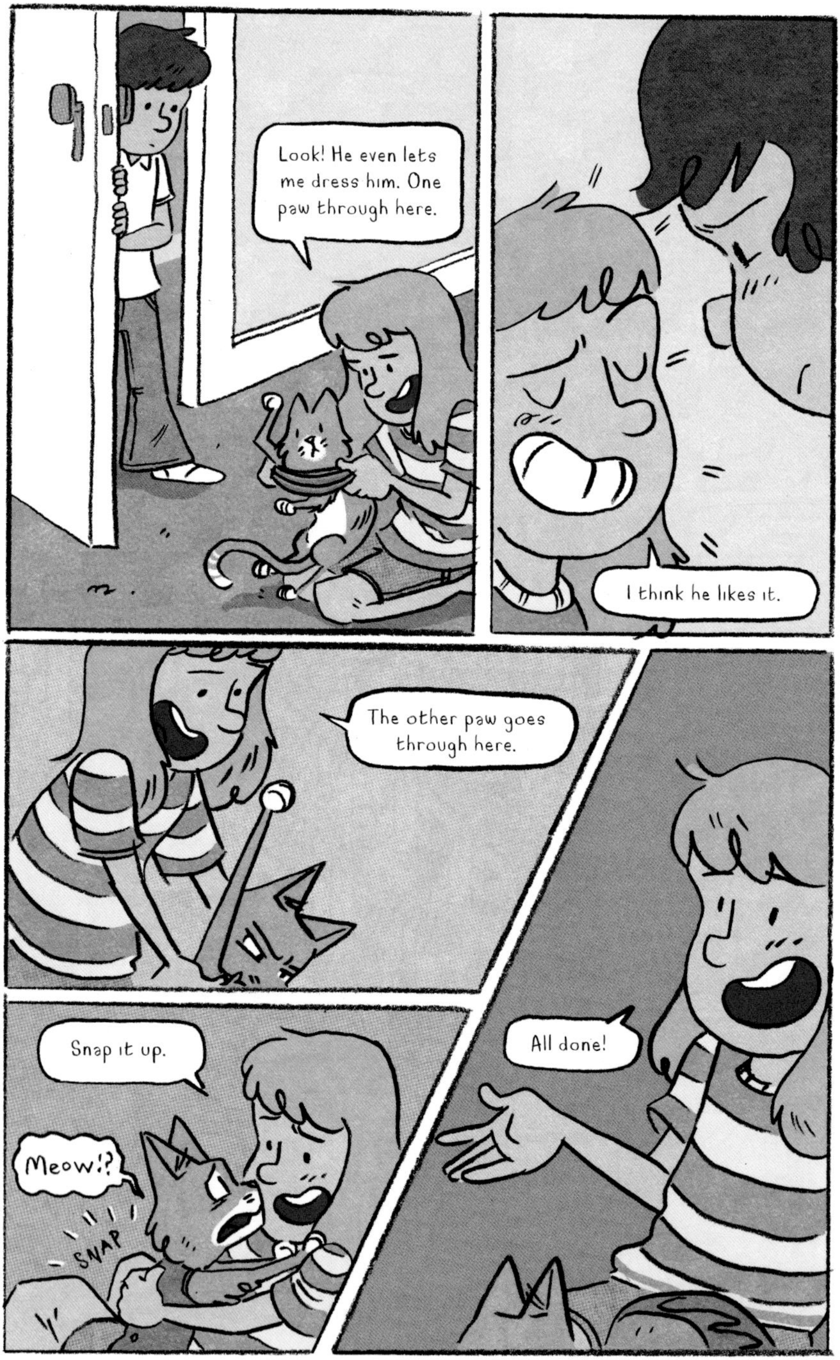
Look! He even lets me dress him. One paw through here.
I think he likes it.
The other paw goes through here.
Snap it up.
Meow!?
SNAP
All done!

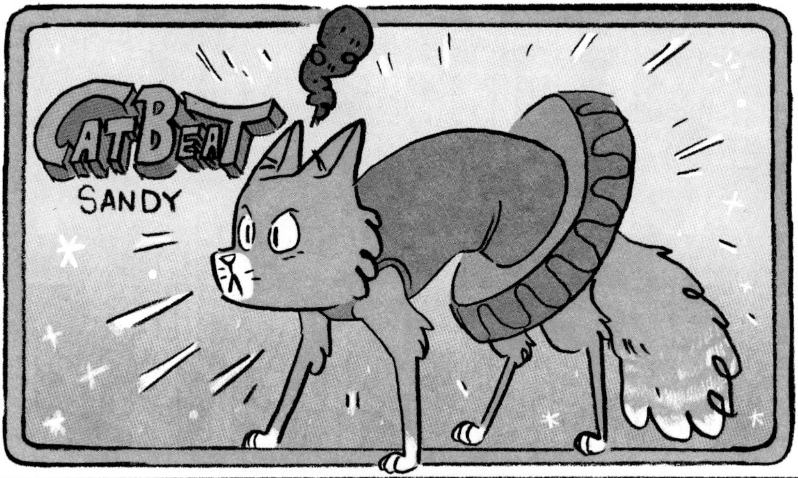
CATBEAT
SANDY

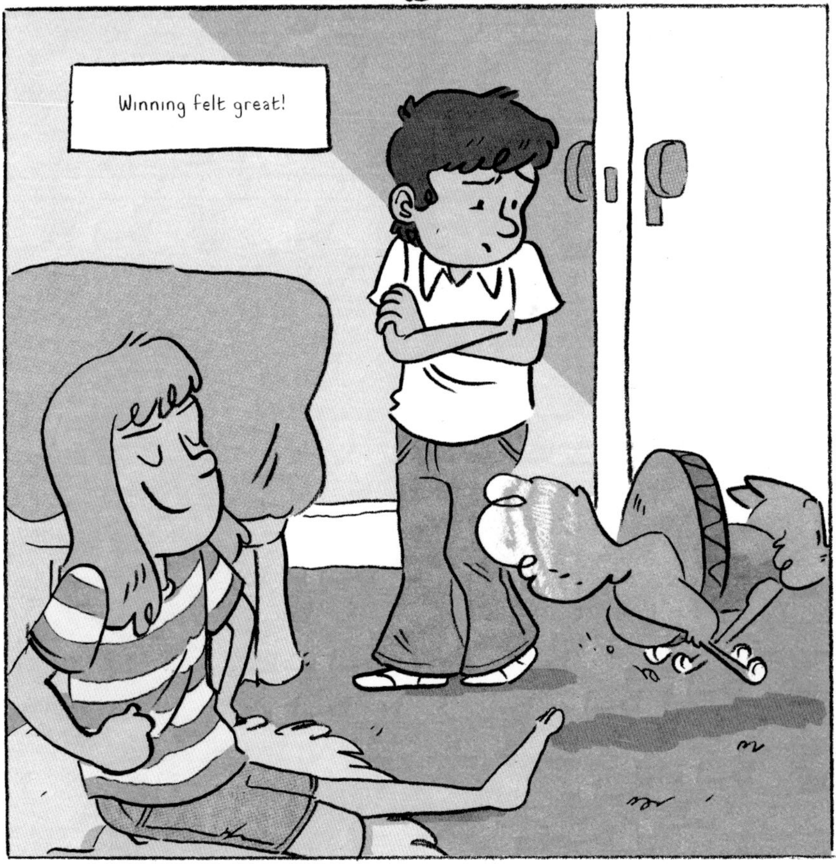
Winning felt great!

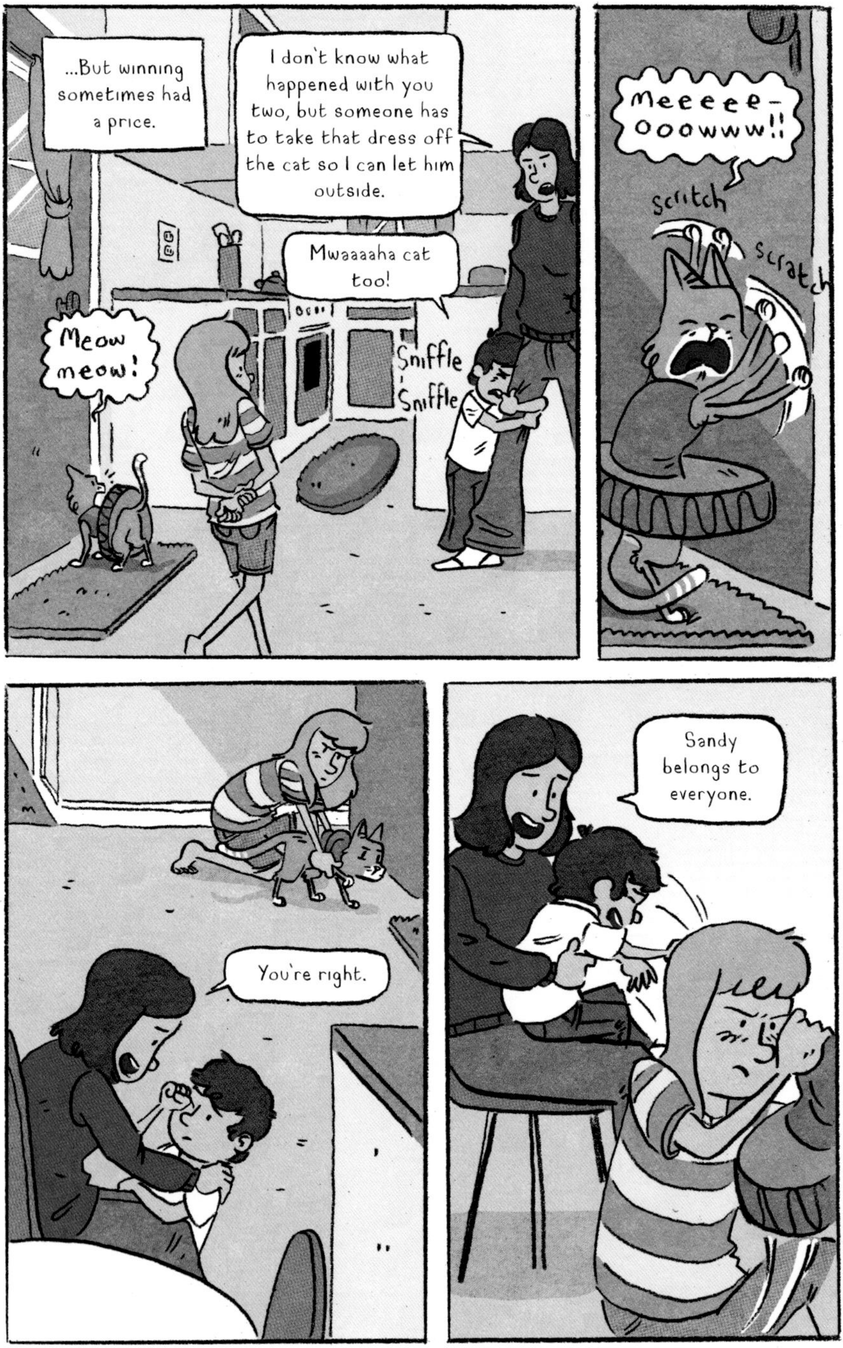
...But winning sometimes had a price.
I don't know what happened with you two, but someone has to take that dress off the cat so I can let him outside.
Mwaaaaha cat too!
Meow meow!
Sniffle Sniffle
Meeeee-ooowww!!
scritch
scratch
You're right.
Sandy belongs to everyone.

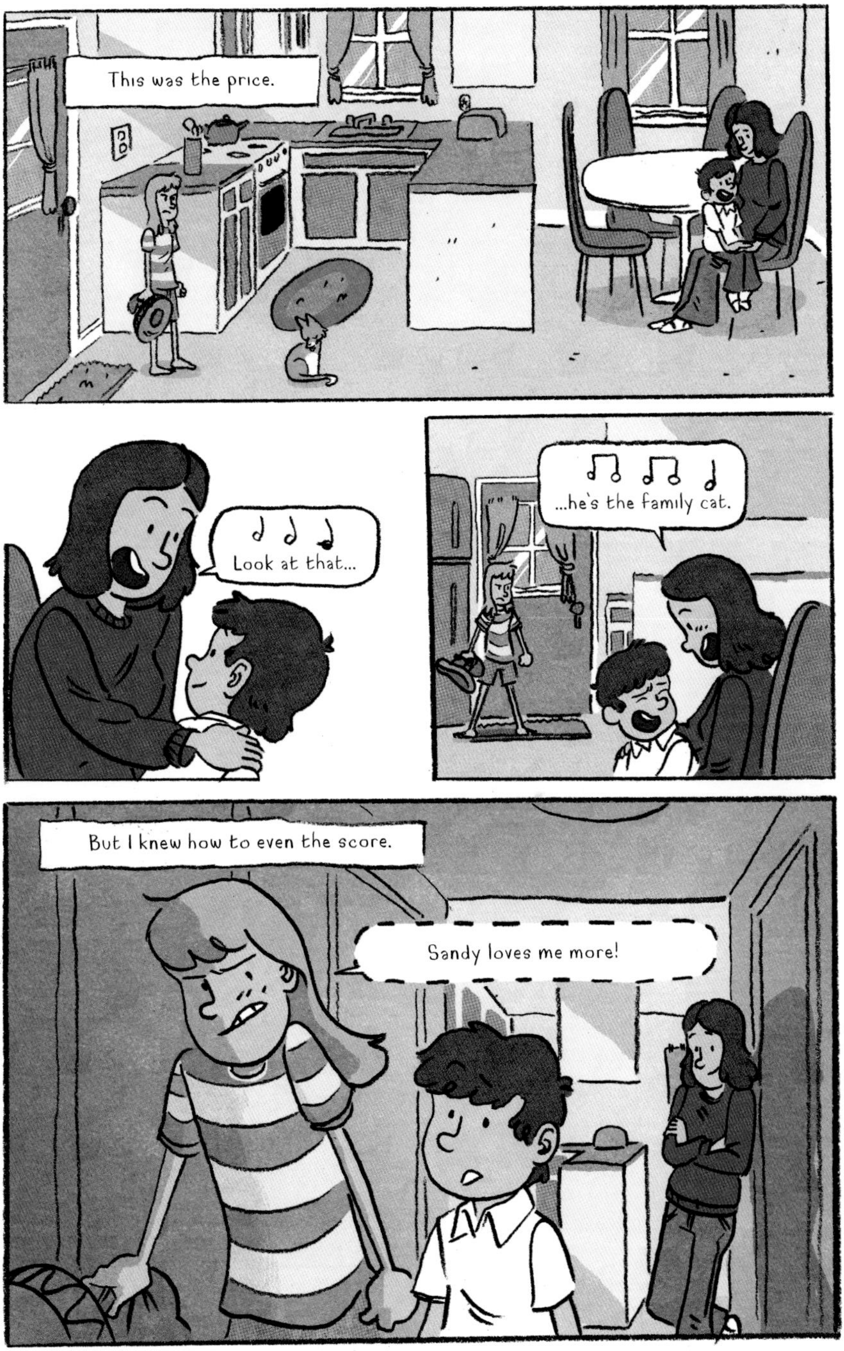
This was the price.
Look at that...
...he's the family cat.
But I knew how to even the score.
Sandy loves me more!

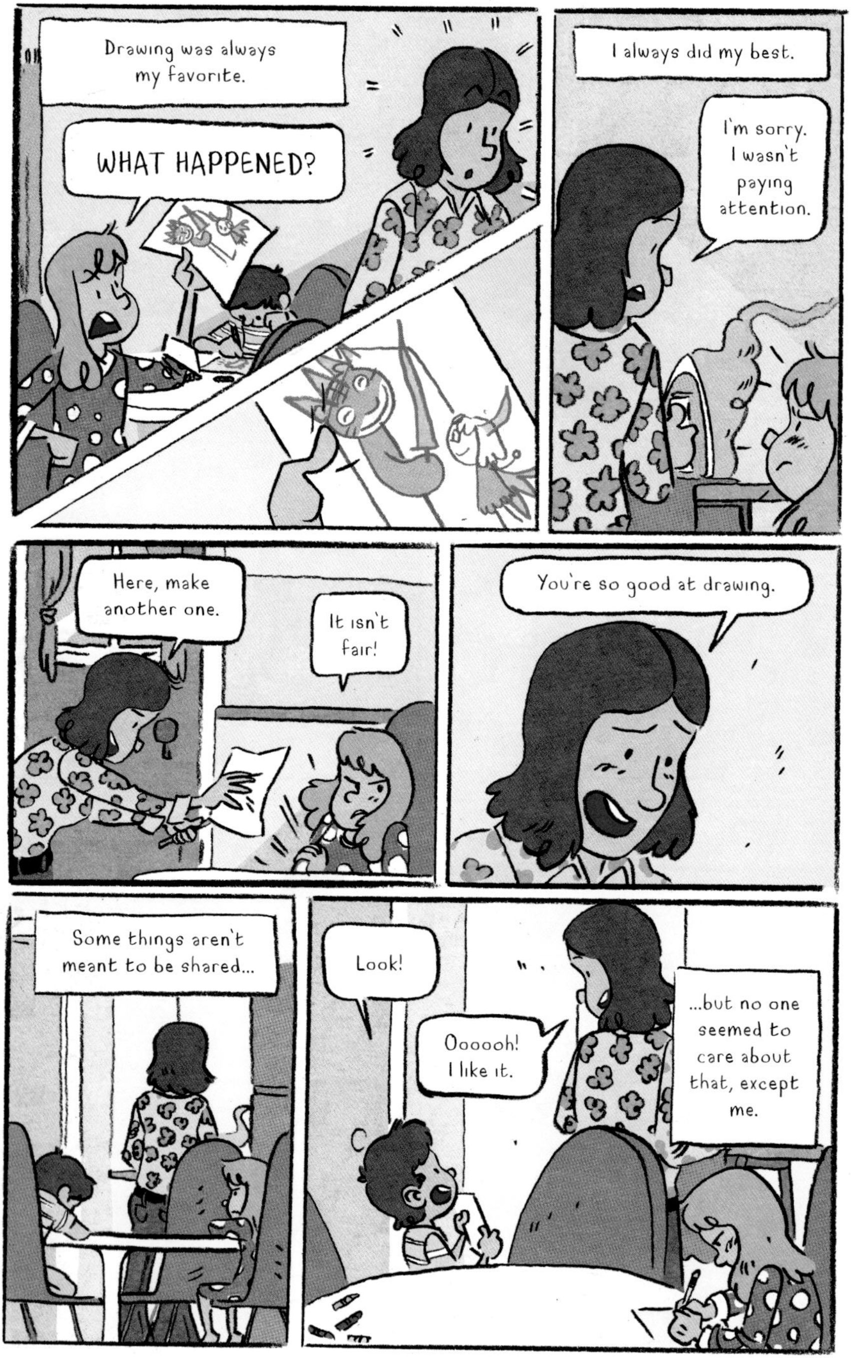

Drawing was always my favorite.
WHAT HAPPENED?
I always did my best.
I'm sorry. I wasn't paying attention.
Here, make another one.
It isn't fair!
You're so good at drawing.
Some things aren't meant to be shared...
Look!
Oooooh! I like it.
...but no one seemed to care about that, except me.

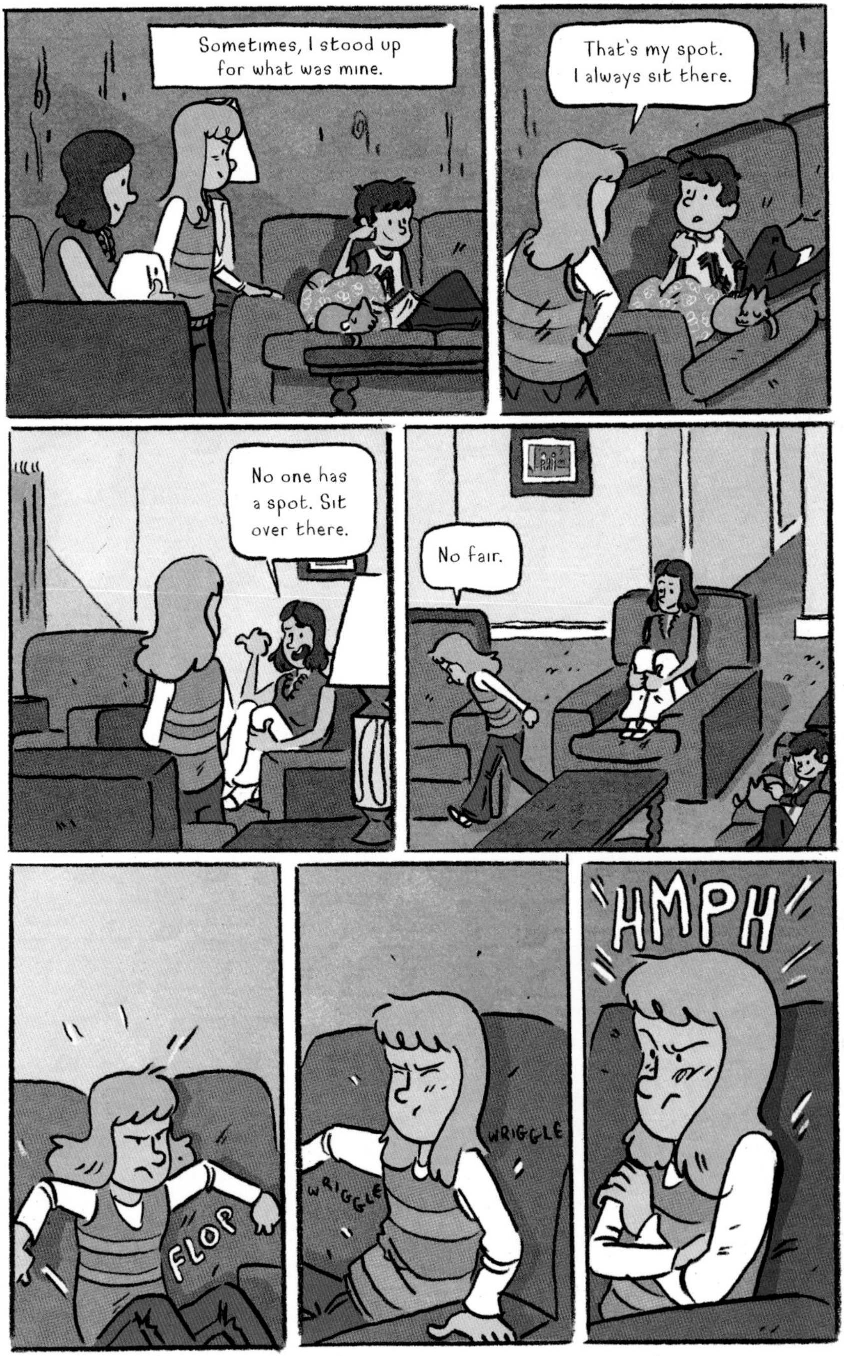
Sometimes, I stood up
for what was mine.
That's my spot.
I always sit there.
No one has
a spot. Sit
over there.
No fair.
FLOP
WRIGGLE
WRIGGLE
HMPH

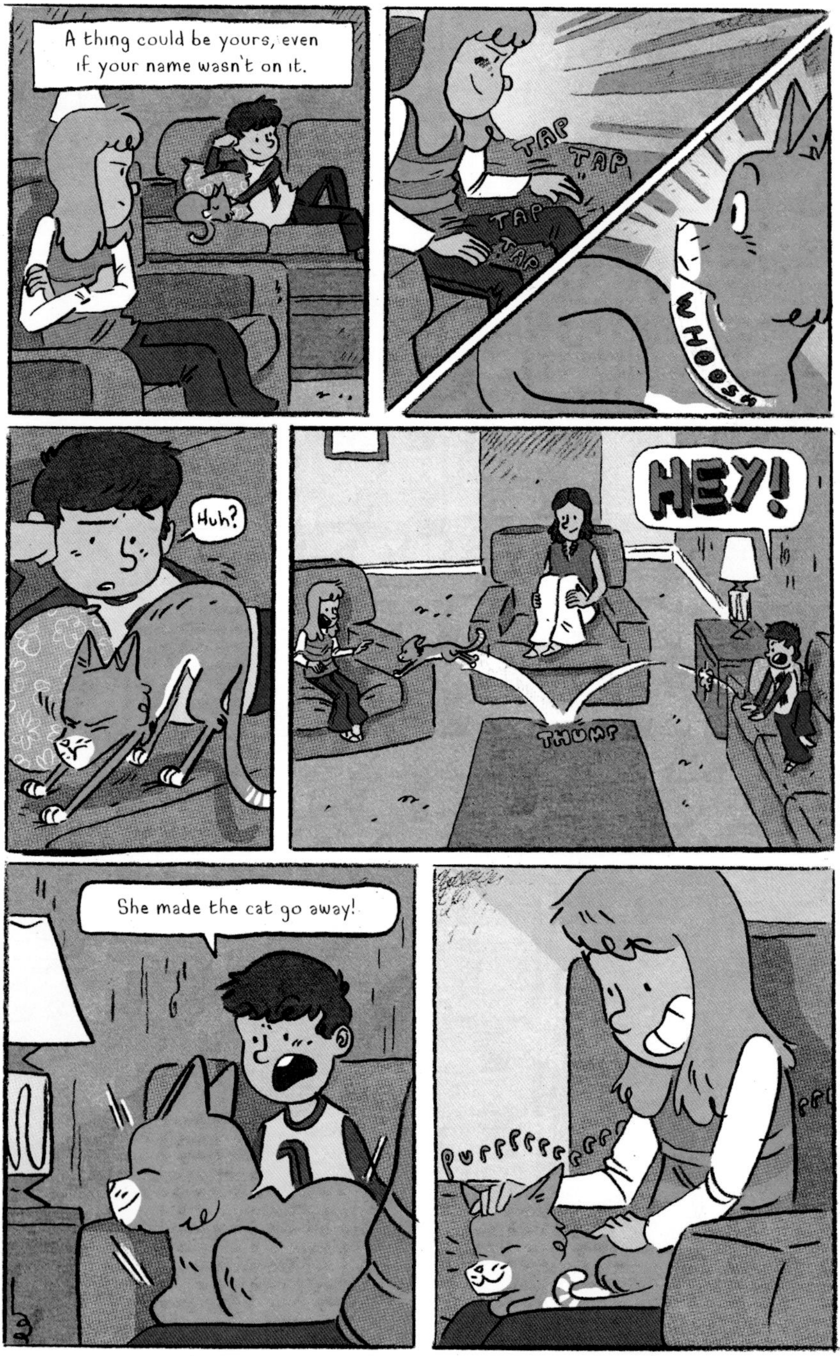
A thing could be yours, even if your name wasn't on it.
TAP TAP
TAP TAP
WHOOSH
Huh?
HEY!
THUMP
She made the cat go away!
purrrrrrrrr
prr

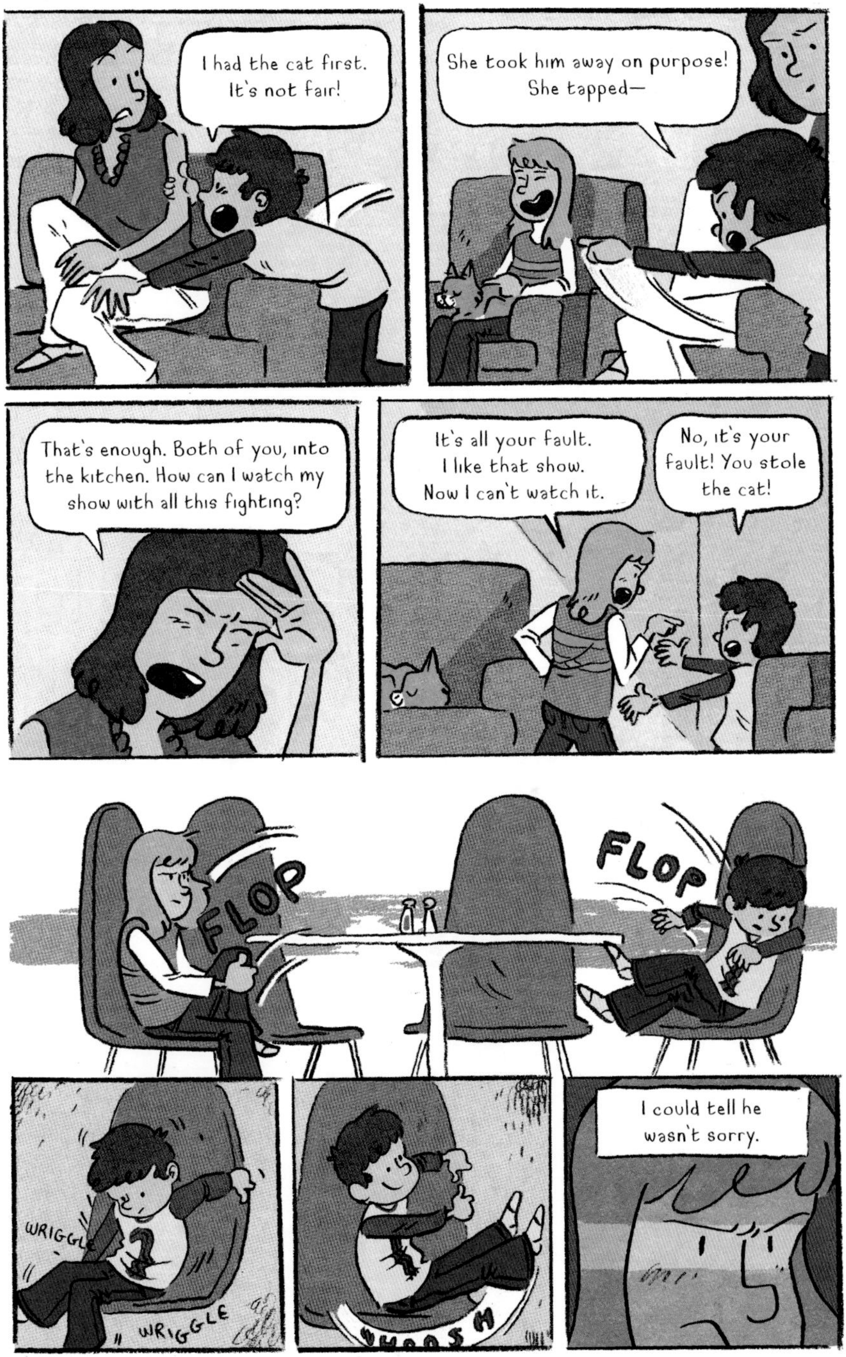
I had the cat first. It's not fair!
She took him away on purpose! She tapped—
That's enough. Both of you, into the kitchen. How can I watch my show with all this fighting?
It's all your fault. I like that show. Now I can't watch it.
No, it's your fault! You stole the cat!
FLOP
FLOP
WRIGGLE
WRIGGLE
WHOOSH
I could tell he wasn't sorry.

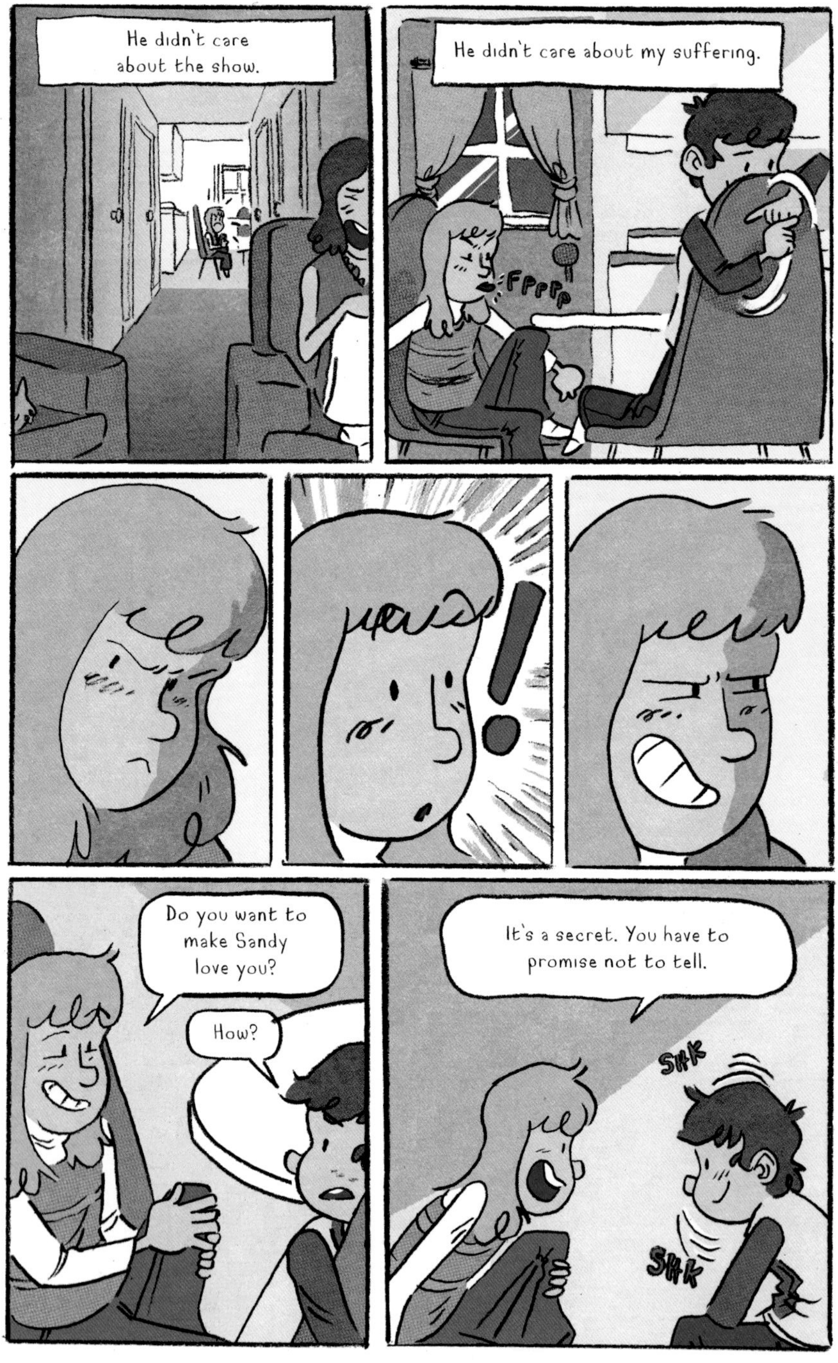
He didn't care about the show.
He didn't care about my suffering.
FFFFP
Do you want to make Sandy love you?
How?
It's a secret. You have to promise not to tell.
SHK
SHK

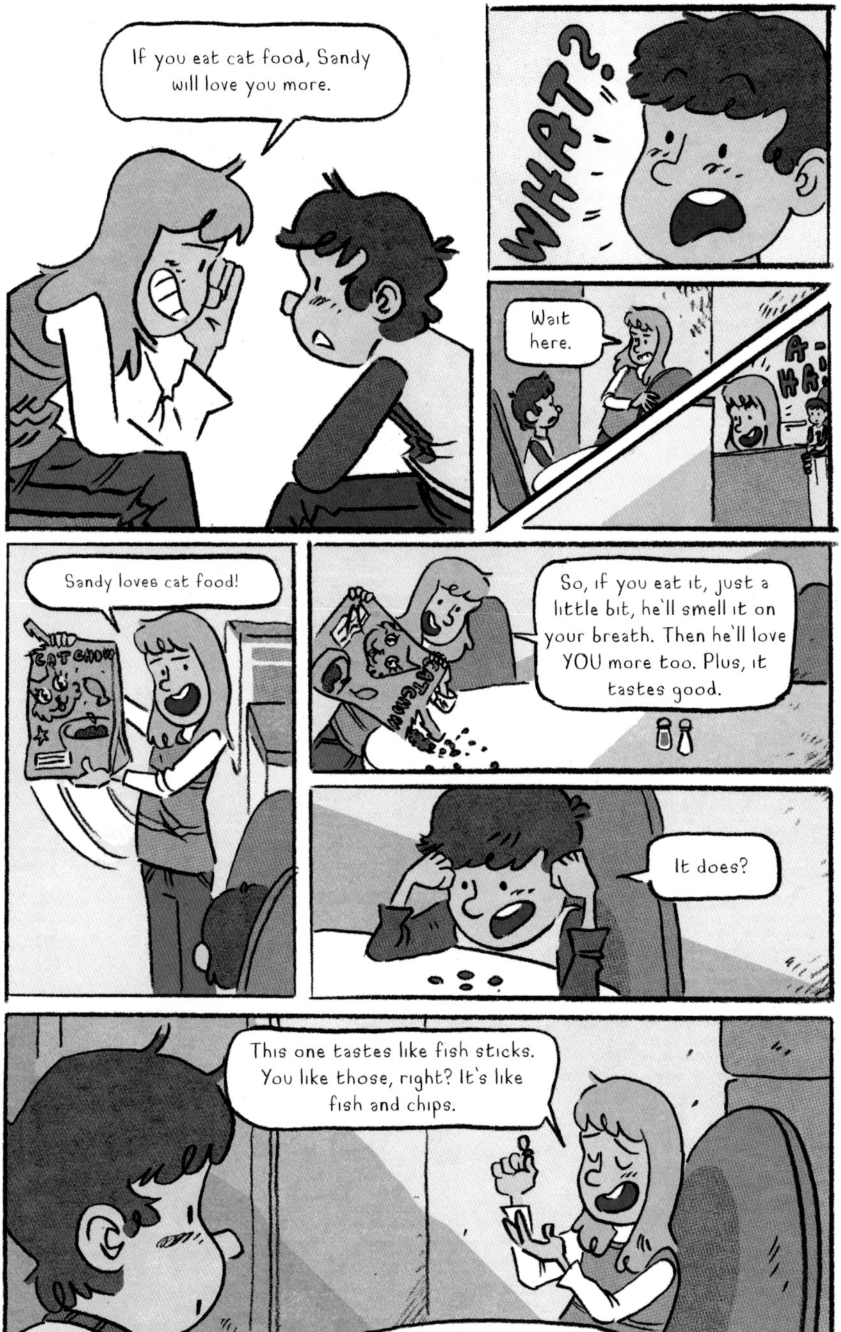
If you eat cat food, Sandy will love you more.
WHAT?
Wait here.
A-HA!
Sandy loves cat food!
CAT CHOW
So, if you eat it, just a little bit, he'll smell it on your breath. Then he'll love YOU more too. Plus, it tastes good.
It does?
This one tastes like fish sticks. You like those, right? It's like fish and chips.

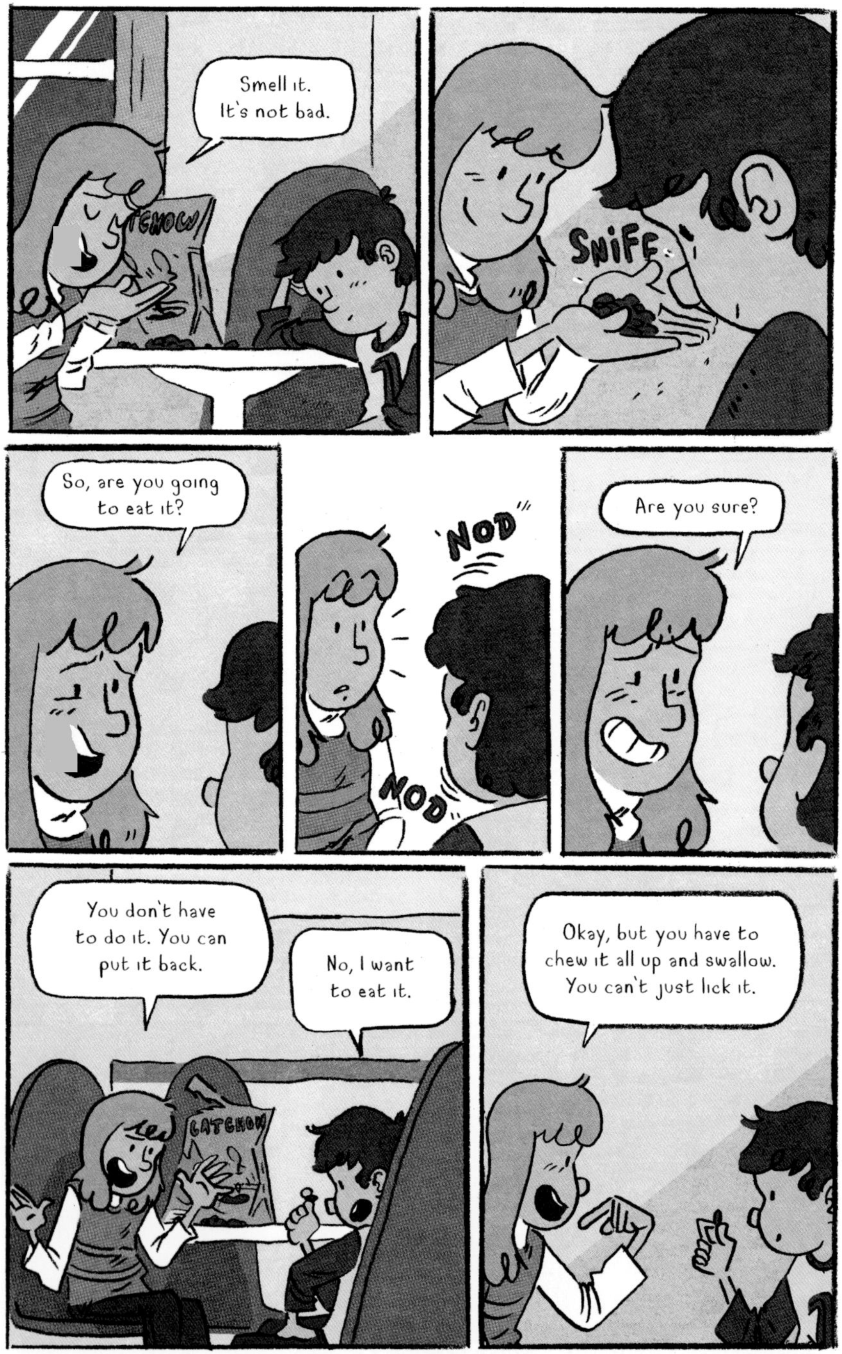
Smell it. It's not bad.
CATCHOW
SNIFF
So, are you going to eat it?
NOD
NOD
Are you sure?
You don't have to do it. You can put it back.
No, I want to eat it.
CATCHOW
Okay, but you have to chew it all up and swallow. You can't just lick it.

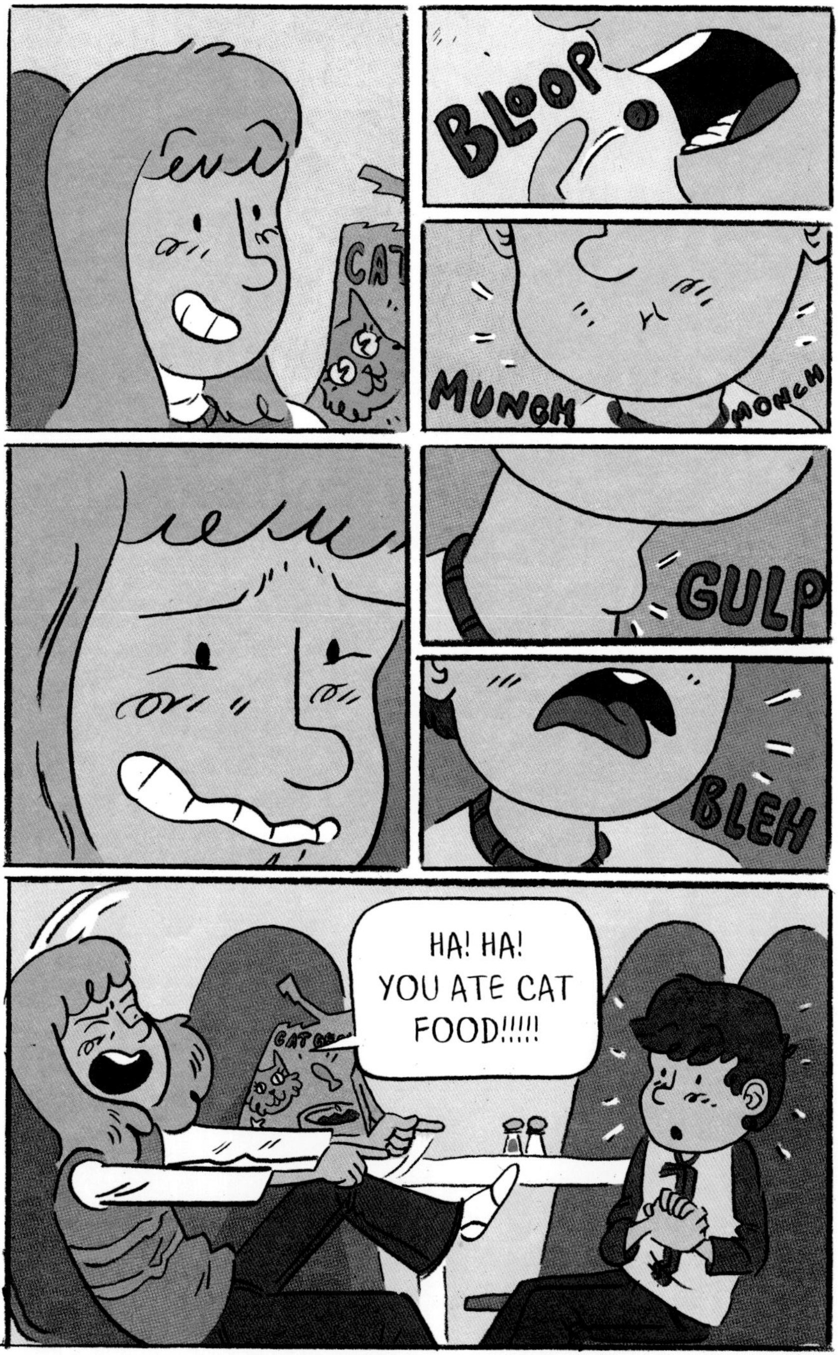
CAT
BLOOP
MUNCH
MONCH
GULP
BLEH
HA! HA!
YOU ATE CAT
FOOD!!!!!

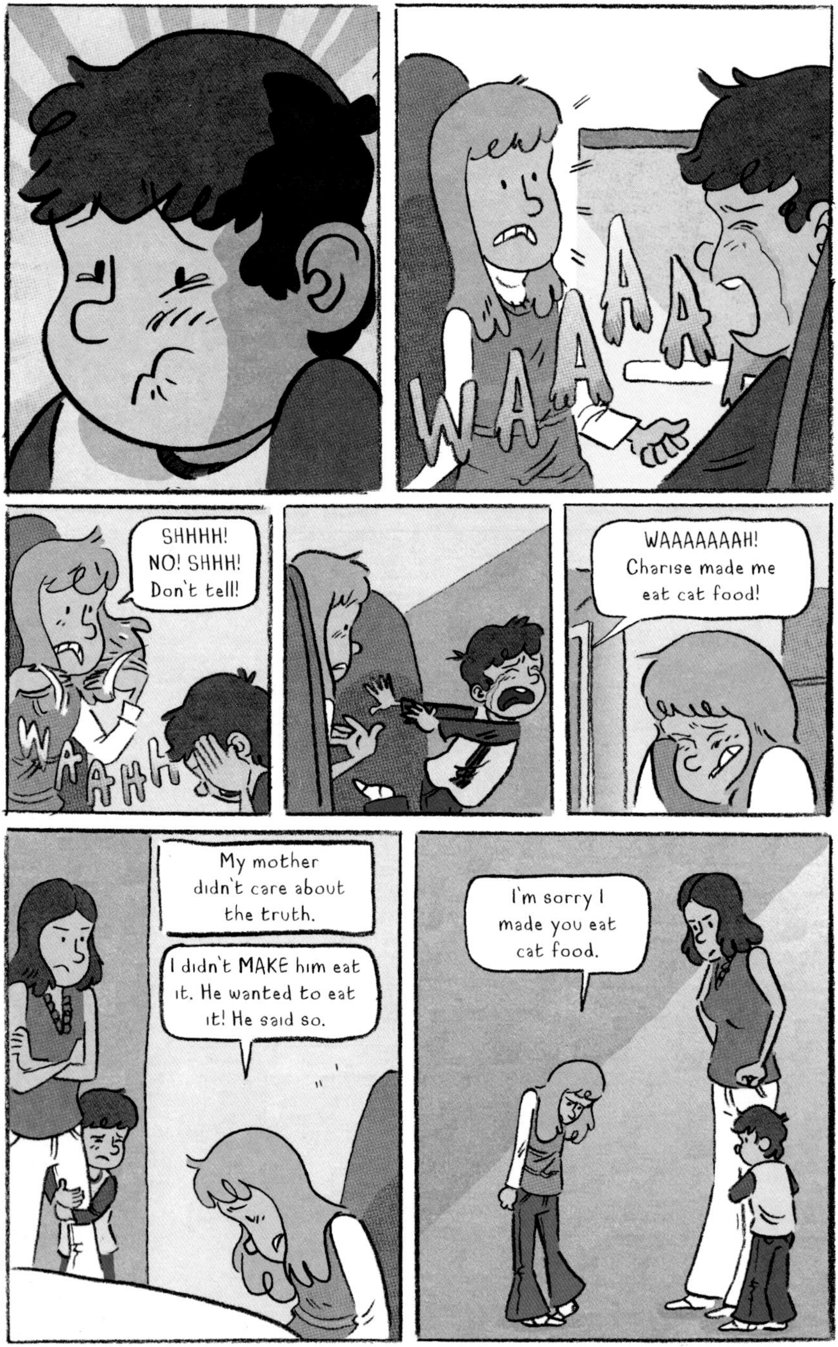

WAAAAA
SHHHH! NO! SHHH! Don't tell!
WAAHH
WAAAAAAAH! Charise made me eat cat food!
My mother didn't care about the truth.
I didn't MAKE him eat it. He wanted to eat it! He said so.
I'm sorry I made you eat cat food.

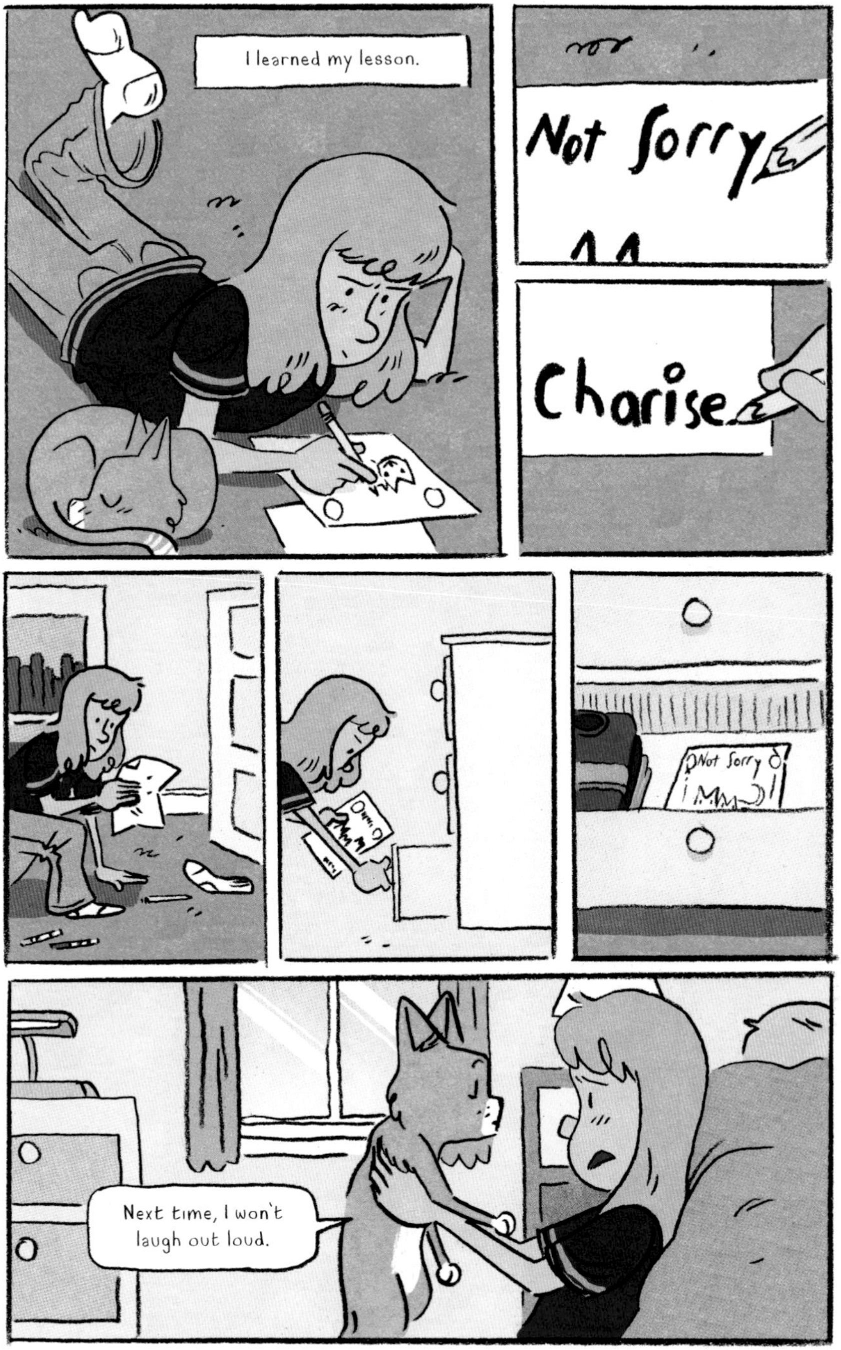
I learned my lesson.
Not Sorry
Charise
Not Sorry
Next time, I won't laugh out loud.

The Power of Seeing
and Knowing

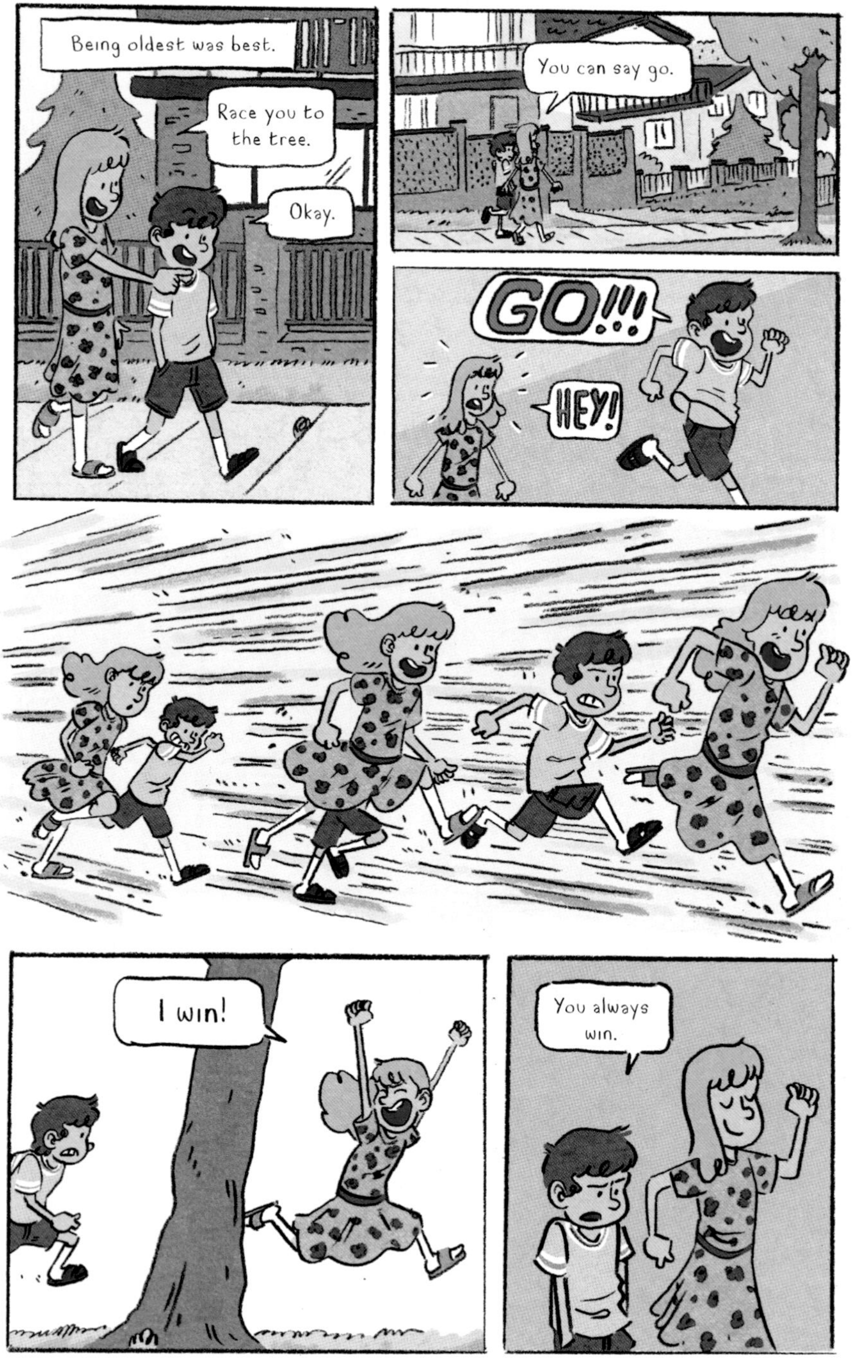
Being oldest was best.
Race you to the tree.
Okay.
You can say go.
GO!!!
HEY!
I win!
You always win.

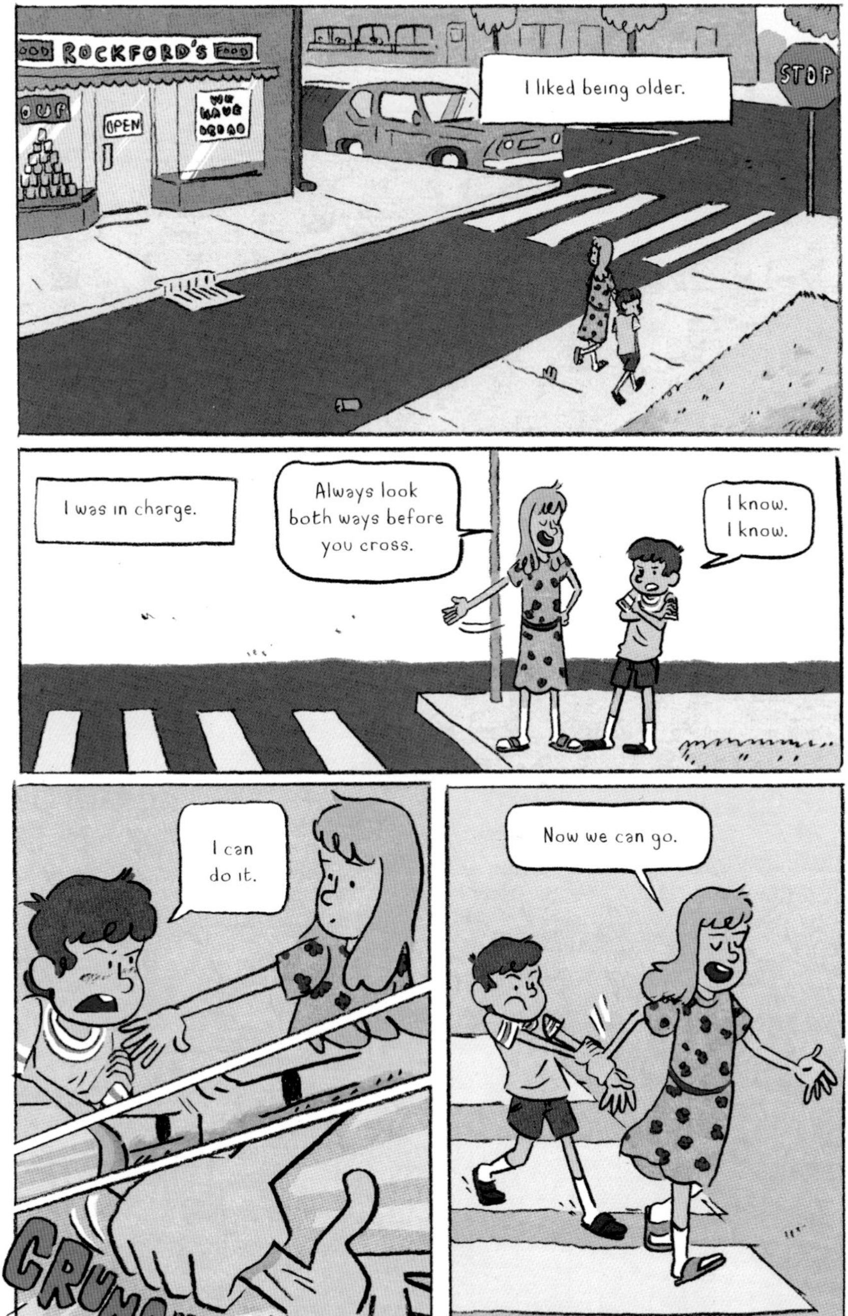
ROCKFORD'S
OPEN
I liked being older.
STOP
I was in charge.
Always look both ways before you cross.
I know. I know.
I can do it.
CRUNCH
Now we can go.

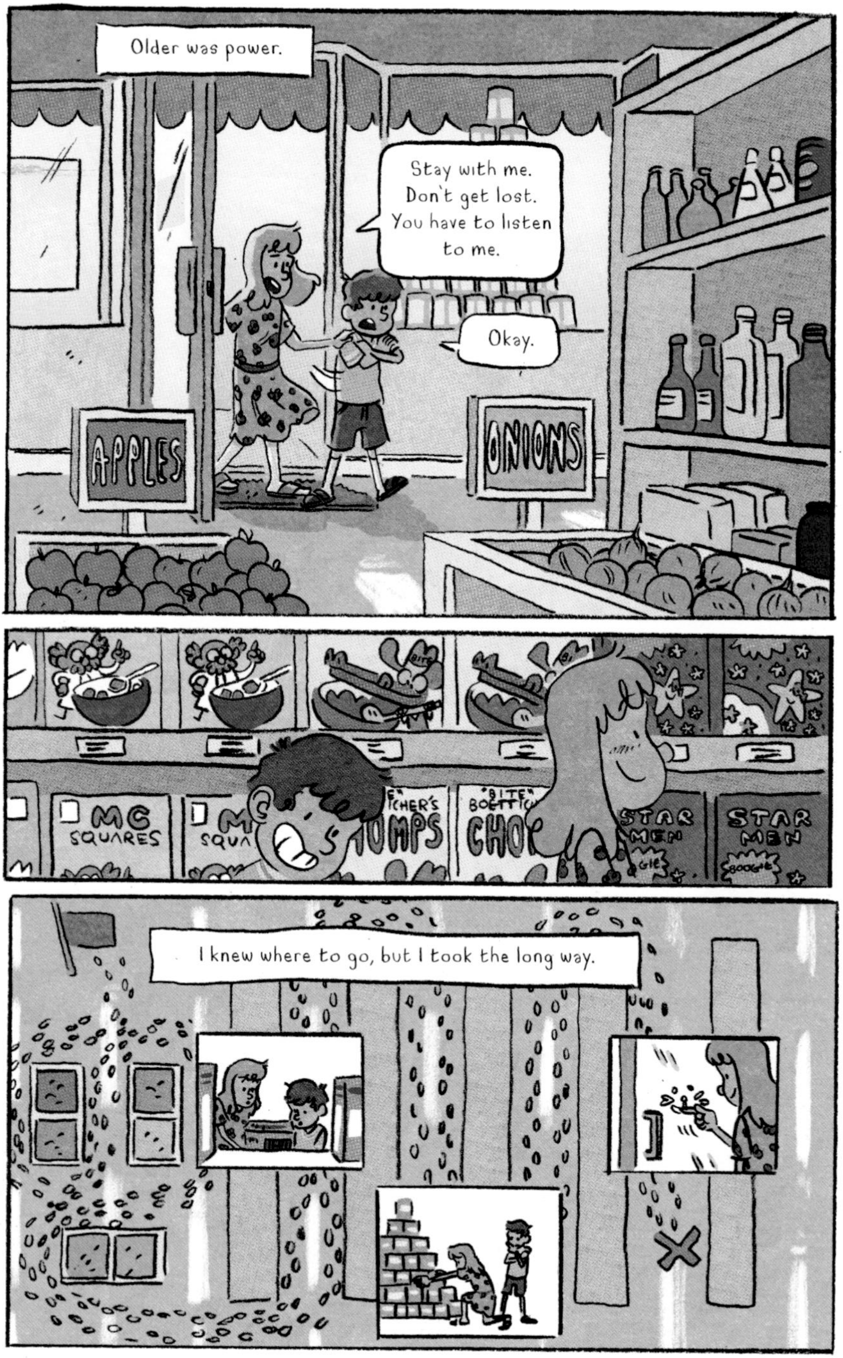

Older was power.
APPLES
ONIONS
Stay with me. Don't get lost. You have to listen to me.
Okay.
MC SQUARES
STAR MEN
STAR MEN
I knew where to go, but I took the long way.

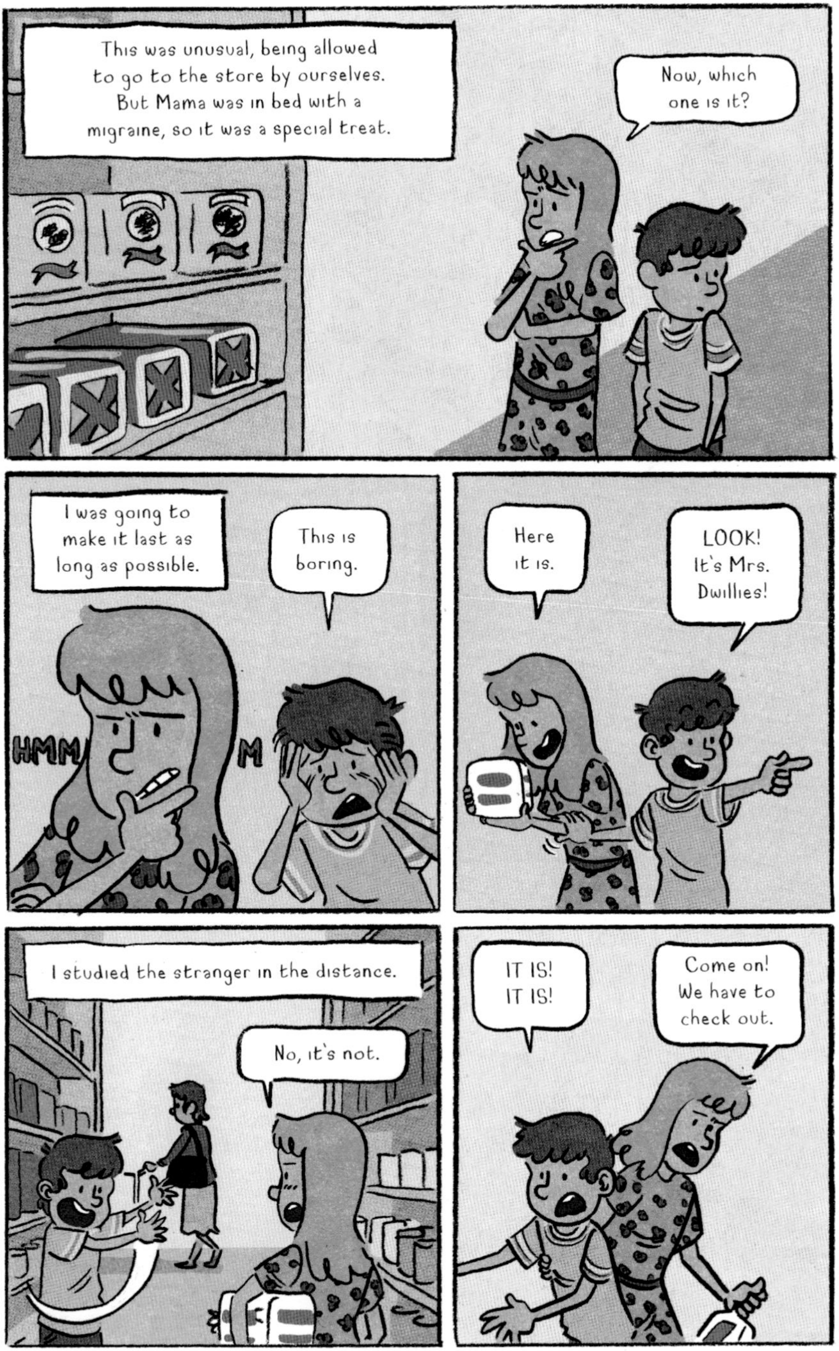
This was unusual, being allowed to go to the store by ourselves. But Mama was in bed with a migraine, so it was a special treat.
Now, which one is it?
I was going to make it last as long as possible.
This is boring.
HMMM
Here it is.
LOOK! It's Mrs. Dwillies!
I studied the stranger in the distance.
No, it's not.
IT IS! IT IS!
Come on! We have to check out.

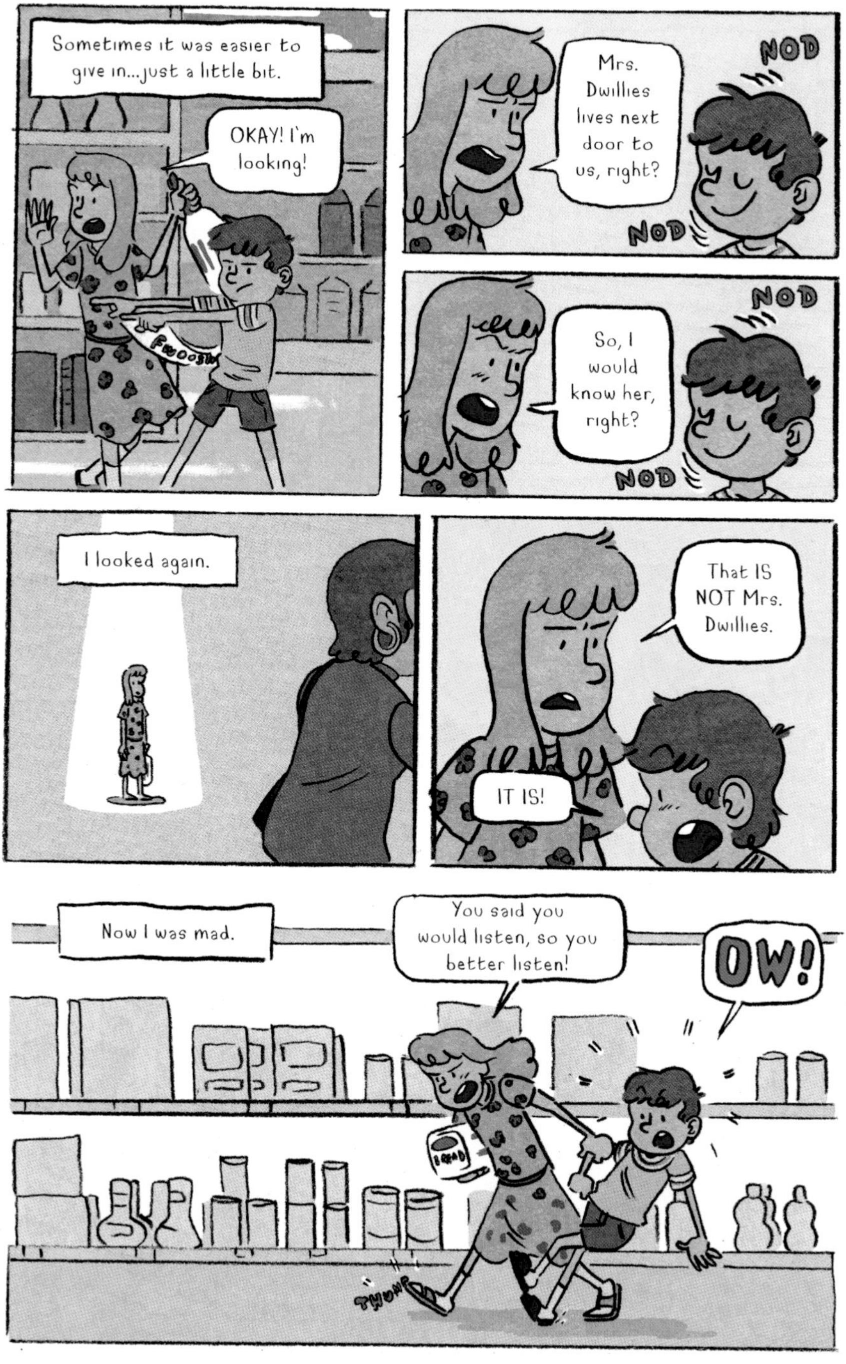
Sometimes it was easier to give in...just a little bit.
OKAY! I'm looking!
Mrs. Dwillies lives next door to us, right?
NOD
NOD
So, I would know her, right?
NOD
NOD
I looked again.
That IS NOT Mrs. Dwillies.
IT IS!
Now I was mad.
You said you would listen, so you better listen!
OW!

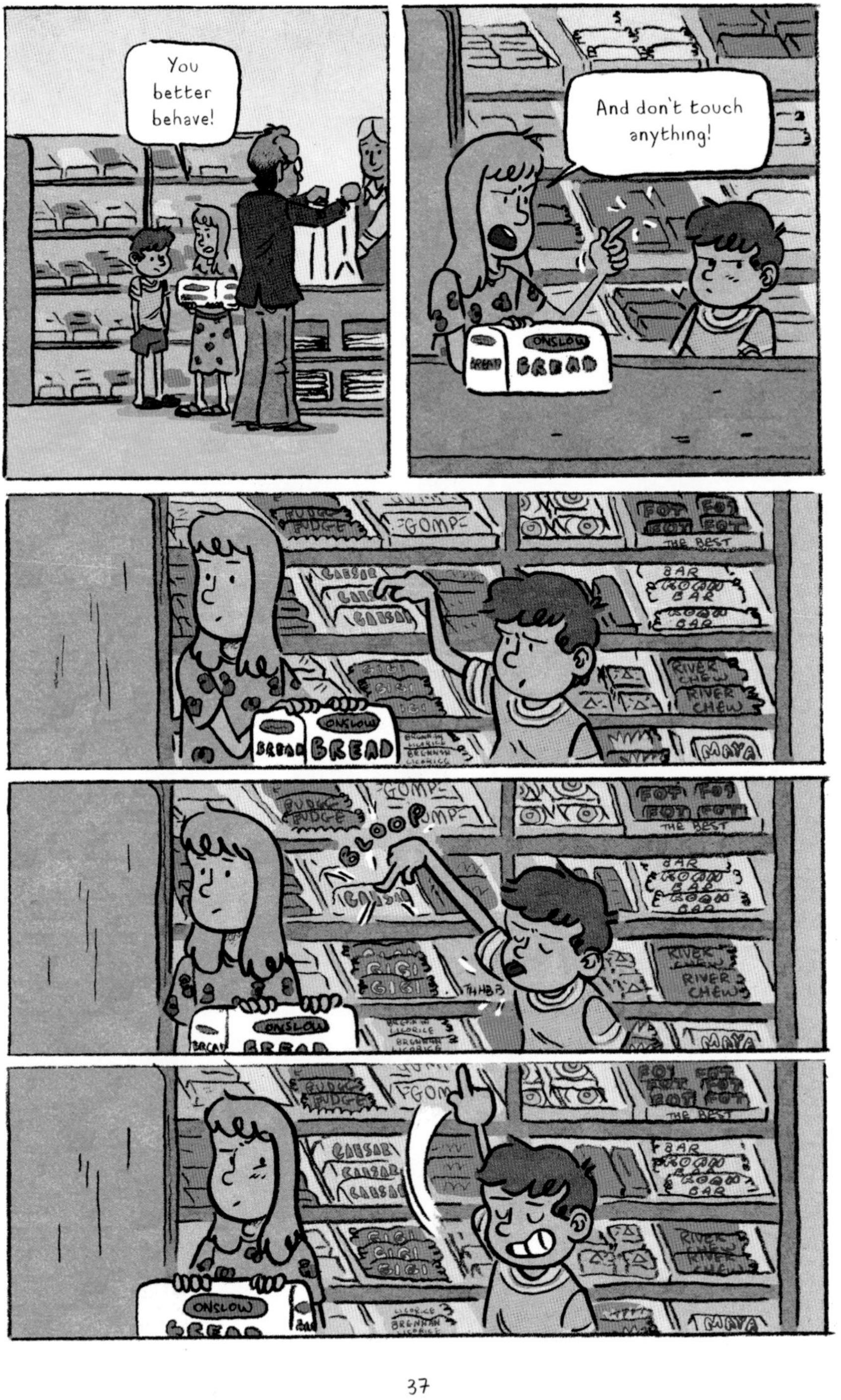
You better behave!
And don't touch anything!
ONSLOW
BREAD
GOMP
FUDGE
CAESAR
GIGI
FOT
THE BEST
BAR
RIVER CHEW
MAYA
BRENNAN LICORICE
BLOOP
THBB

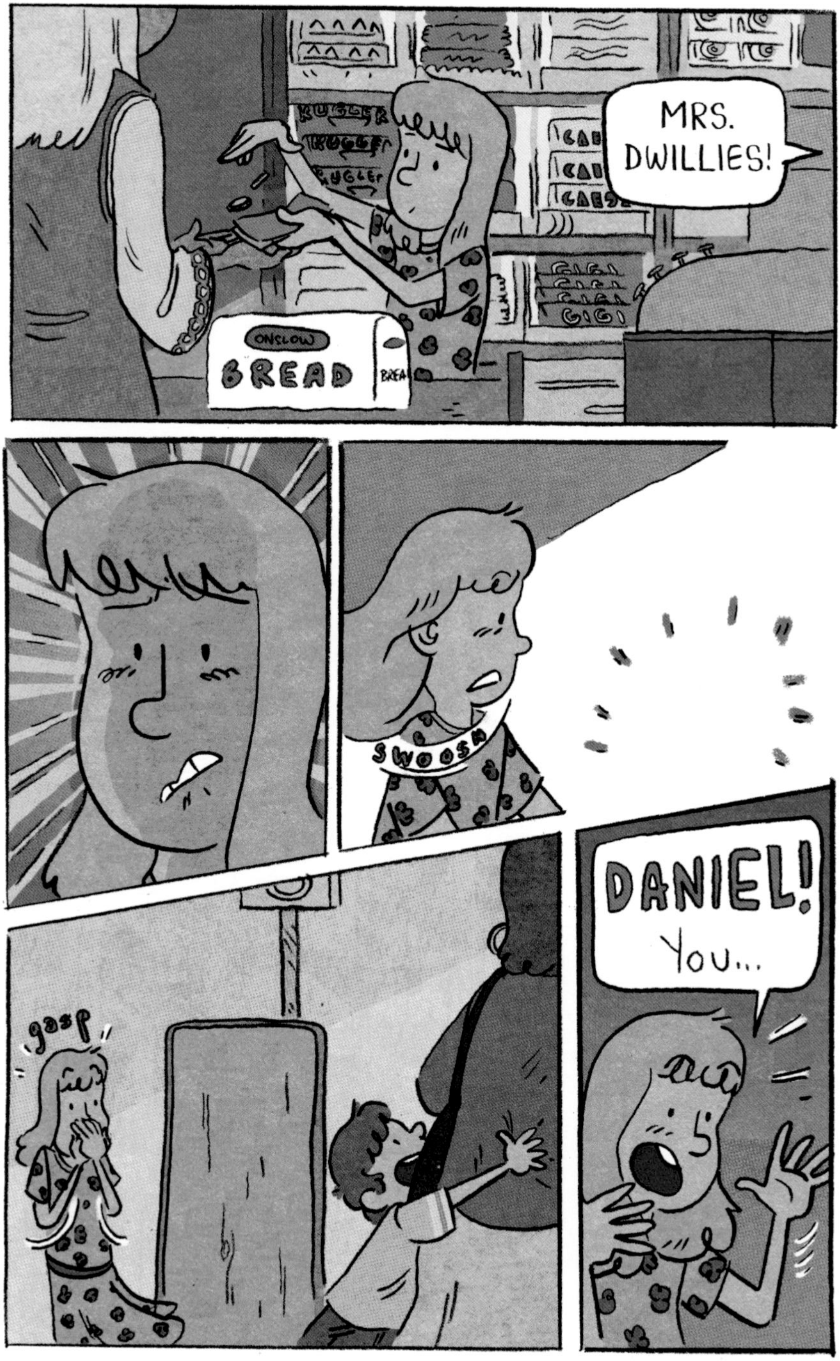
MRS. DWILLIES!
ONSLOW
BREAD
SWOOSH
gasp
DANIEL!
You...

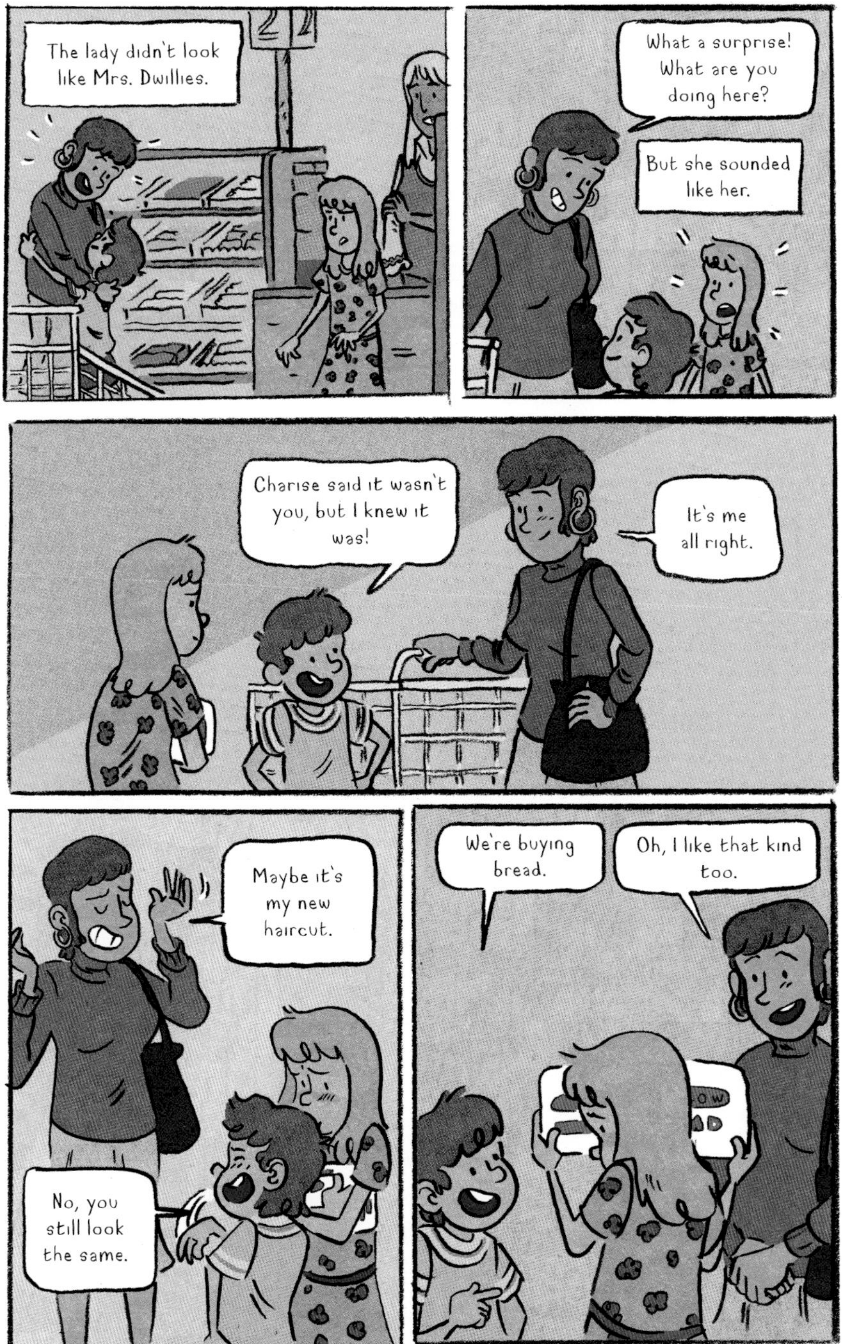
The lady didn't look like Mrs. Dwillies.
What a surprise! What are you doing here?
But she sounded like her.
Charise said it wasn't you, but I knew it was!
It's me all right.
Maybe it's my new haircut.
No, you still look the same.
We're buying bread.
Oh, I like that kind too.

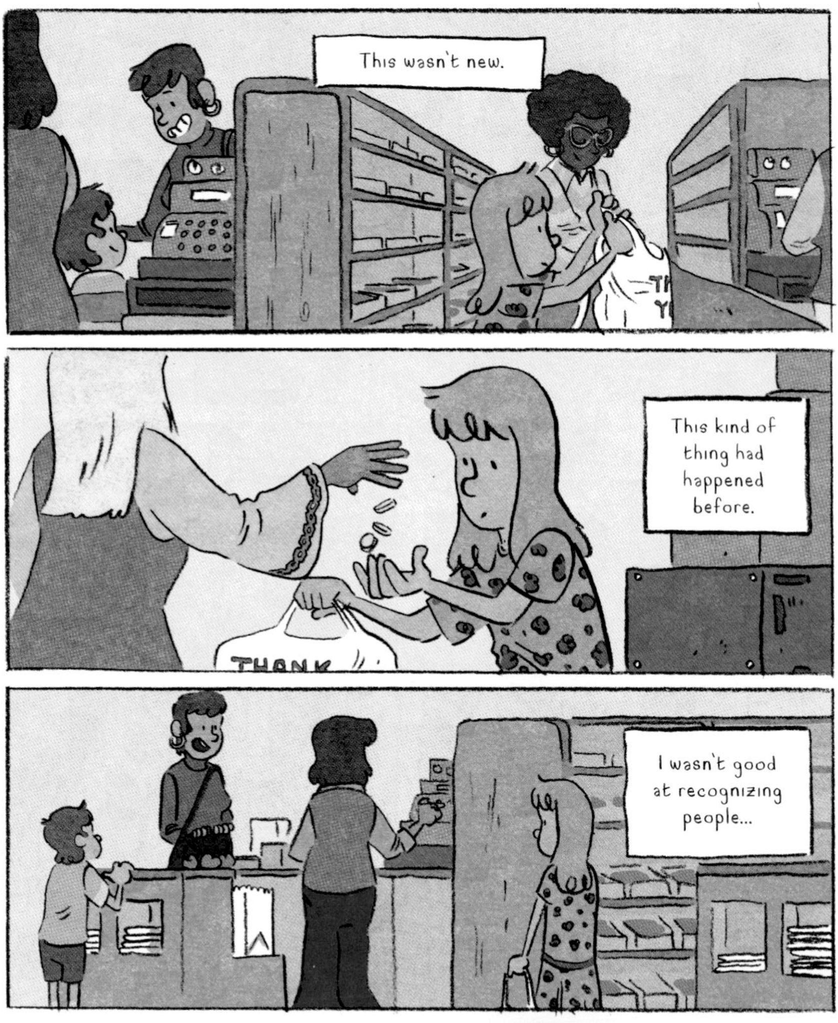
This wasn't new.
This kind of thing had happened before.
THANK
I wasn't good at recognizing people...
...but Daniel was.

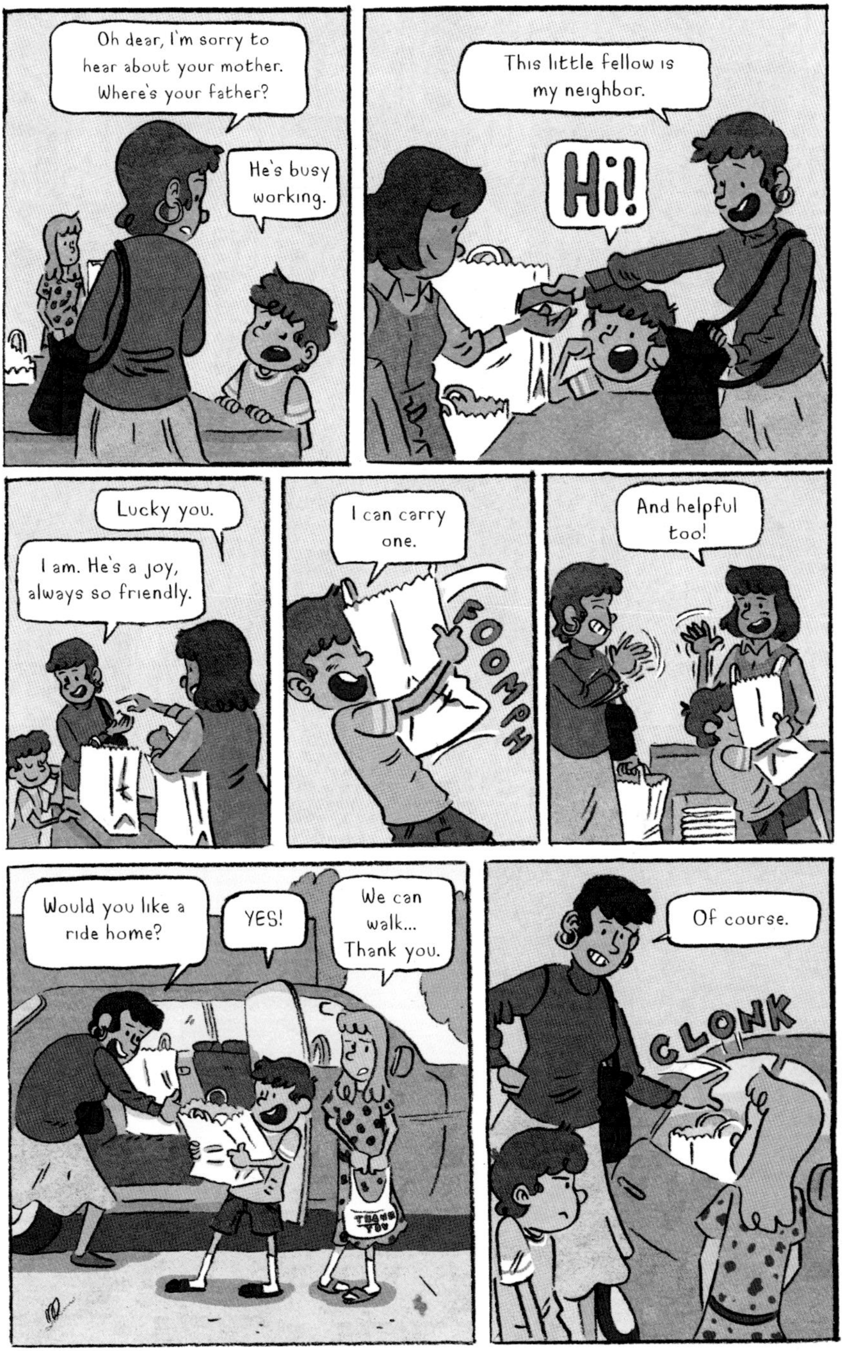

Oh dear, I'm sorry to hear about your mother. Where's your father?
He's busy working.
This little fellow is my neighbor.
Hi!
Lucky you.
I am. He's a joy, always so friendly.
I can carry one.
FOOOMPH
And helpful too!
Would you like a ride home?
YES!
We can walk... Thank you.
Of course.
CLONK

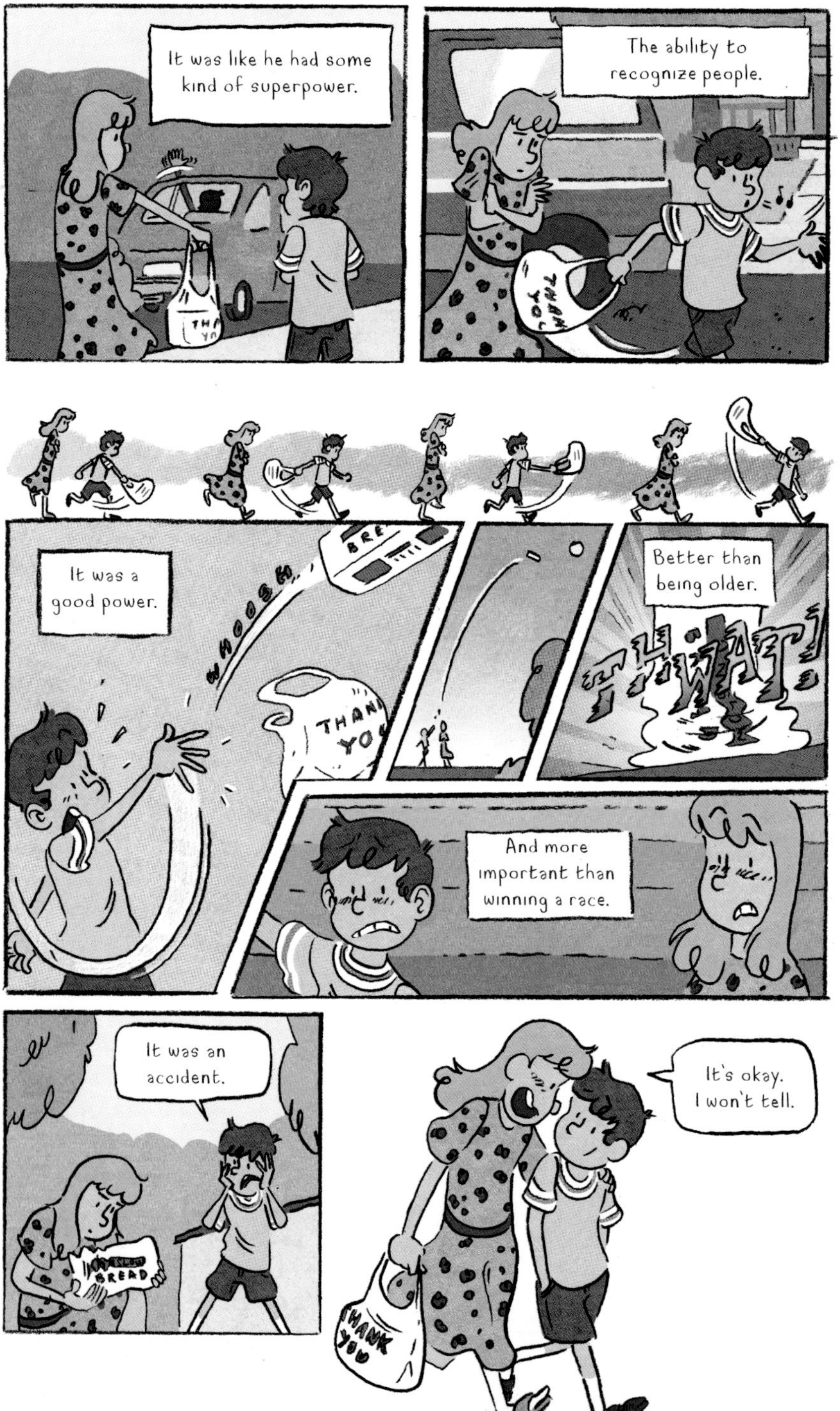
It was like he had some kind of superpower.
The ability to recognize people.
It was a good power.
WHOOSH...
THANK YOU
Better than being older.
THWAT!
And more important than winning a race.
It was an accident.
BREAD
It's okay. I won't tell.
THANK YOU

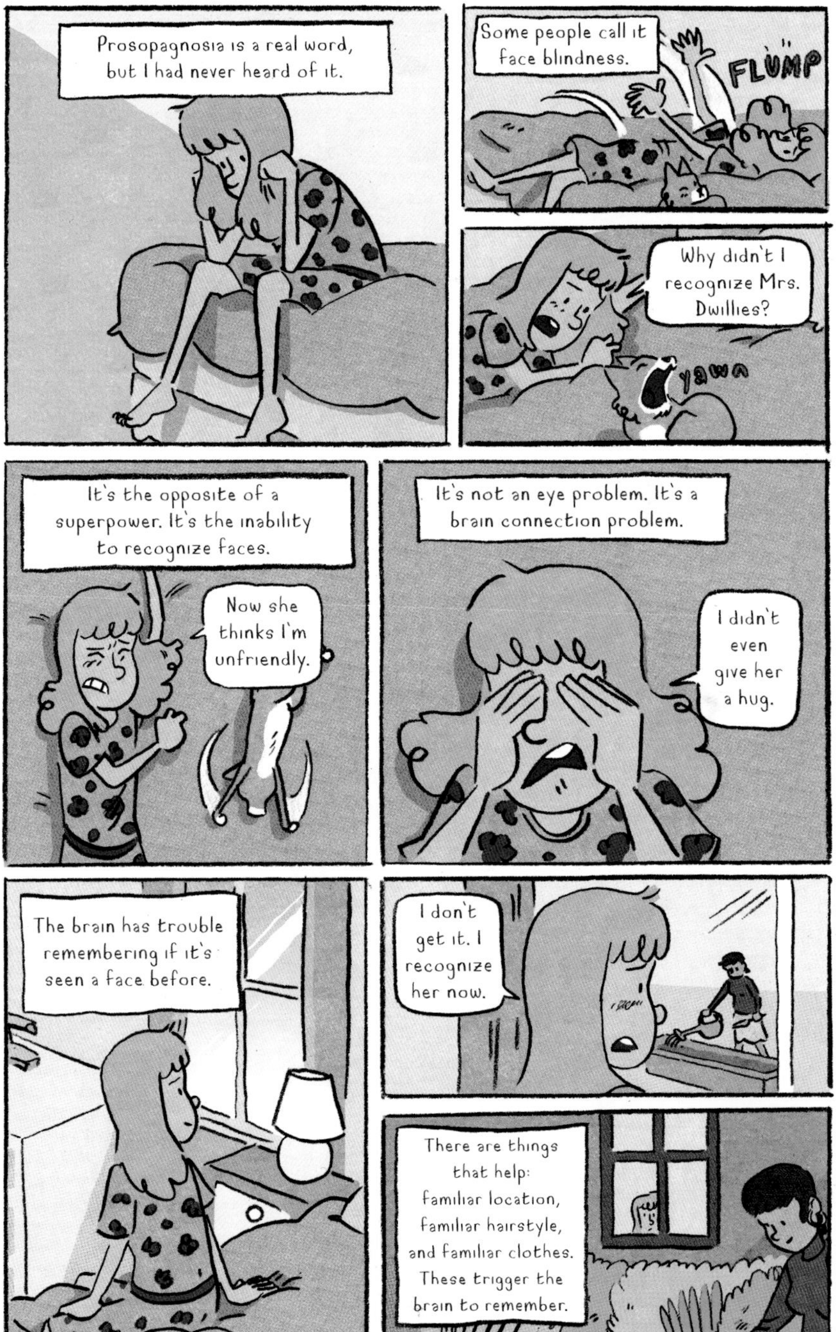
Prosopagnosia is a real word, but I had never heard of it.
Some people call it face blindness.
FLUMP
Why didn't I recognize Mrs. Dwillies?
yawn
It's the opposite of a superpower. It's the inability to recognize faces.
Now she thinks I'm unfriendly.
It's not an eye problem. It's a brain connection problem.
I didn't even give her a hug.
The brain has trouble remembering if it's seen a face before.
I don't get it. I recognize her now.
There are things that help: familiar location, familiar hairstyle, and familiar clothes. These trigger the brain to remember.

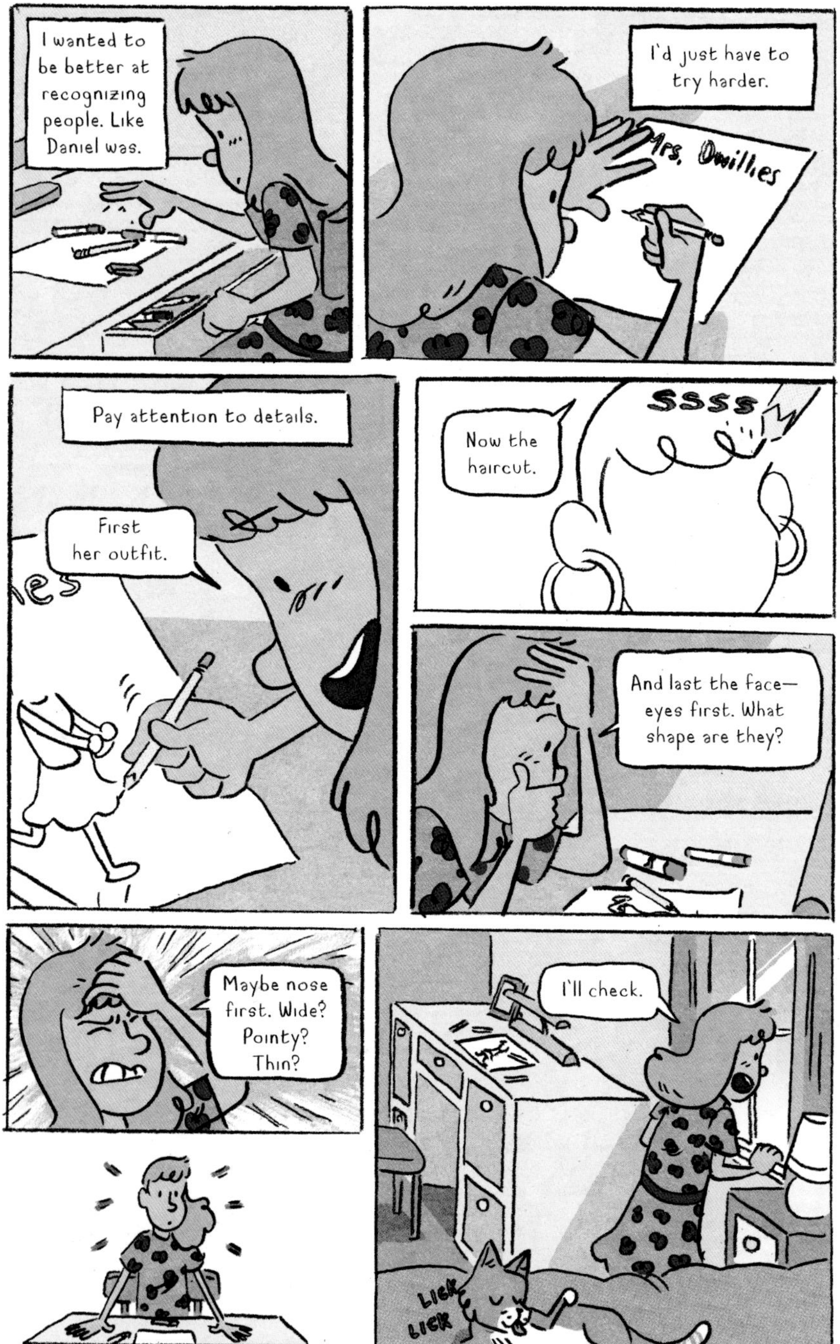
I wanted to be better at recognizing people. Like Daniel was.
I'd just have to try harder.
Mrs. Dwillies
Pay attention to details.
First her outfit.
Now the haircut.
SSSS
And last the face— eyes first. What shape are they?
Maybe nose first. Wide? Pointy? Thin?
I'll check.
LICK
LICK

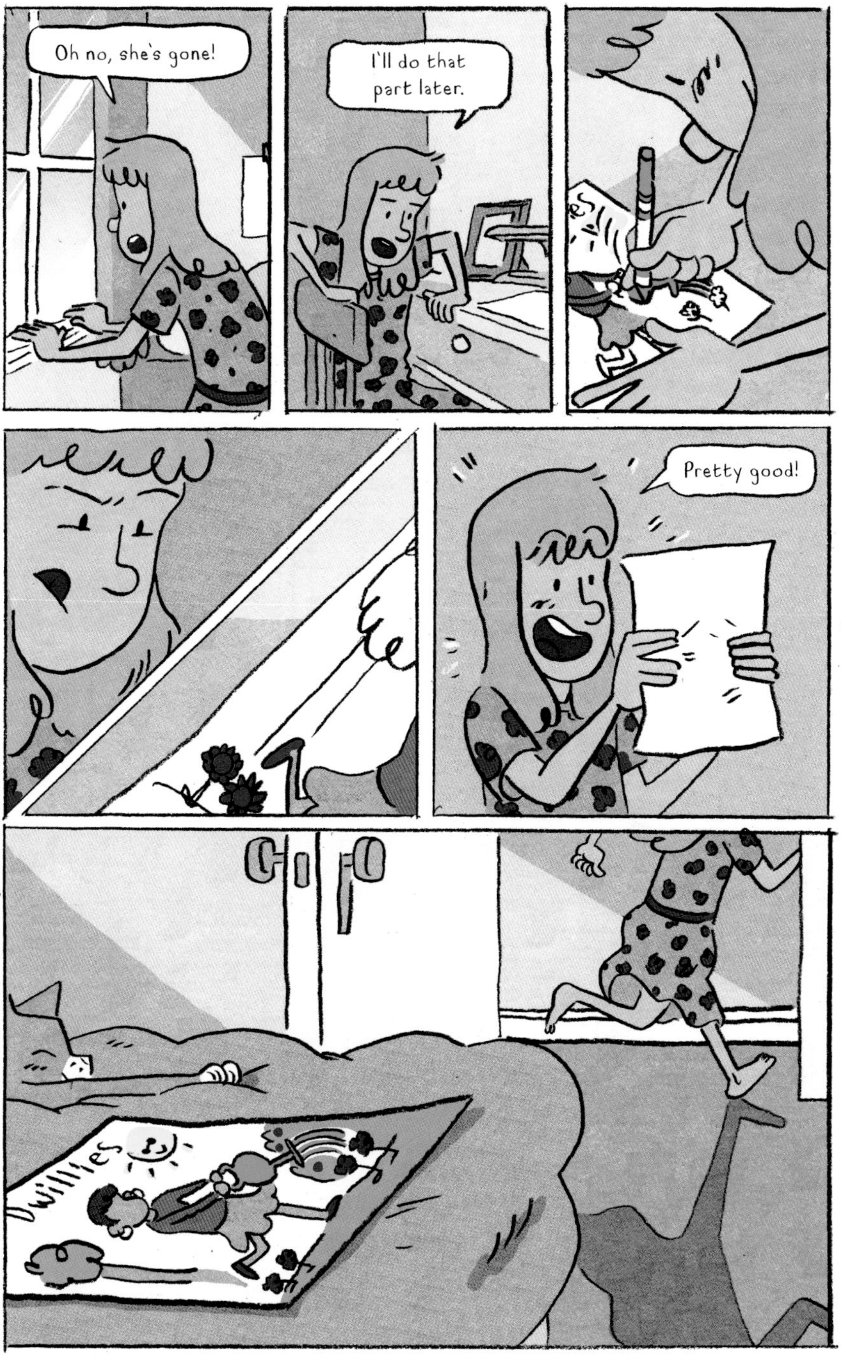
Oh no, she's gone!
I'll do that part later.
Pretty good!

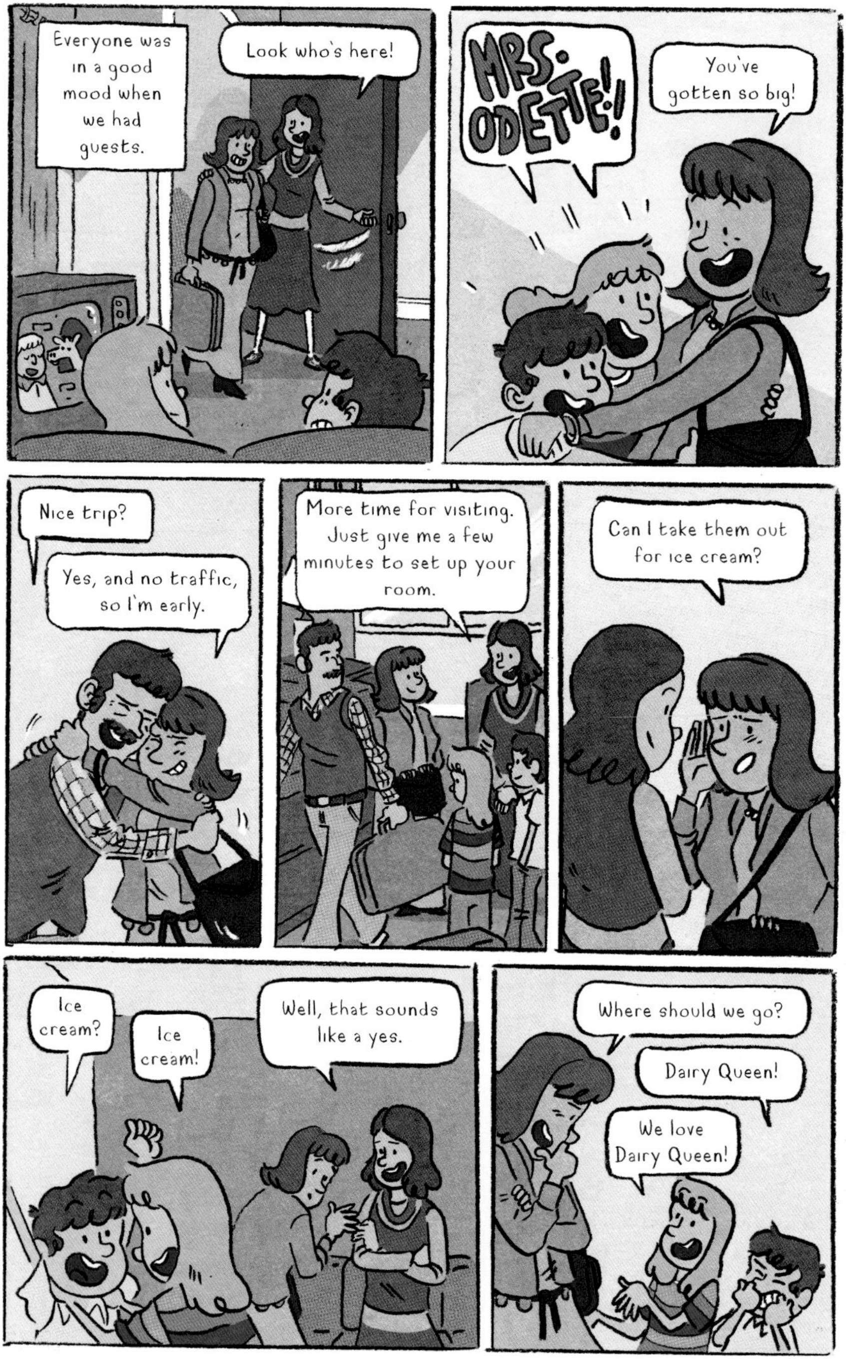
Everyone was in a good mood when we had guests.
Look who's here!
MRS. ODETTE!!
You've gotten so big!
Nice trip?
Yes, and no traffic, so I'm early.
More time for visiting. Just give me a few minutes to set up your room.
Can I take them out for ice cream?
Ice cream?
Ice cream!
Well, that sounds like a yes.
Where should we go?
Dairy Queen!
We love Dairy Queen!

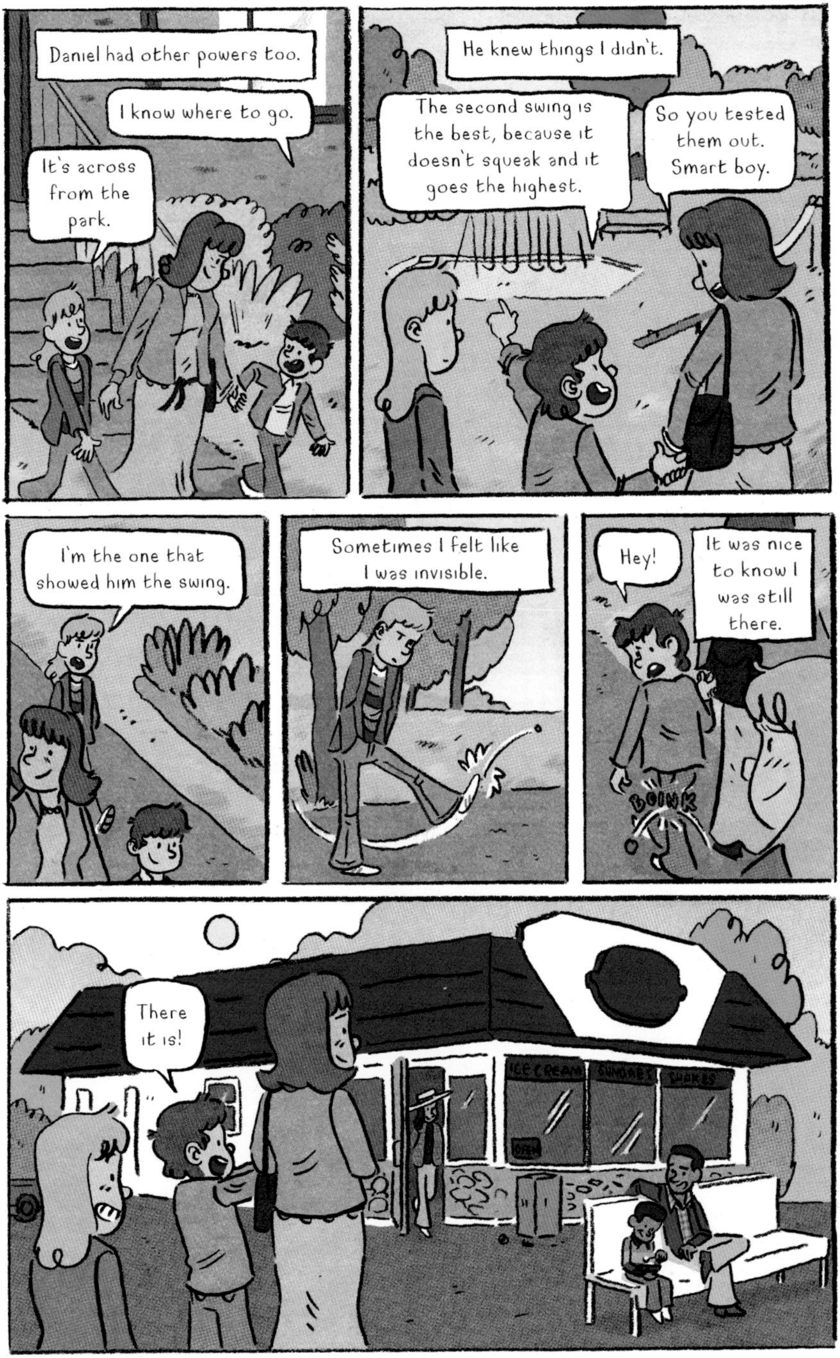
Daniel had other powers too.
I know where to go.
It's across from the park.
He knew things I didn't.
The second swing is the best, because it doesn't squeak and it goes the highest.
So you tested them out. Smart boy.
I'm the one that showed him the swing.
Sometimes I felt like I was invisible.
Hey!
It was nice to know I was still there.
BOINK
There it is!
ICE CREAM
SUNDAES
SHAKES

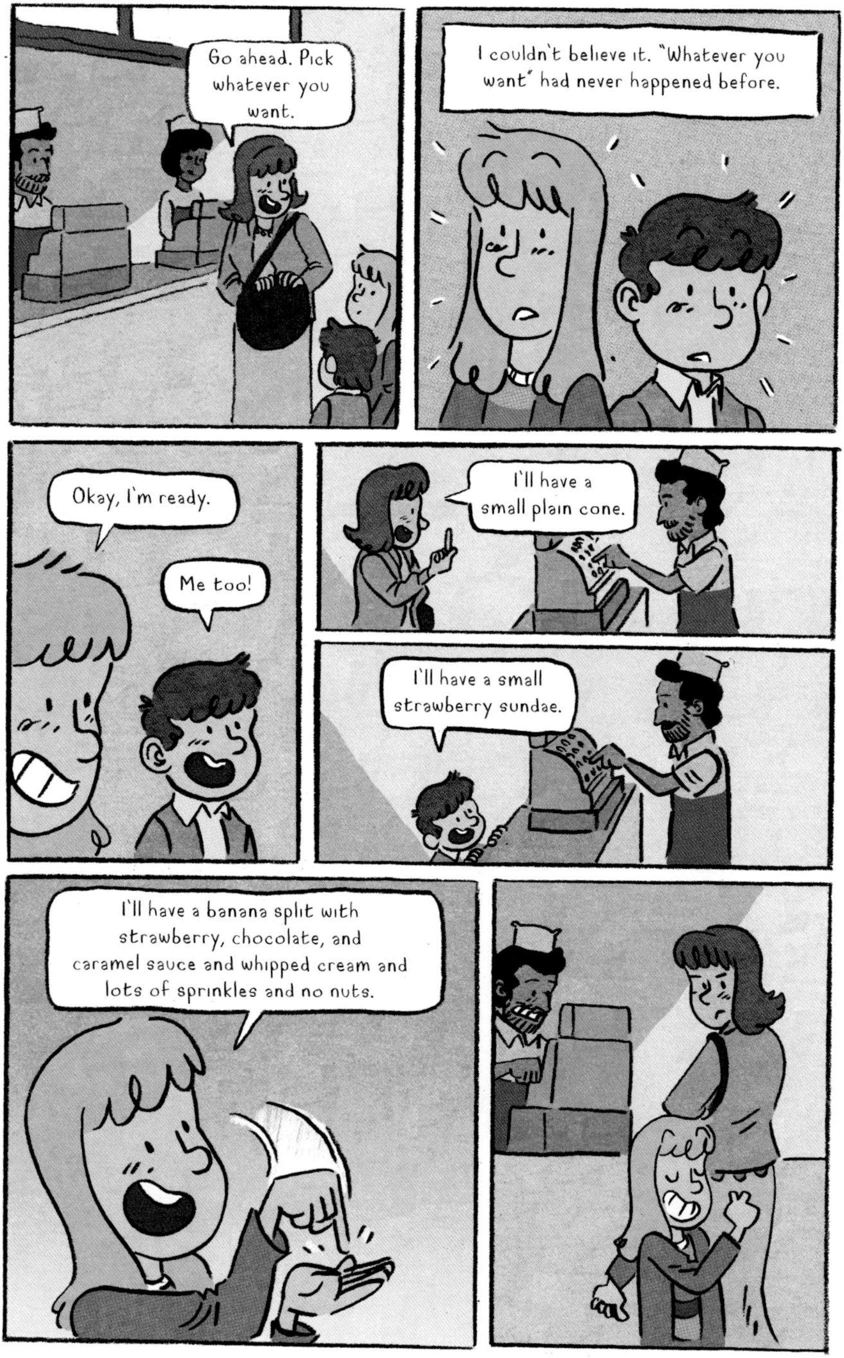
Go ahead. Pick whatever you want.
I couldn't believe it. "Whatever you want" had never happened before.
Okay, I'm ready.
Me too!
I'll have a small plain cone.
I'll have a small strawberry sundae.
I'll have a banana split with strawberry, chocolate, and caramel sauce and whipped cream and lots of sprinkles and no nuts.

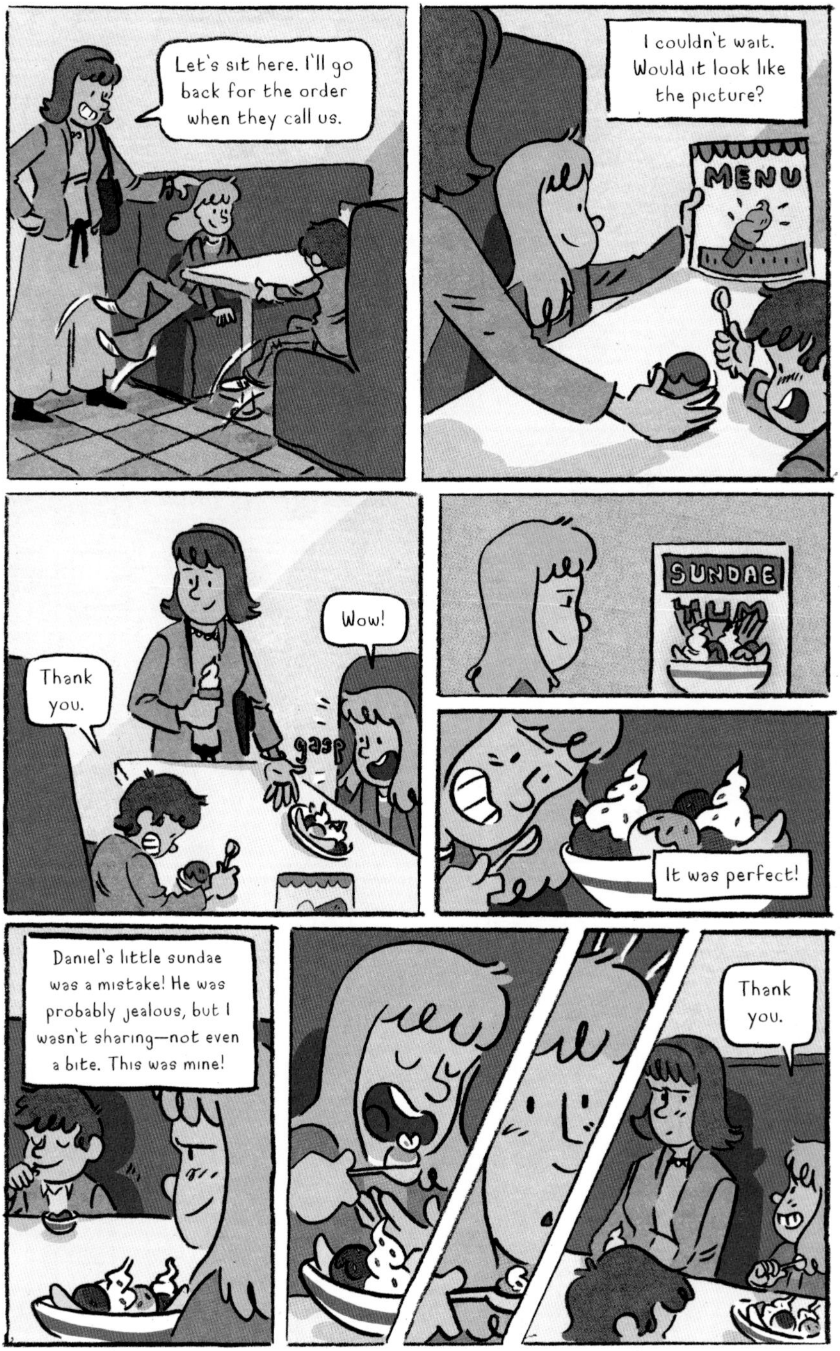
Let's sit here. I'll go back for the order when they call us.
I couldn't wait. Would it look like the picture?
MENU
Thank you.
Wow!
gasp
SUNDAE
It was perfect!
Daniel's little sundae was a mistake! He was probably jealous, but I wasn't sharing—not even a bite. This was mine!
Thank you.

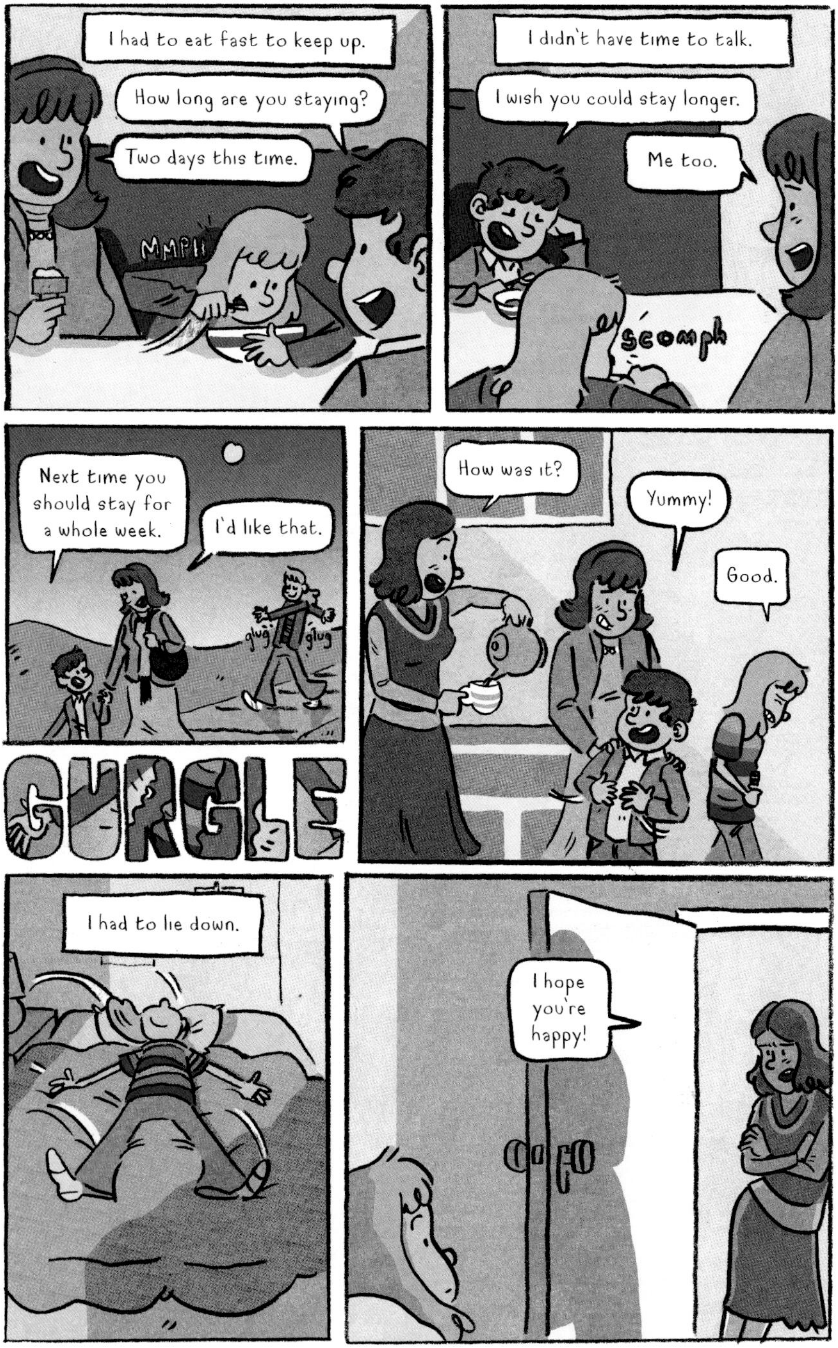
I had to eat fast to keep up.
How long are you staying?
Two days this time.
MMPH
I didn't have time to talk.
I wish you could stay longer.
Me too.
scomph
Next time you should stay for a whole week.
I'd like that.
glug
glug
GURGLE
How was it?
Yummy!
Good.
I had to lie down.
I hope you're happy!

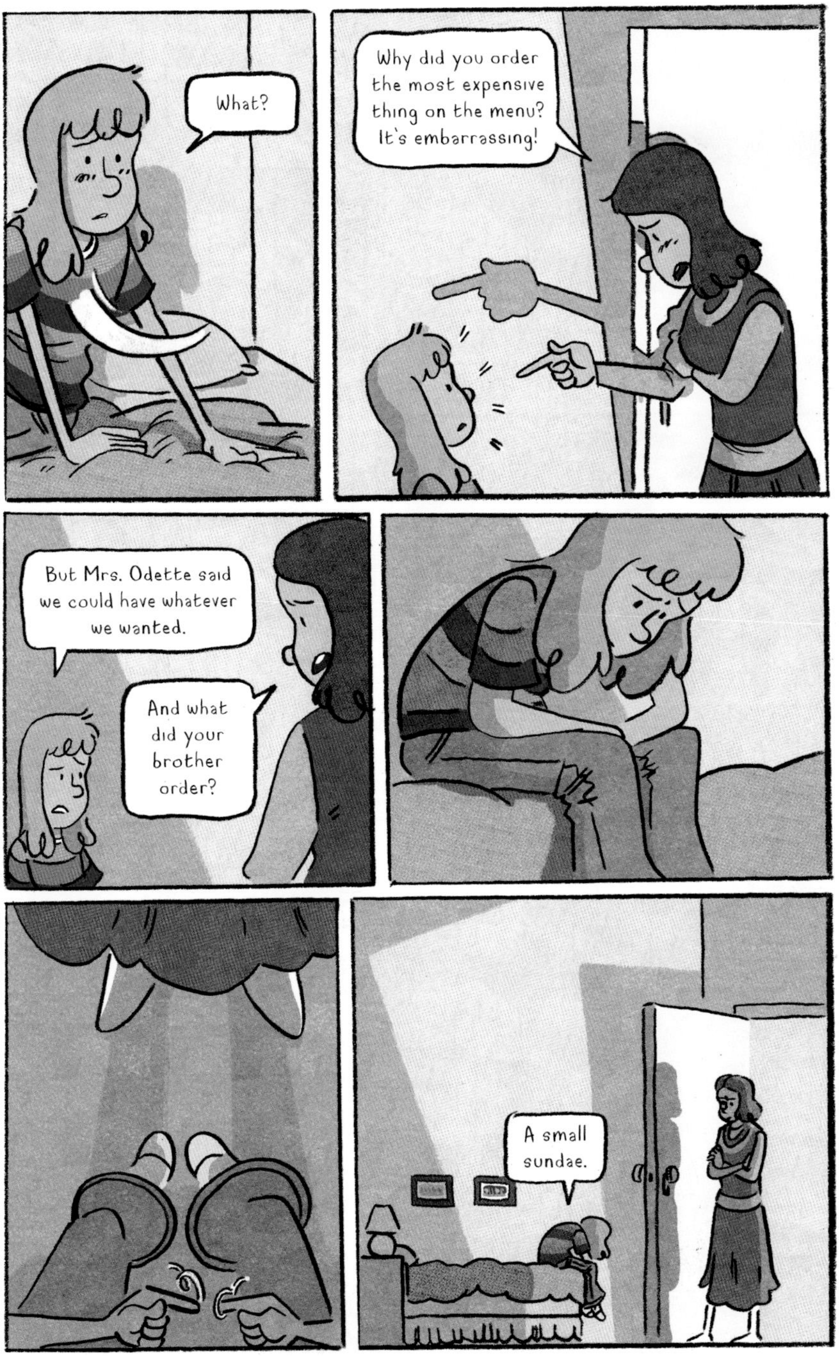
What?
Why did you order the most expensive thing on the menu? It's embarrassing!
But Mrs. Odette said we could have whatever we wanted.
And what did your brother order?
A small sundae.

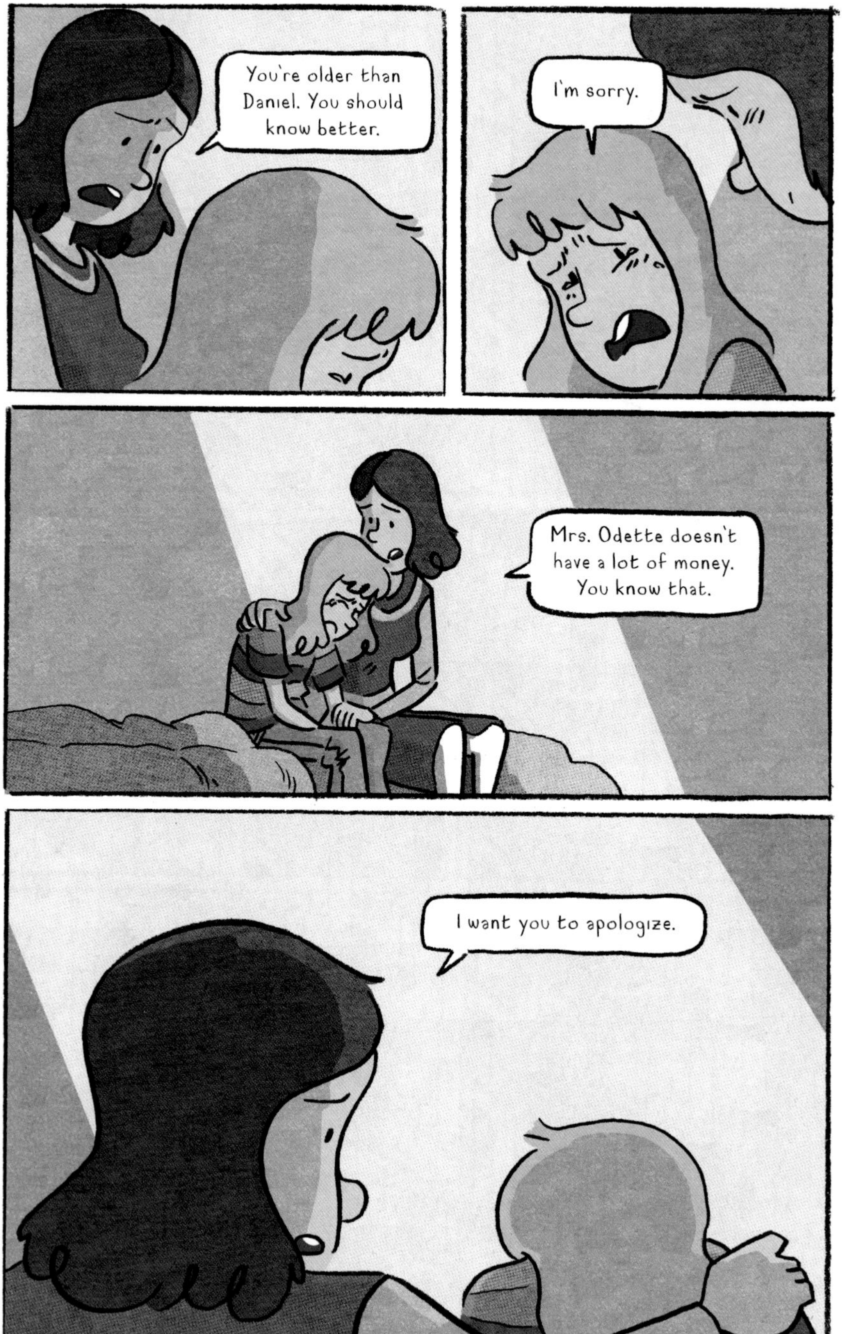
You're older than Daniel. You should know better.
I'm sorry.
Mrs. Odette doesn't have a lot of money. You know that.
I want you to apologize.

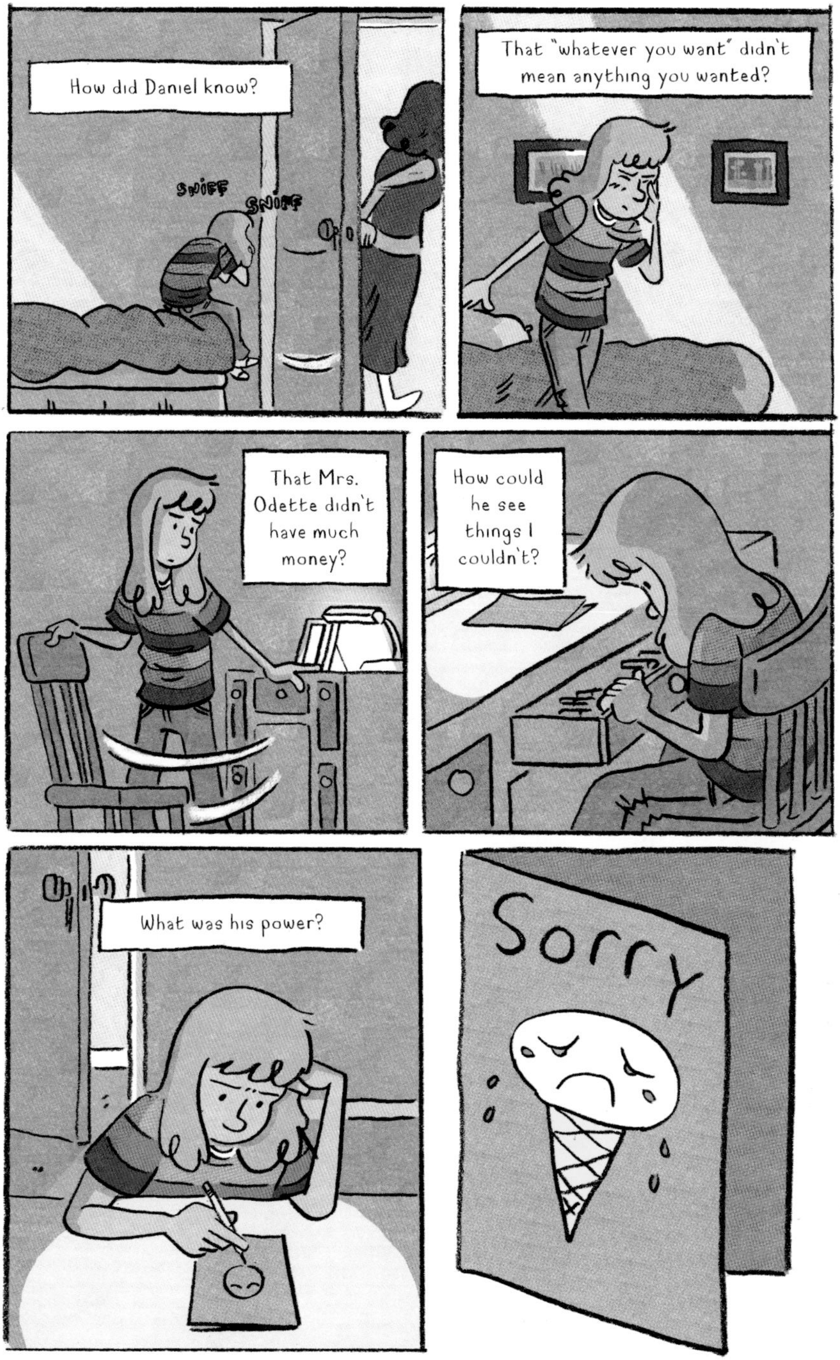
How did Daniel know?
SNIFF
SNIFF
That "whatever you want" didn't mean anything you wanted?
That Mrs. Odette didn't have much money?
How could he see things I couldn't?
What was his power?
Sorry

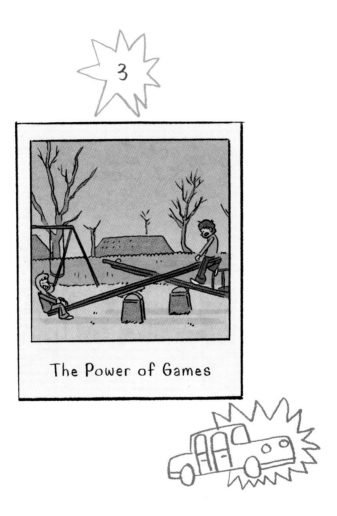

3

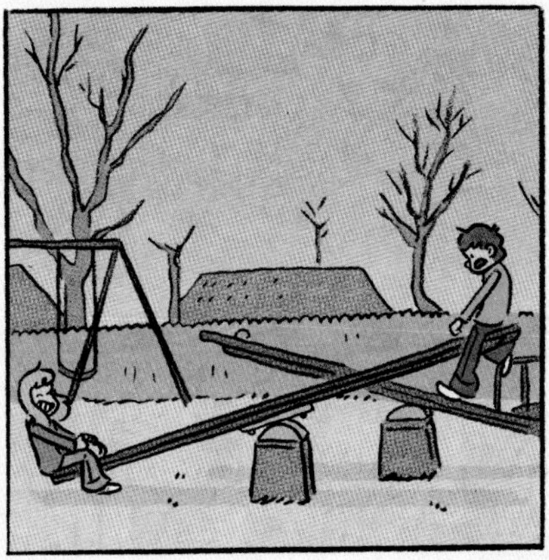

The Power of Games

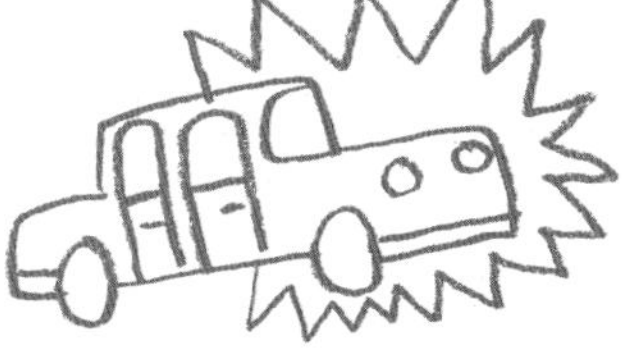

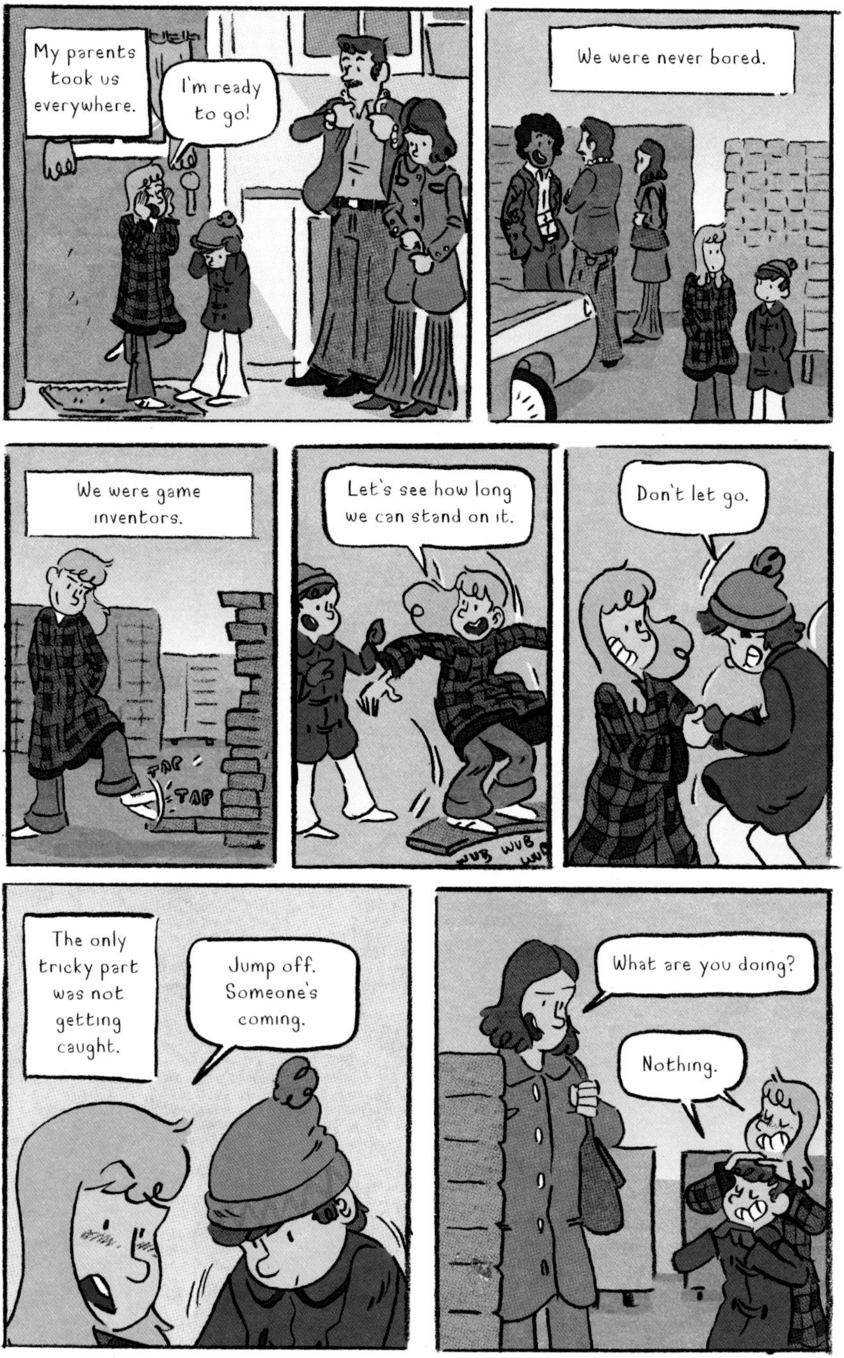
My parents took us everywhere.
I'm ready to go!
We were never bored.
We were game inventors.
TAP
TAP
Let's see how long we can stand on it.
WUB WUB
Don't let go.
The only tricky part was not getting caught.
Jump off. Someone's coming.
What are you doing?
Nothing.

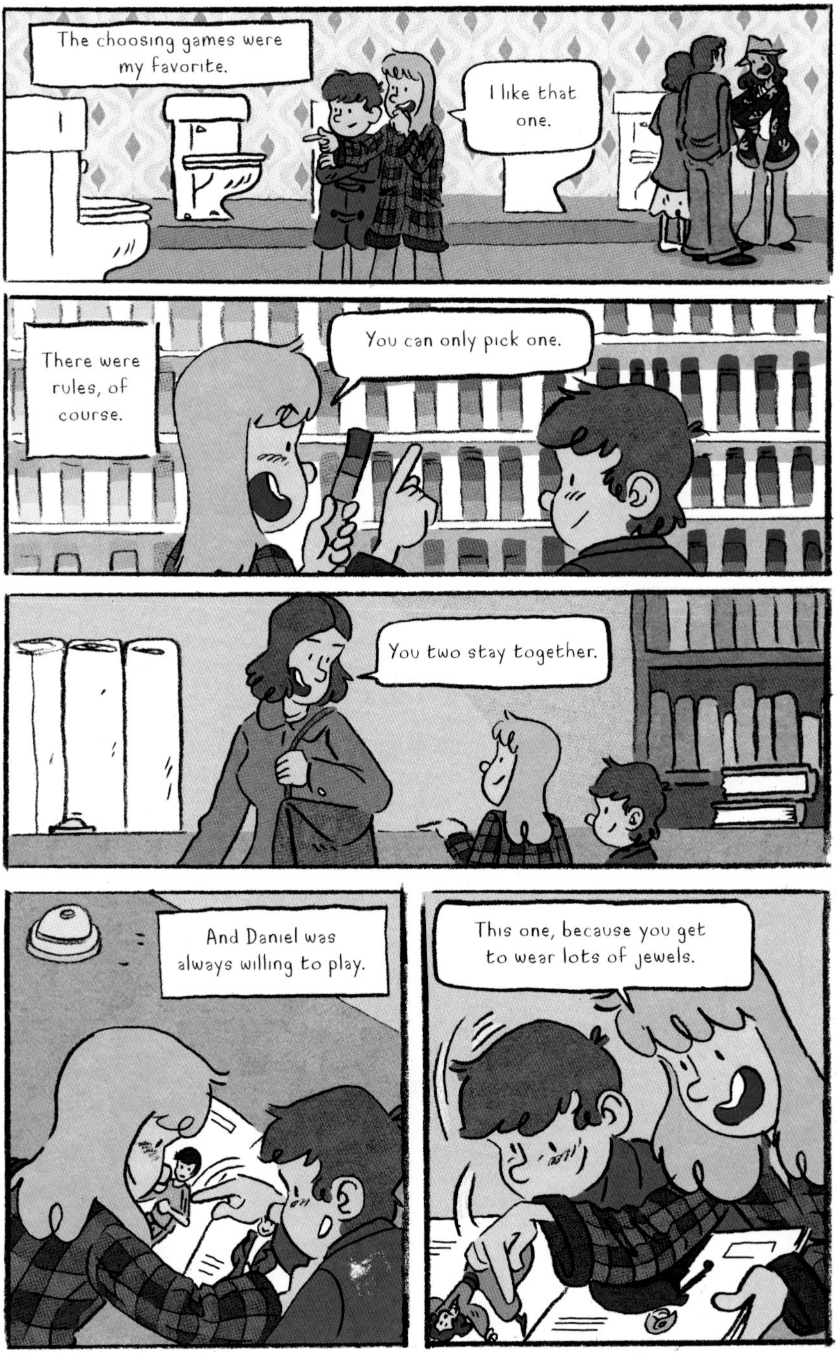
The choosing games were my favorite.
I like that one.
There were rules, of course.
You can only pick one.
You two stay together.
And Daniel was always willing to play.
This one, because you get to wear lots of jewels.

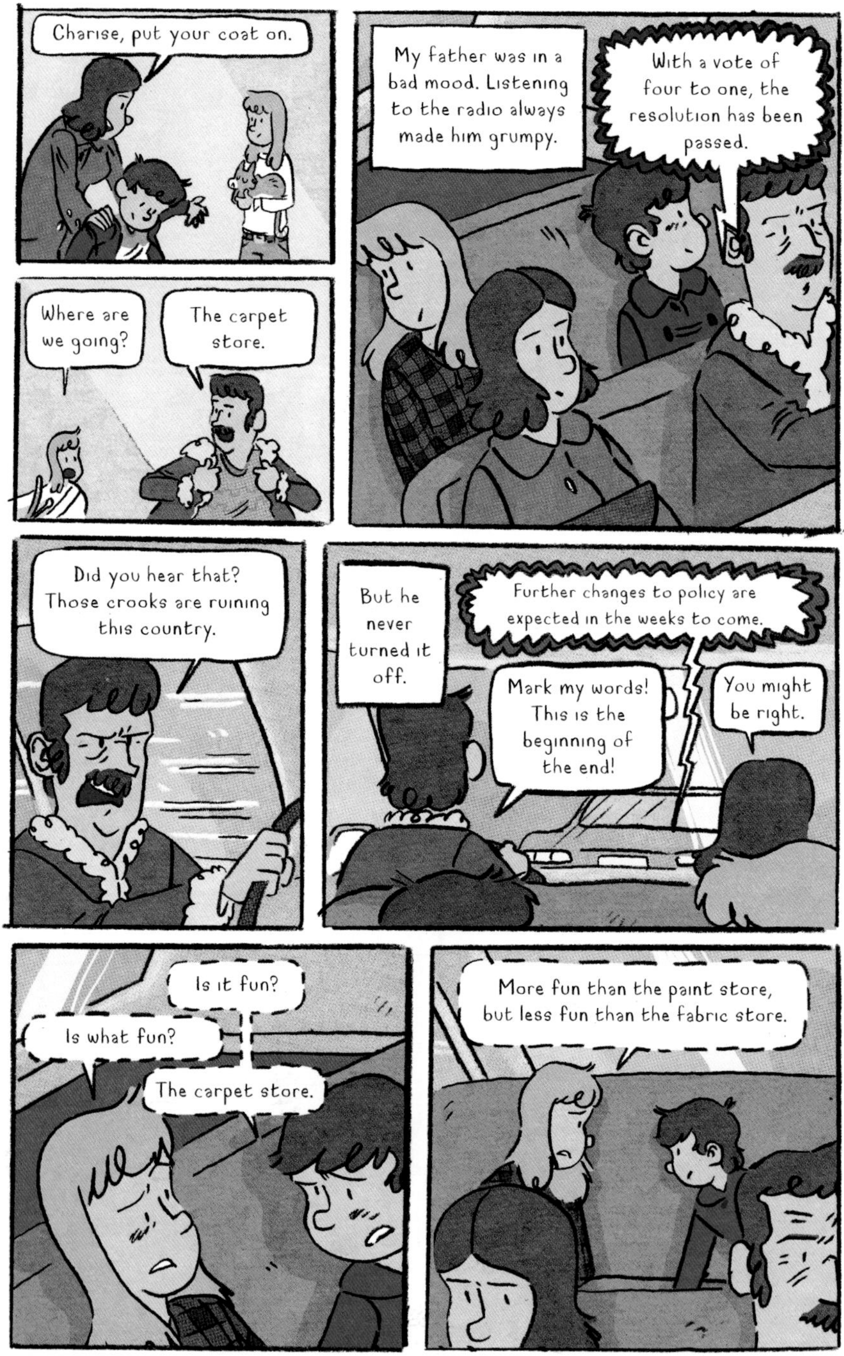
Charise, put your coat on.
Where are we going?
The carpet store.
My father was in a bad mood. Listening to the radio always made him grumpy.
With a vote of four to one, the resolution has been passed.
Did you hear that? Those crooks are ruining this country.
But he never turned it off.
Further changes to policy are expected in the weeks to come.
Mark my words! This is the beginning of the end!
You might be right.
Is it fun?
Is what fun?
The carpet store.
More fun than the paint store, but less fun than the fabric store.

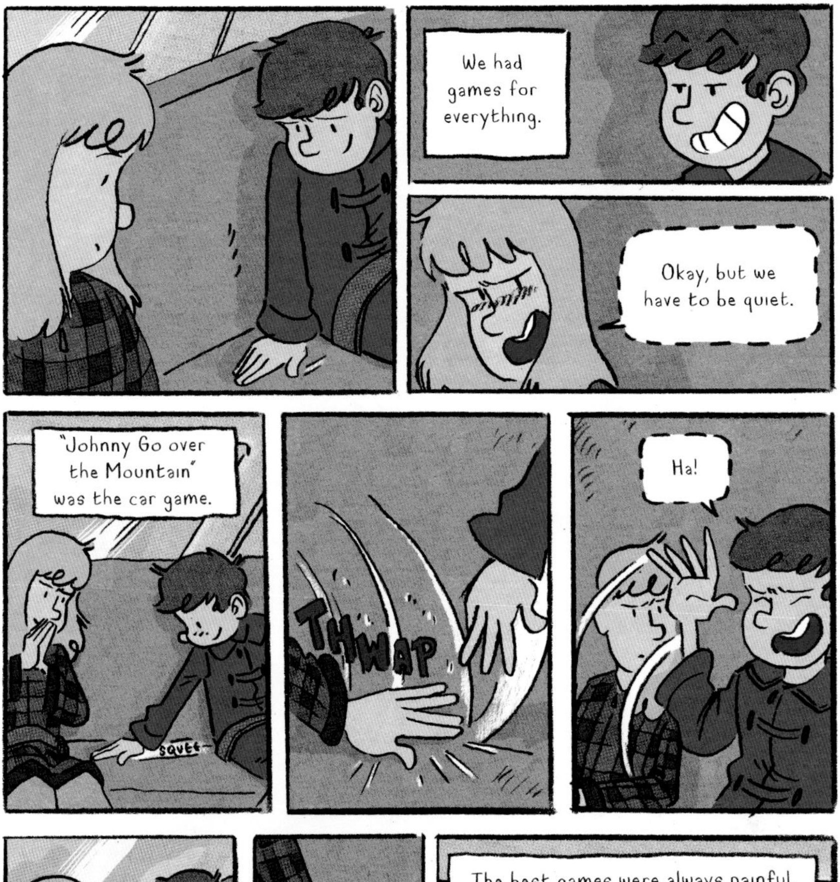

We had games for everything.
Okay, but we have to be quiet.
"Johnny Go over the Mountain" was the car game.
SQUEE
THWAP
Ha!
CRAAACK!!!
The best games were always painful.
YAH!
Eeeh!
TWINKLE

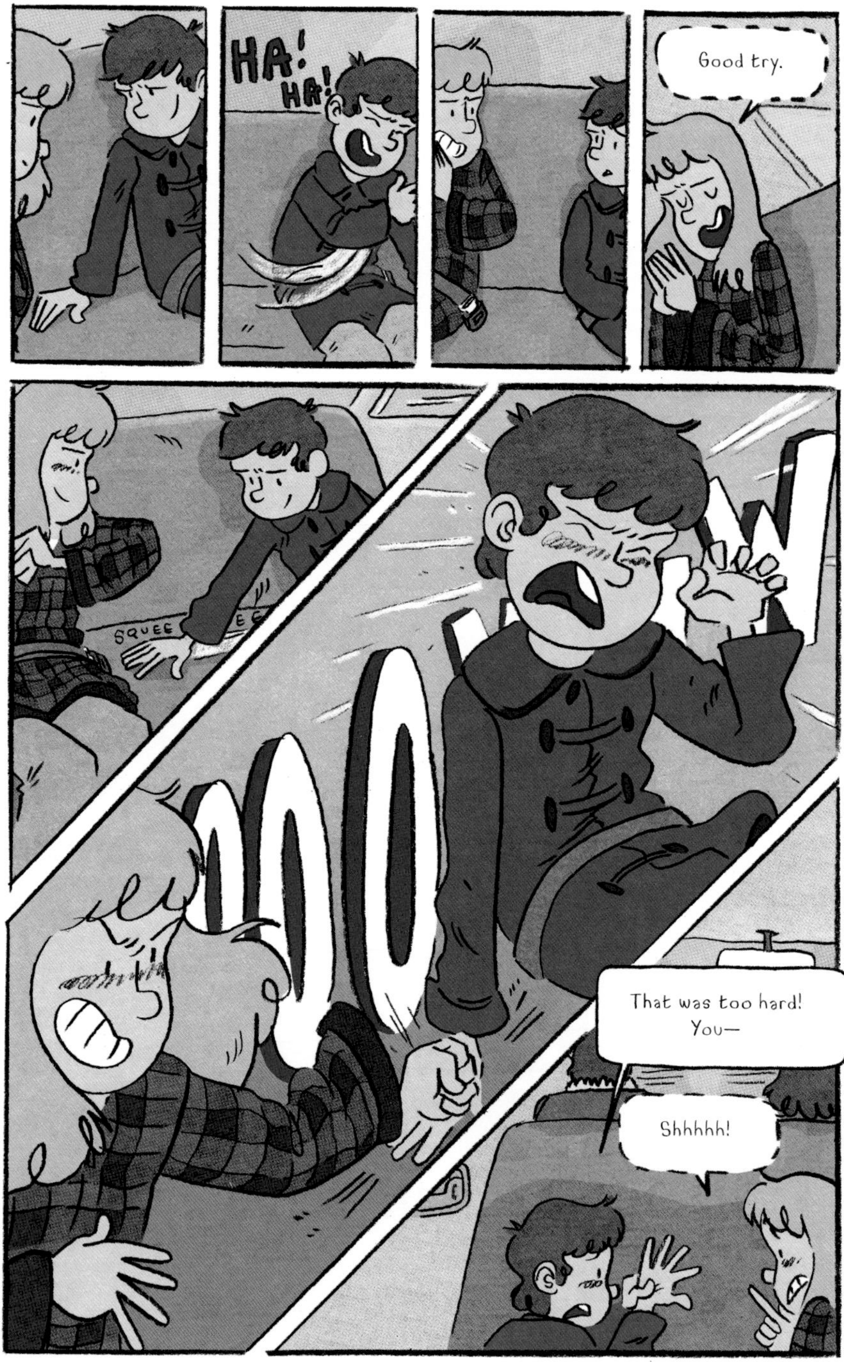
HA! HA!
Good try.
SQUEE
That was too hard! You—
Shhhhh!

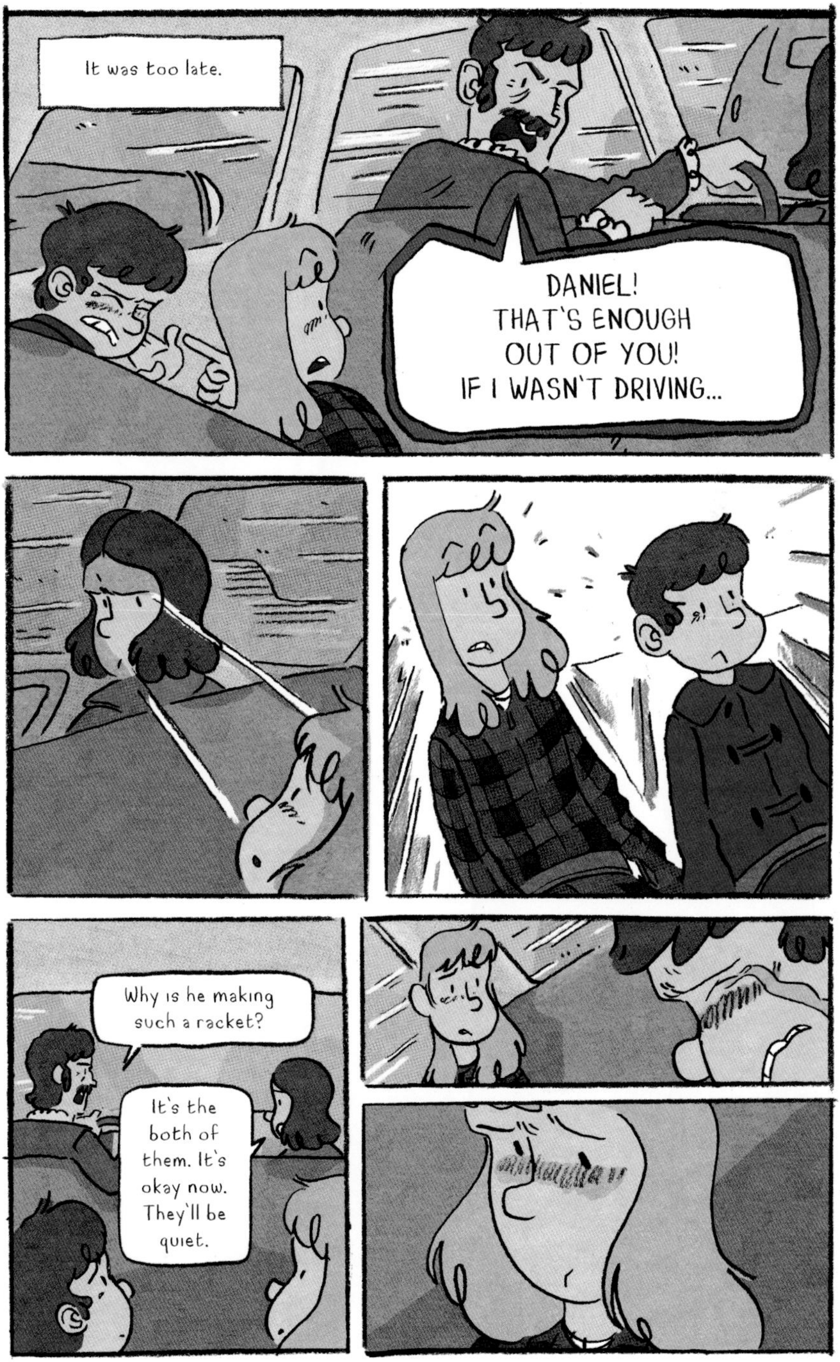
It was too late.
DANIEL! THAT'S ENOUGH OUT OF YOU! IF I WASN'T DRIVING...
Why is he making such a racket?
It's the both of them. It's okay now. They'll be quiet.

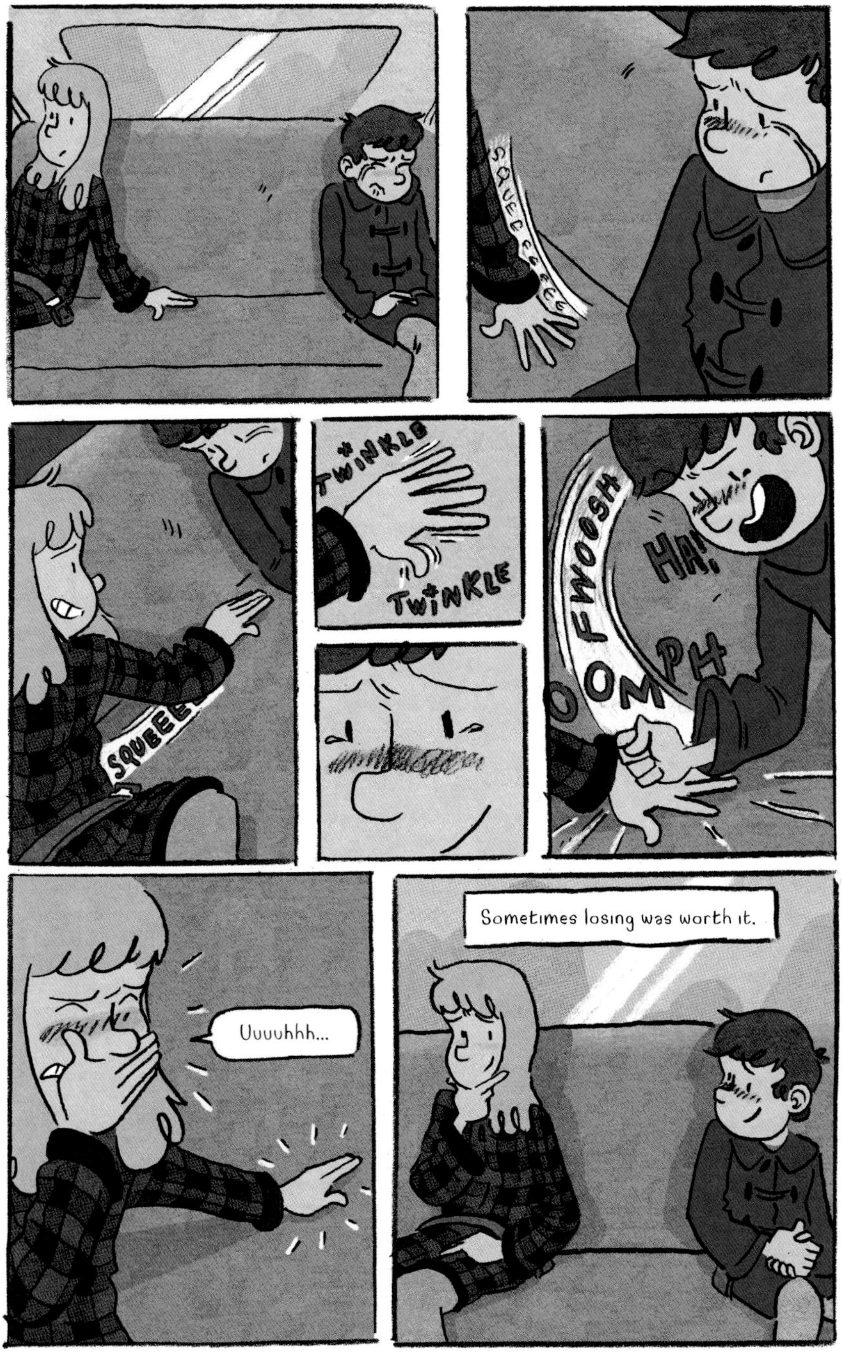
SQUEEEEEEE
SQUEEEE
TWINKLE
TWINKLE
FWOOSH
HA!
OOMPH
Uuuuhhh...
Sometimes losing was worth it.

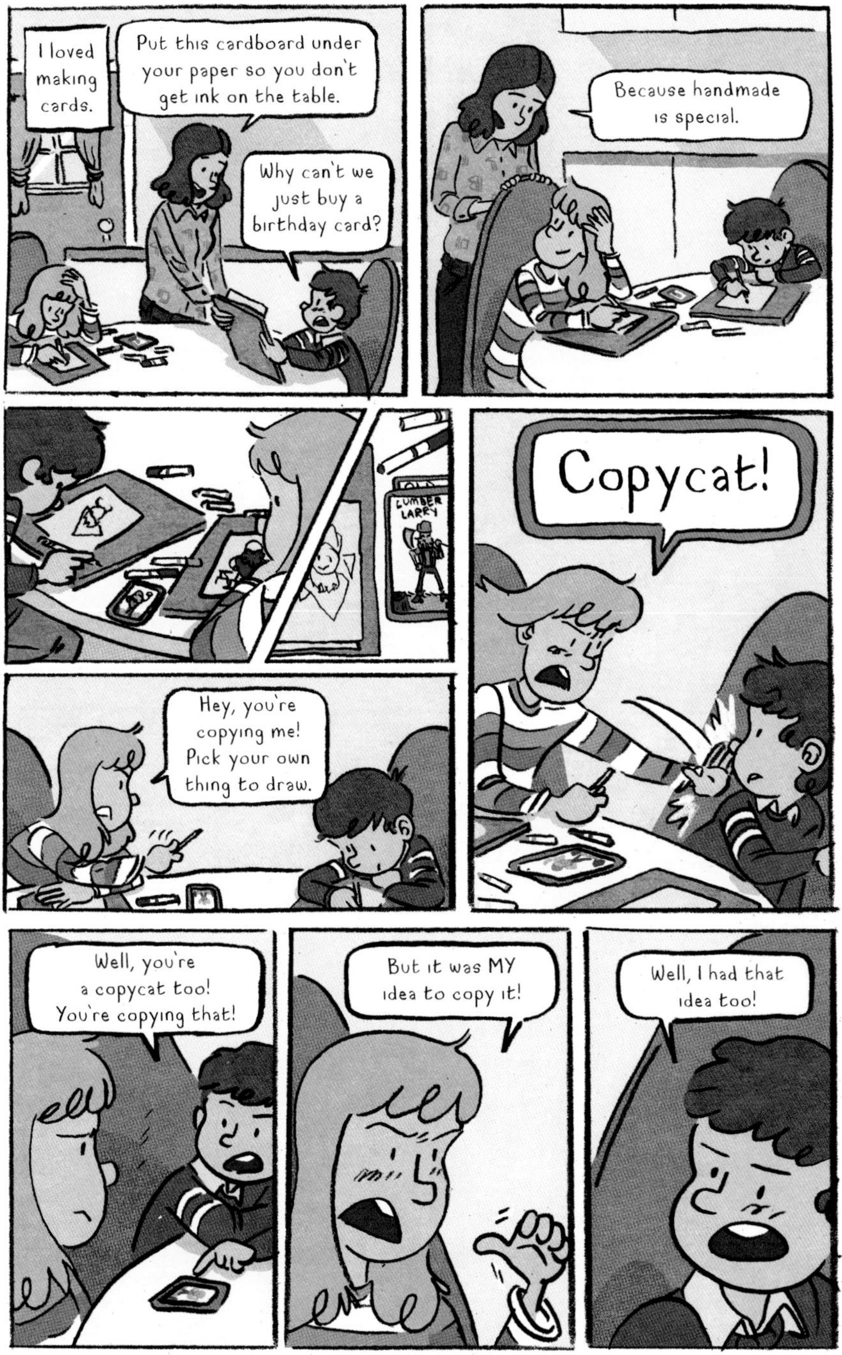
I loved making cards.
Put this cardboard under your paper so you don't get ink on the table.
Why can't we just buy a birthday card?
Because handmade is special.
LUMBER LARRY
Copycat!
Hey, you're copying me! Pick your own thing to draw.
Well, you're a copycat too! You're copying that!
But it was MY idea to copy it!
Well, I had that idea too!

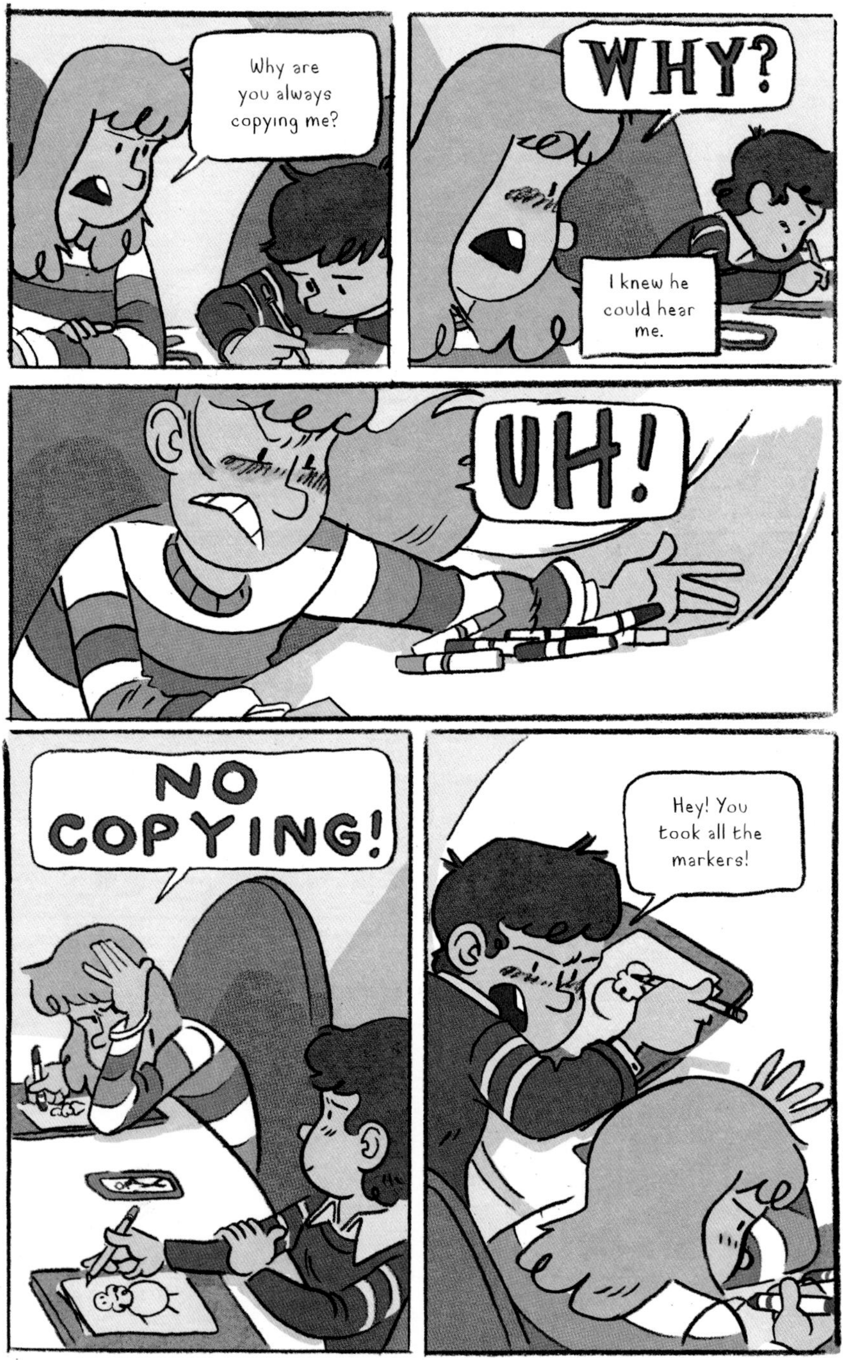
Why are you always copying me?
WHY?
I knew he could hear me.
UH!
NO COPYING!
Hey! You took all the markers!

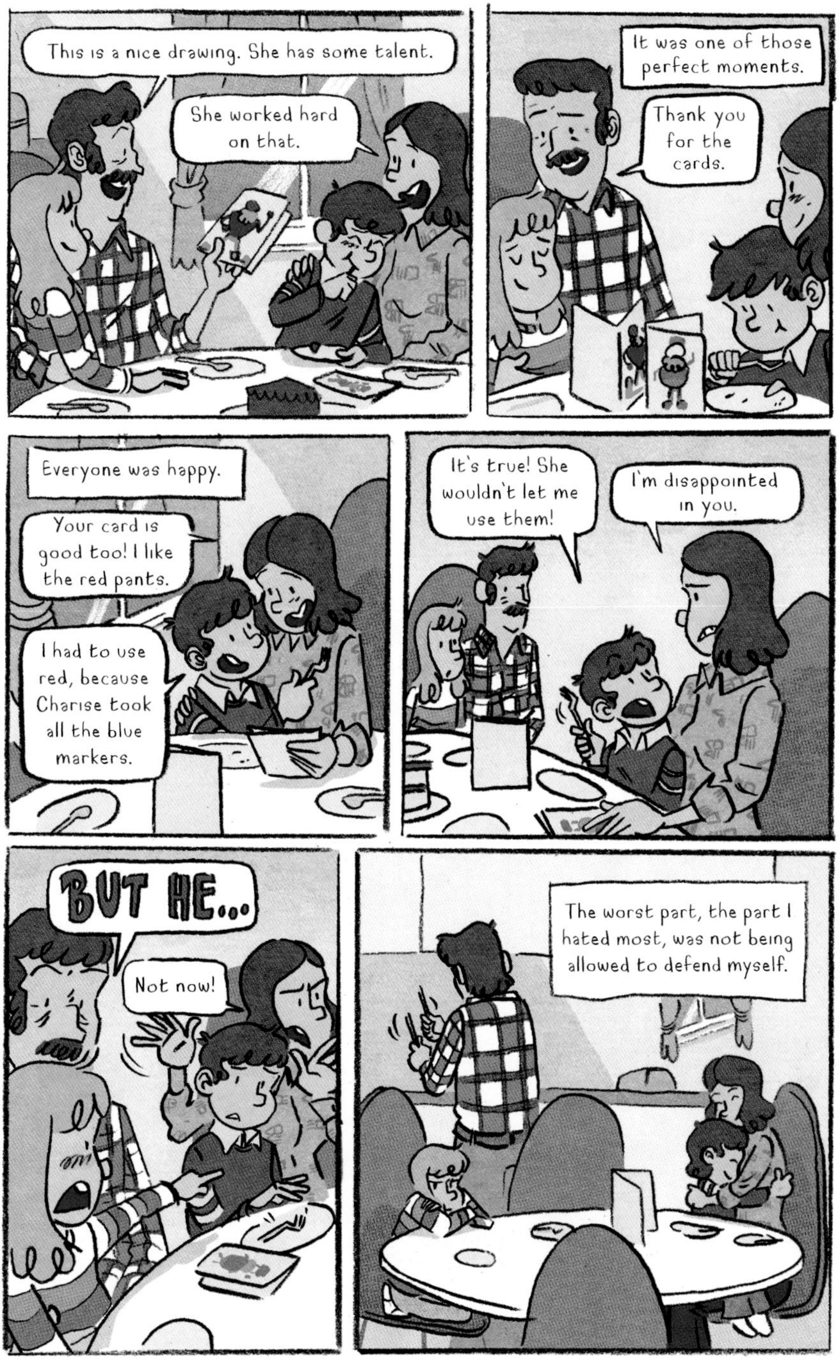
This is a nice drawing. She has some talent.
She worked hard on that.
It was one of those perfect moments.
Thank you for the cards.
Everyone was happy.
Your card is good too! I like the red pants.
I had to use red, because Charise took all the blue markers.
It's true! She wouldn't let me use them!
I'm disappointed in you.
BUT HE...
Not now!
The worst part, the part I hated most, was not being allowed to defend myself.

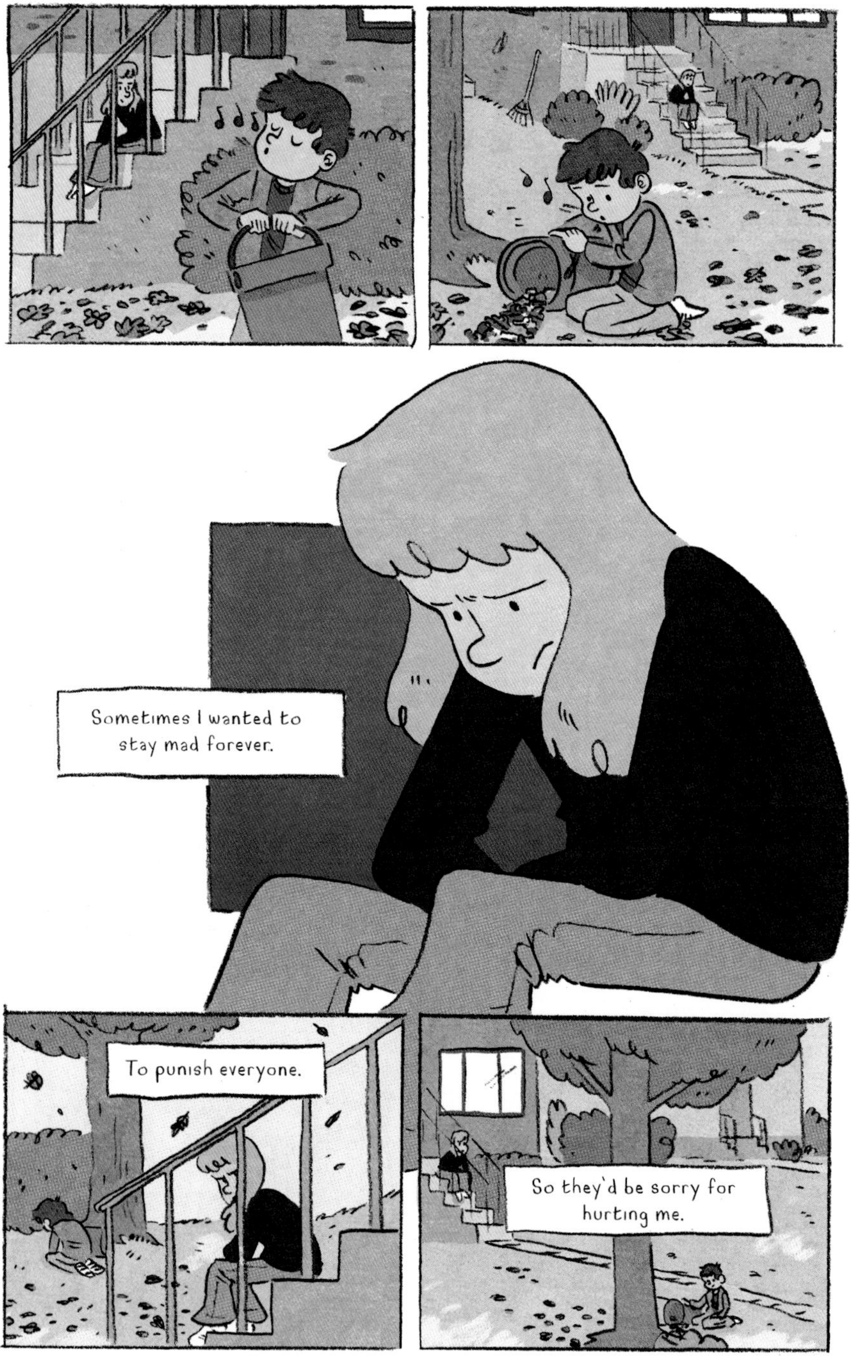
Sometimes I wanted to stay mad forever.
To punish everyone.
So they'd be sorry for hurting me.

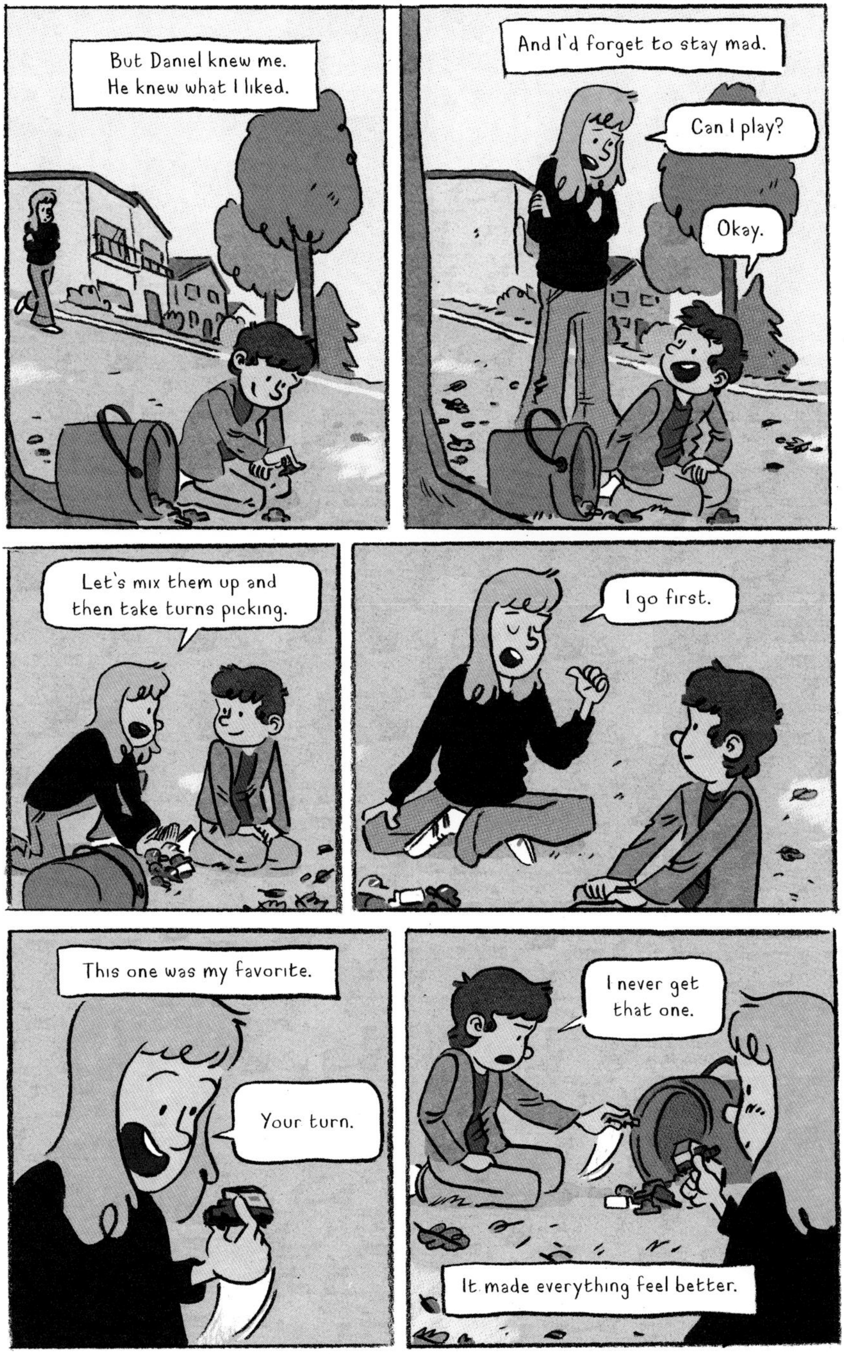
But Daniel knew me.
He knew what I liked.
And I'd forget to stay mad.
Can I play?
Okay.
Let's mix them up and then take turns picking.
I go first.
This one was my favorite.
Your turn.
I never get that one.
It made everything feel better.

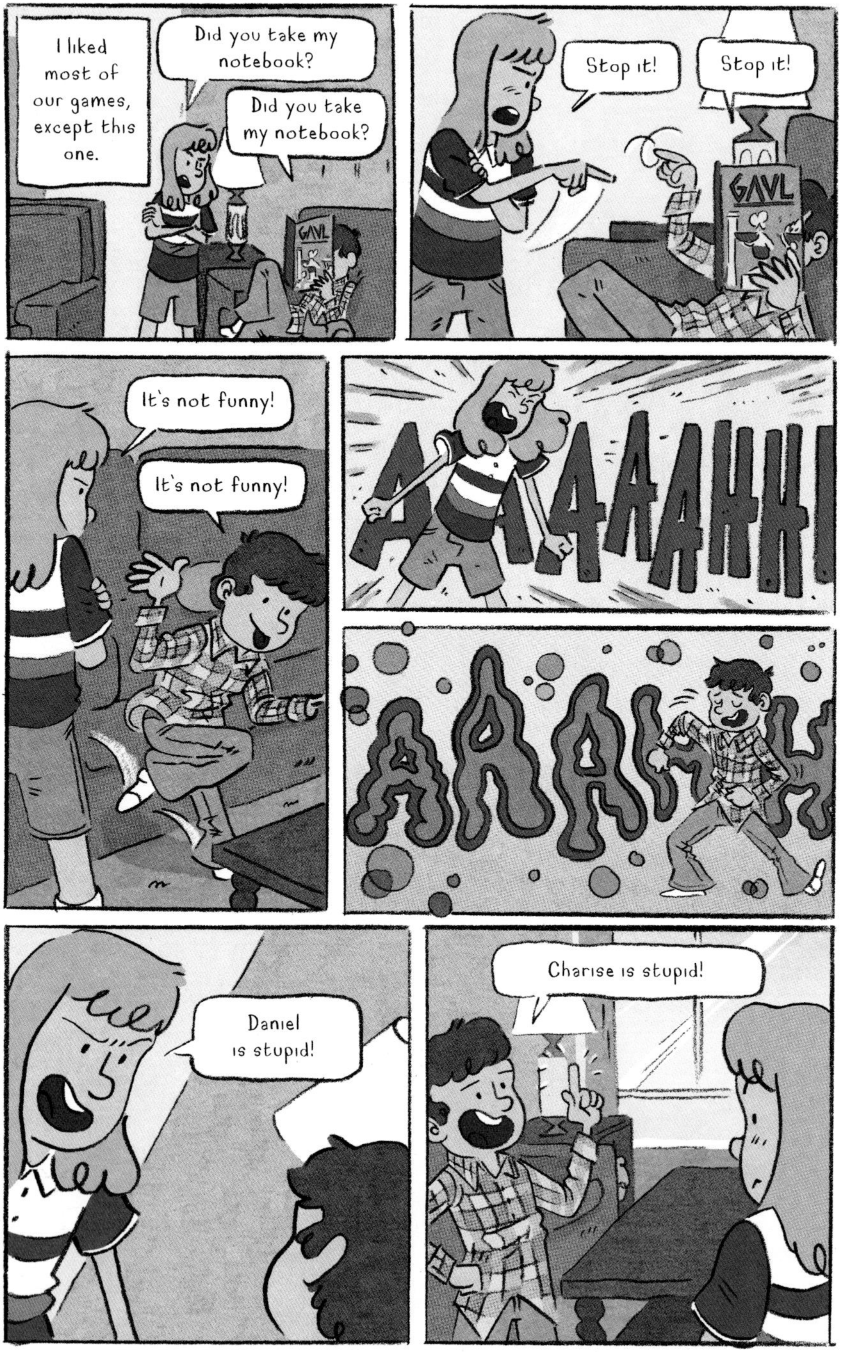
I liked most of our games, except this one.
Did you take my notebook?
Did you take my notebook?
Stop it!
Stop it!
GAVL
It's not funny!
It's not funny!
AAAAHH
AAAH
Daniel is stupid!
Charise is stupid!

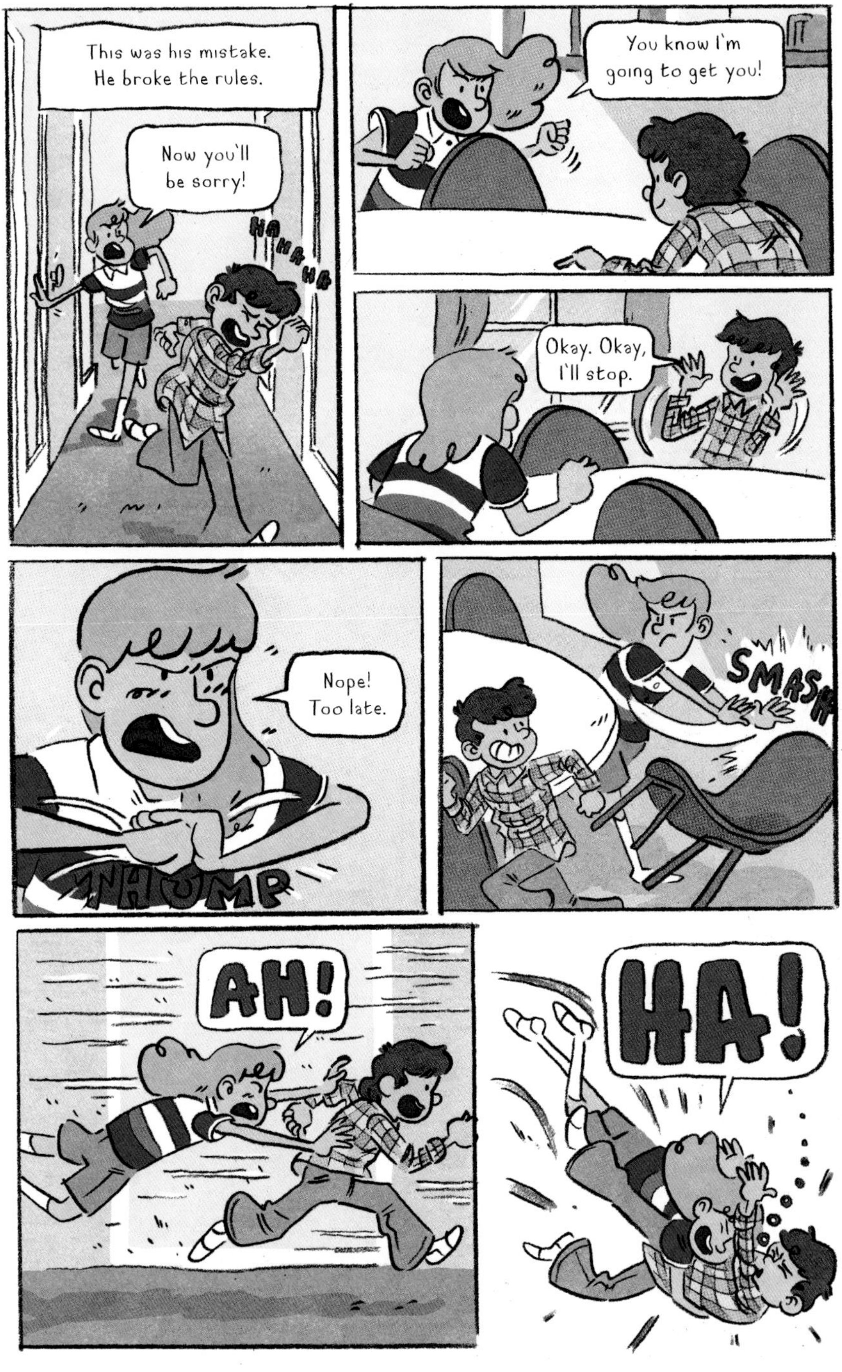
This was his mistake.
He broke the rules.
Now you'll be sorry!
HAHAHAHA
You know I'm going to get you!
Okay. Okay, I'll stop.
Nope! Too late.
WHUMP
SMASH
AH!
HA!

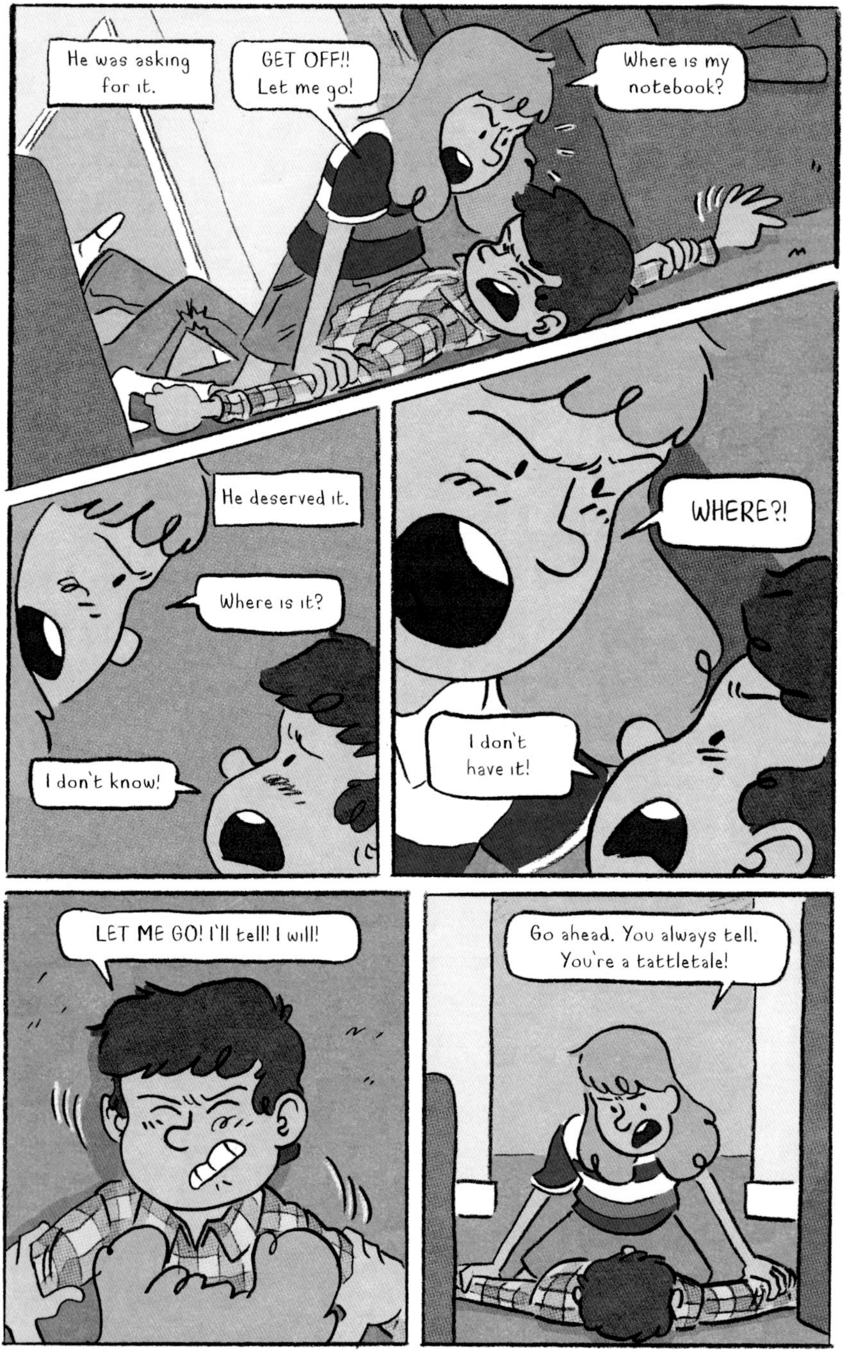
He was asking for it.
GET OFF!! Let me go!
Where is my notebook?
He deserved it.
Where is it?
I don't know!
WHERE?!
I don't have it!
LET ME GO! I'll tell! I will!
Go ahead. You always tell. You're a tattletale!

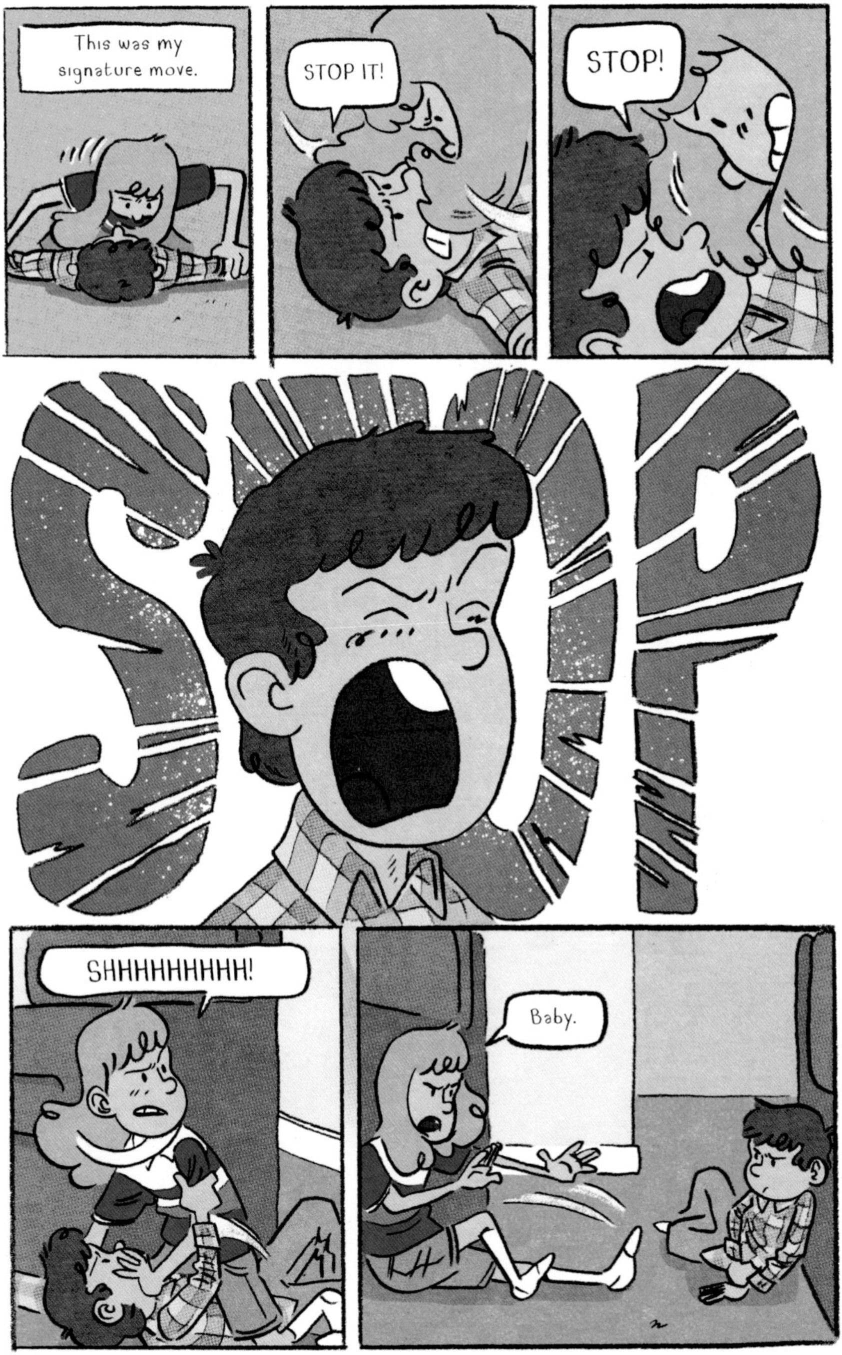
This was my signature move.
STOP IT!
STOP!
STOP
SHHHHHHHHH!
Baby.

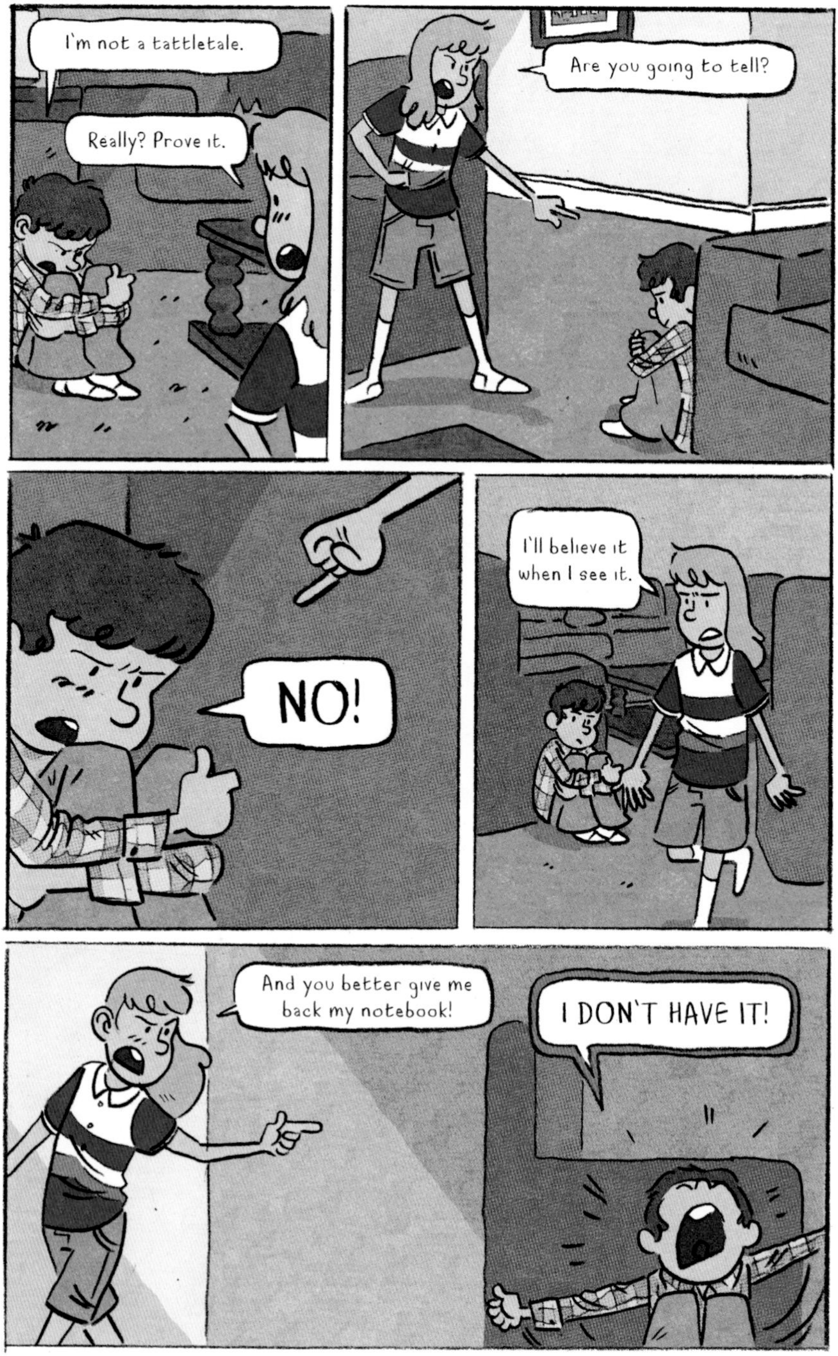
I'm not a tattletale.
Really? Prove it.
Are you going to tell?
NO!
I'll believe it when I see it.
And you better give me back my notebook!
I DON'T HAVE IT!

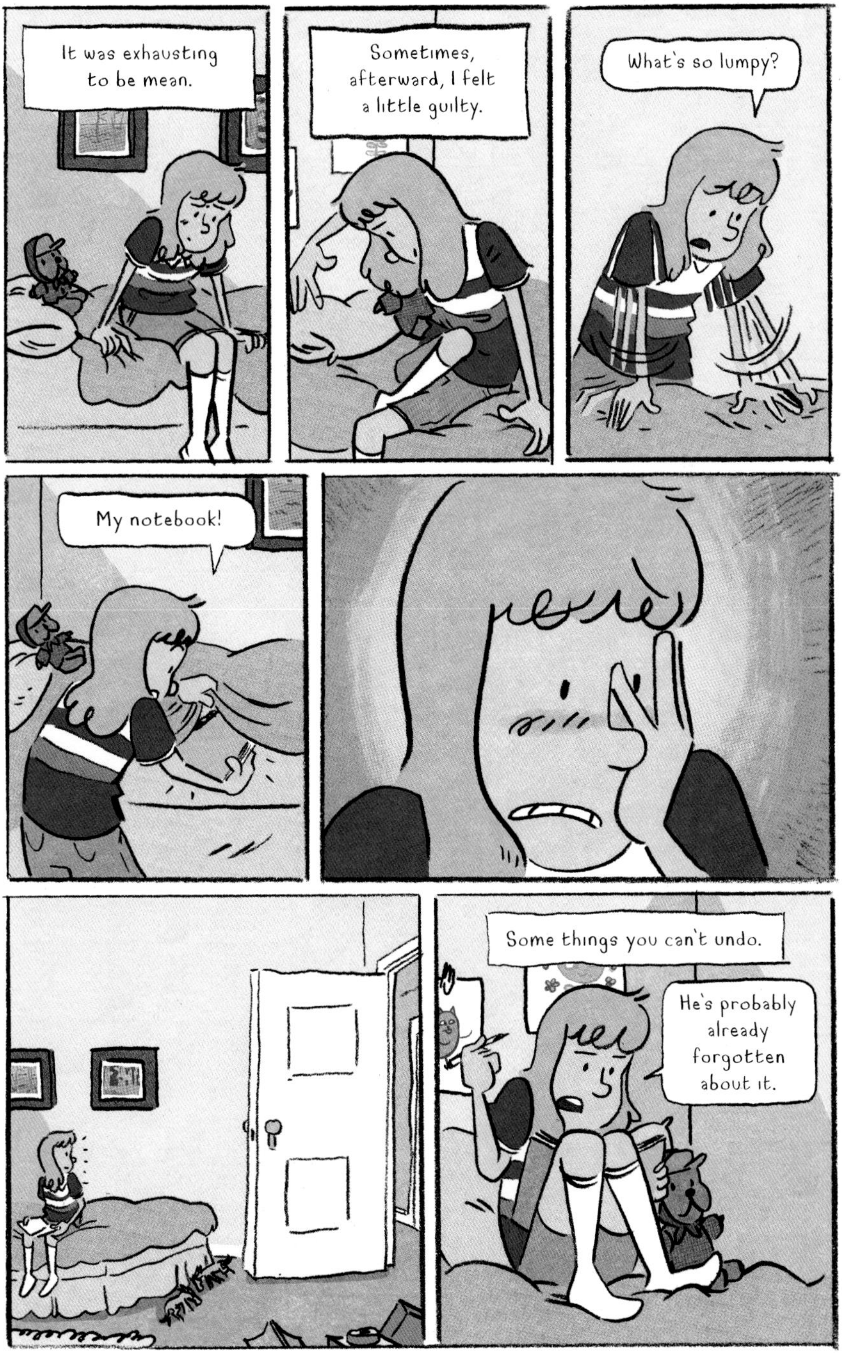
It was exhausting to be mean.
Sometimes, afterward, I felt a little guilty.
What's so lumpy?
My notebook!
Some things you can't undo.
He's probably already forgotten about it.

4

The Power of the Lie

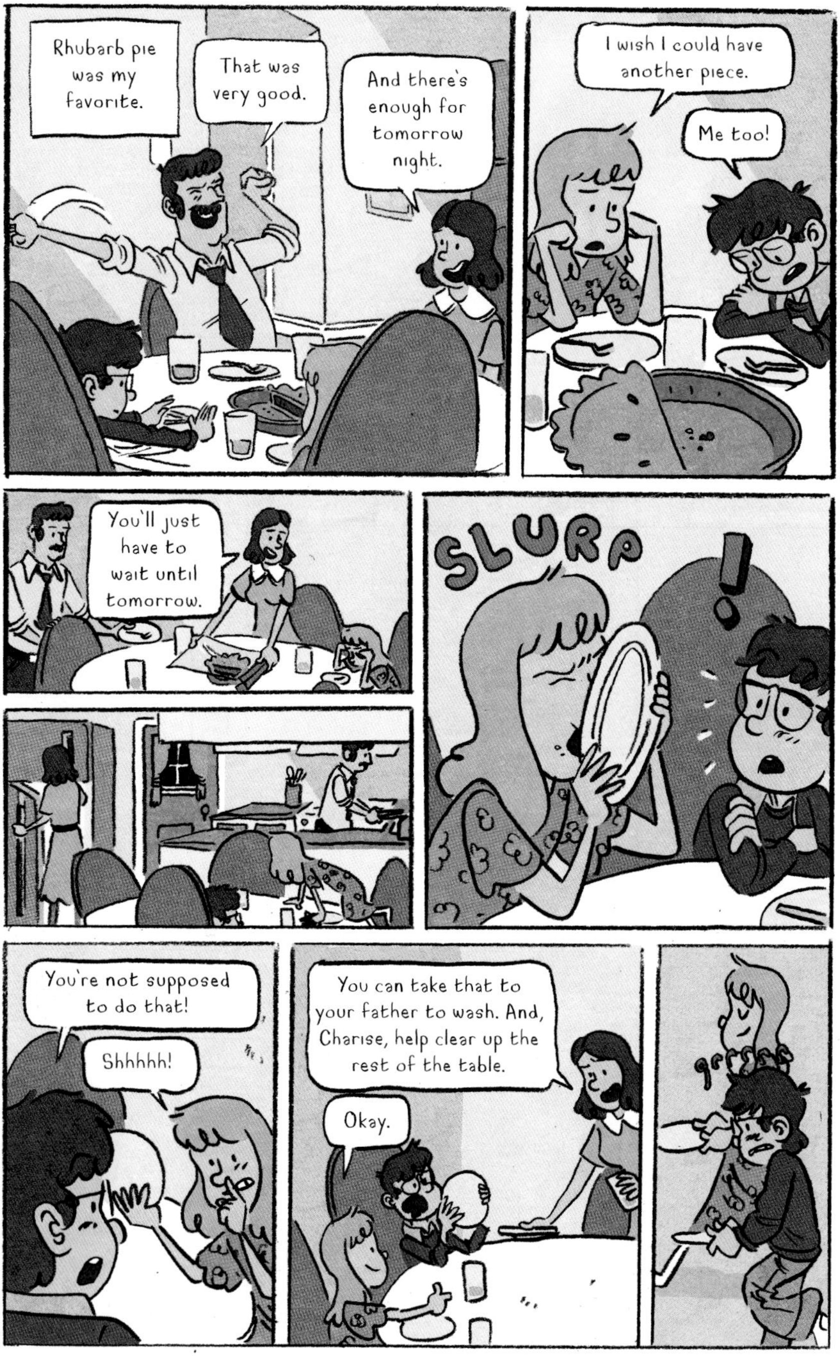
Rhubarb pie was my favorite.
That was very good.
And there's enough for tomorrow night.
I wish I could have another piece.
Me too!
You'll just have to wait until tomorrow.
SLURP
!
You're not supposed to do that!
Shhhhh!
You can take that to your father to wash. And, Charise, help clear up the rest of the table.
Okay.

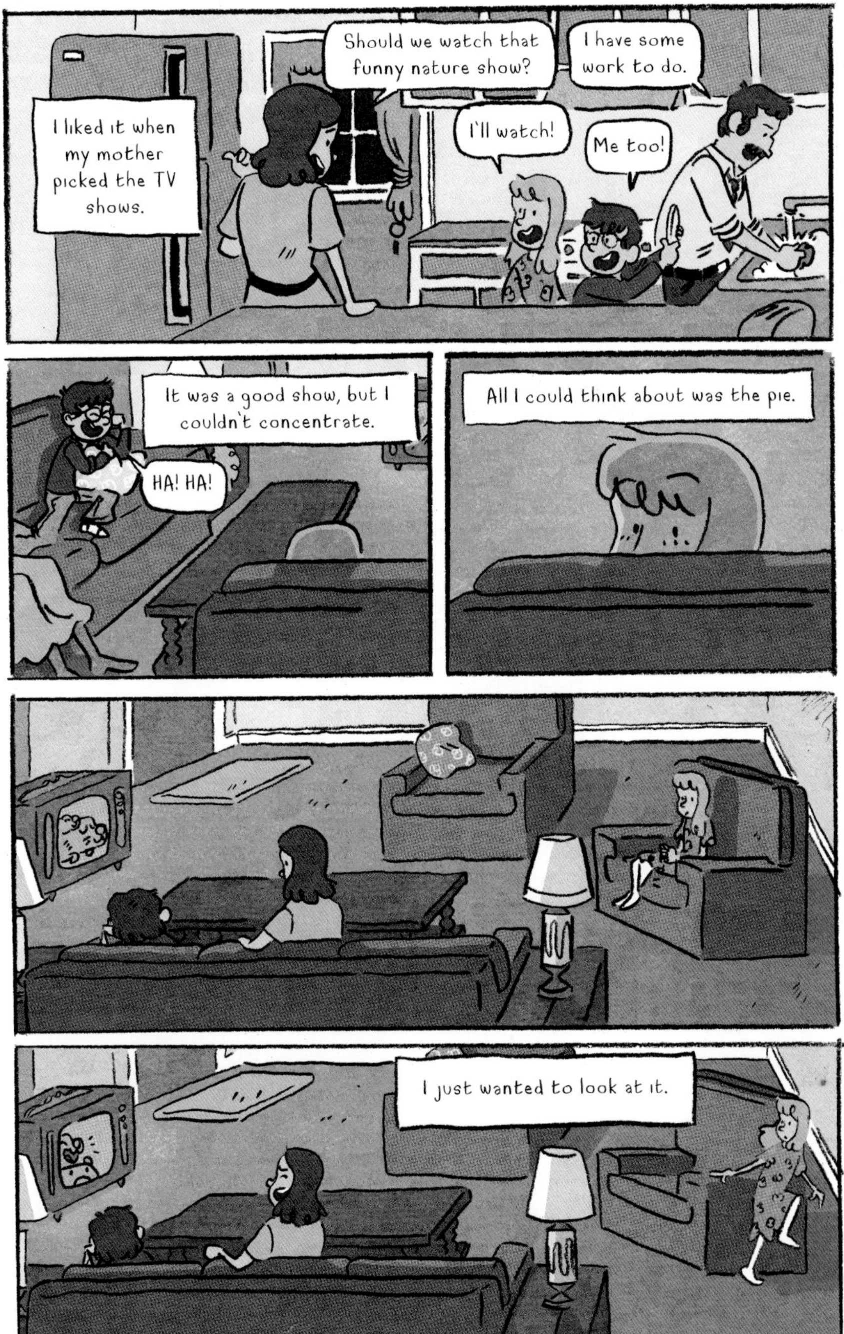
I liked it when my mother picked the TV shows.
Should we watch that funny nature show?
I have some work to do.
I'll watch!
Me too!
It was a good show, but I couldn't concentrate.
HA! HA!
All I could think about was the pie.
I just wanted to look at it.

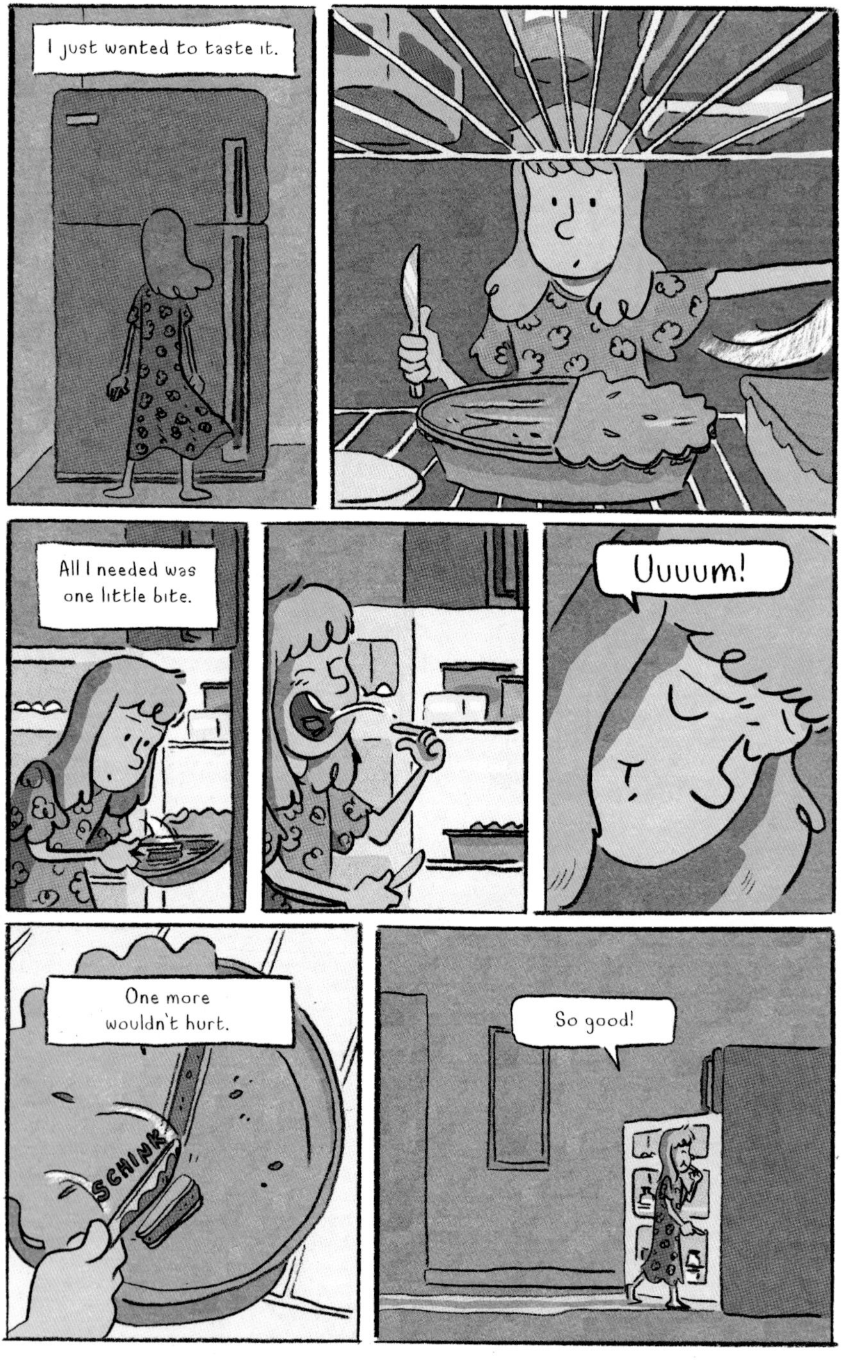
I just wanted to taste it.
All I needed was one little bite.
Uuuum!
One more wouldn't hurt.
SCHINK
So good!

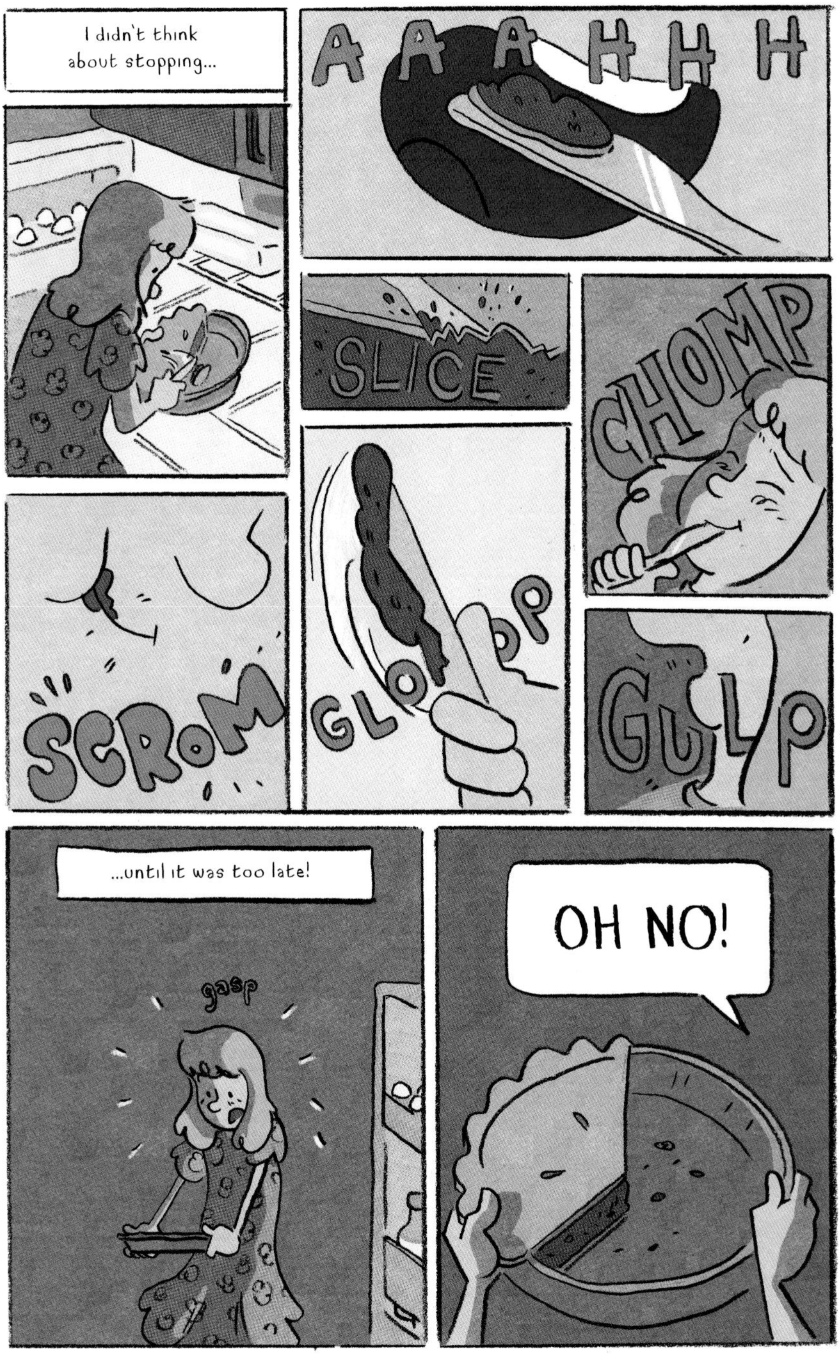
I didn't think about stopping...
AAAHHH
SLICE
CHOMP
SCROM
GLOOP
GULP
...until it was too late!
gasp
OH NO!

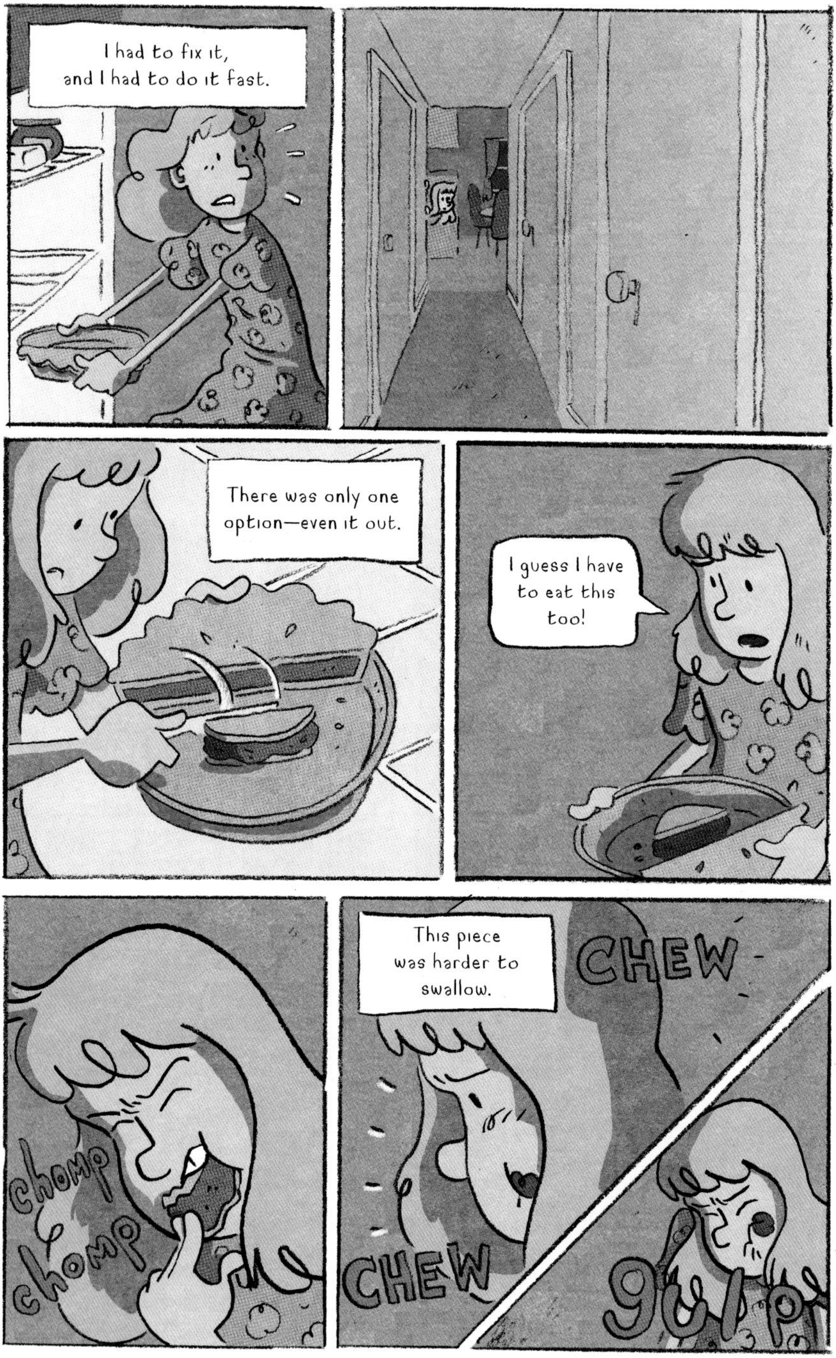
I had to fix it,
and I had to do it fast.
There was only one
option—even it out.
I guess I have
to eat this
too!
chomp
chomp
This piece
was harder to
swallow.
CHEW
CHEW
gulp

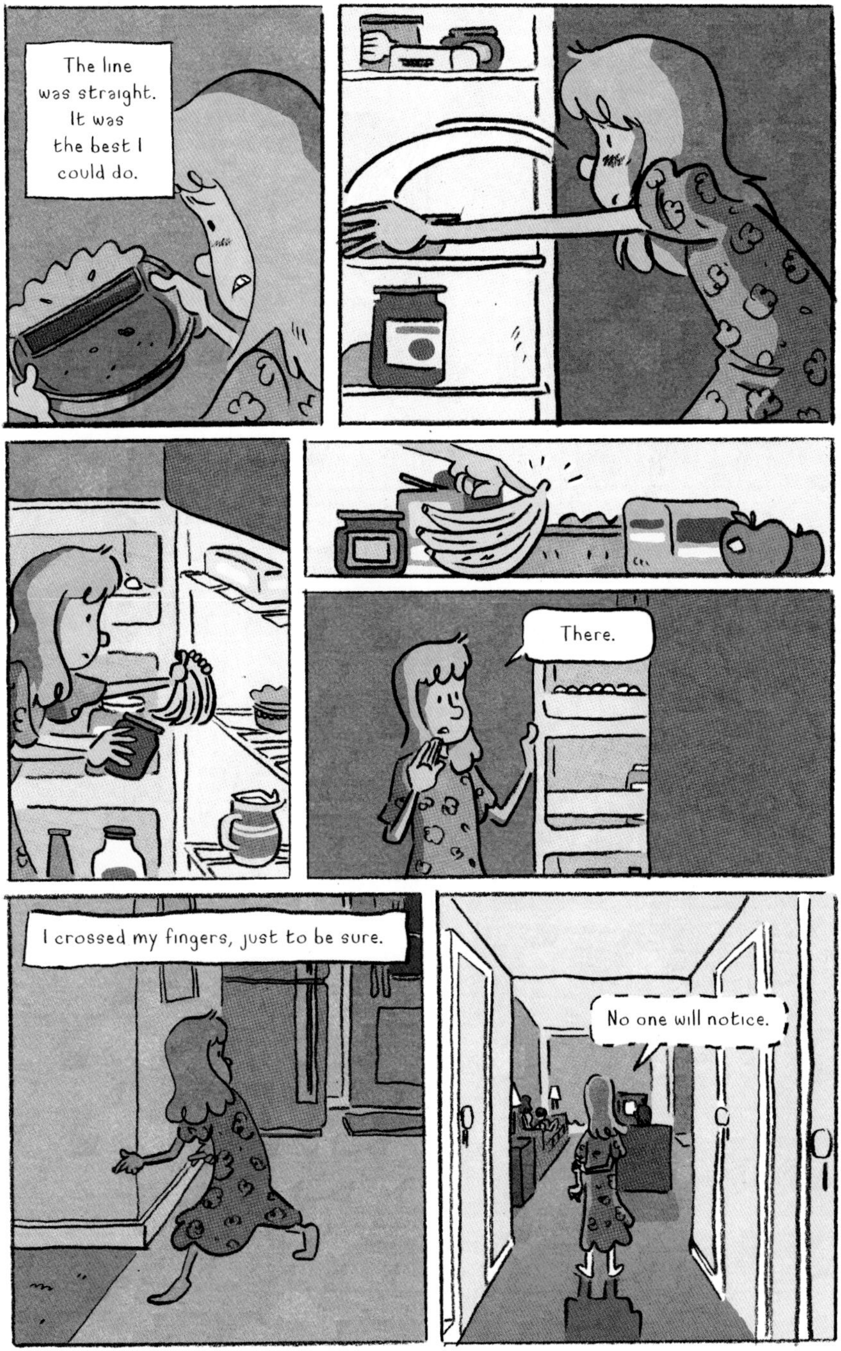
The line
was straight.
It was
the best I
could do.
There.
I crossed my fingers, just to be sure.
No one will notice.

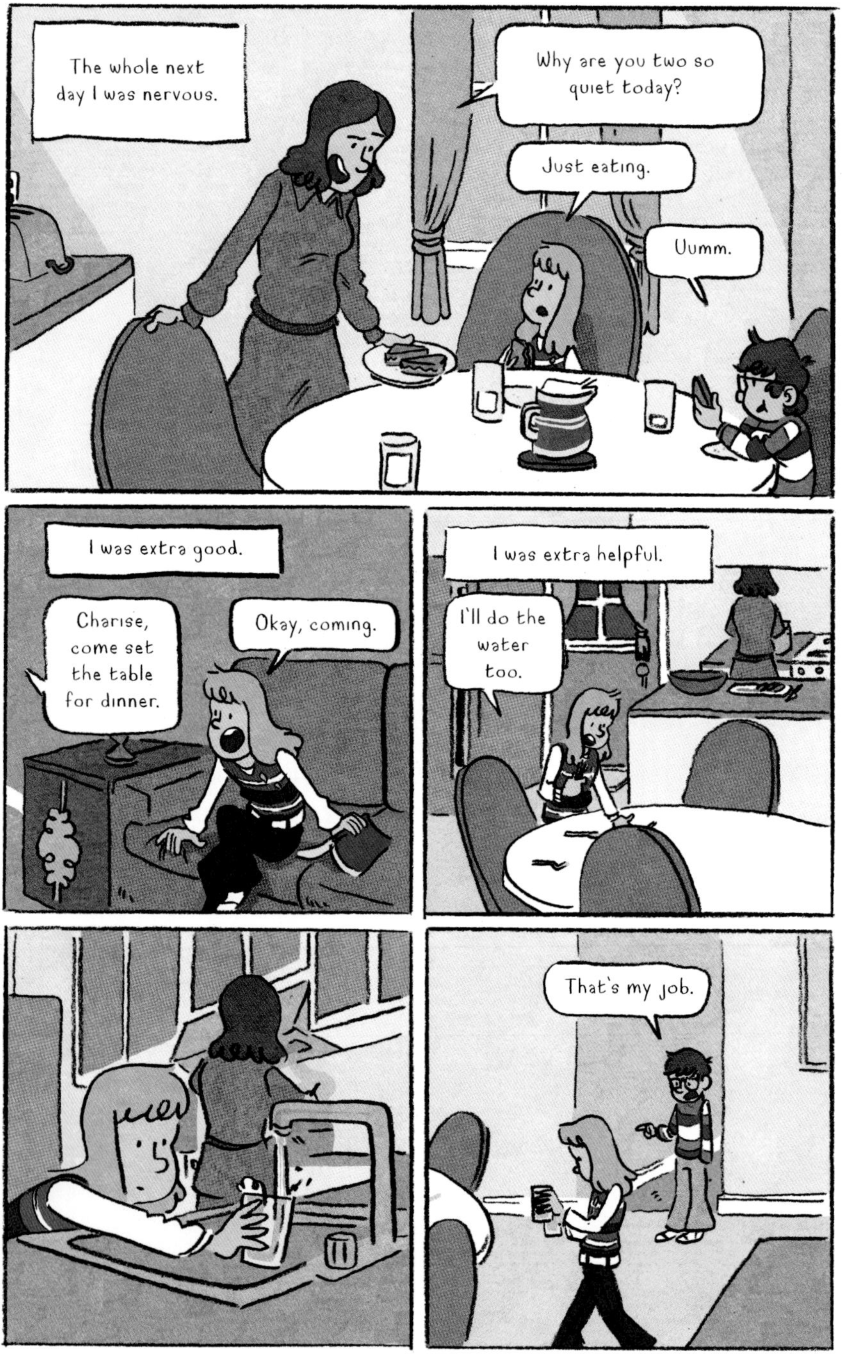
The whole next day I was nervous.
Why are you two so quiet today?
Just eating.
Uumm.
I was extra good.
Charise, come set the table for dinner.
Okay, coming.
I was extra helpful.
I'll do the water too.
That's my job.

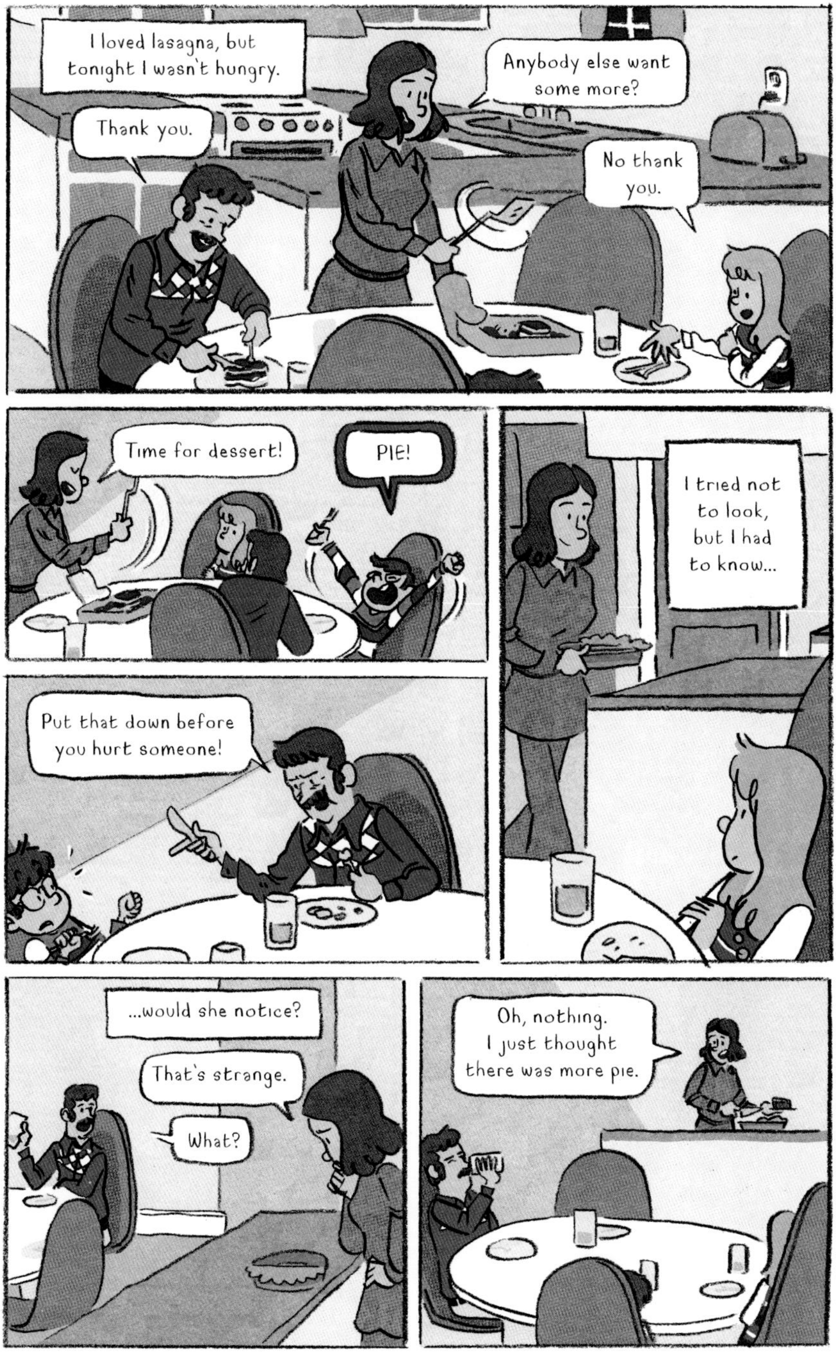
I loved lasagna, but tonight I wasn't hungry.
Anybody else want some more?
Thank you.
No thank you.
Time for dessert!
PIE!
I tried not to look, but I had to know...
Put that down before you hurt someone!
...would she notice?
That's strange.
What?
Oh, nothing. I just thought there was more pie.

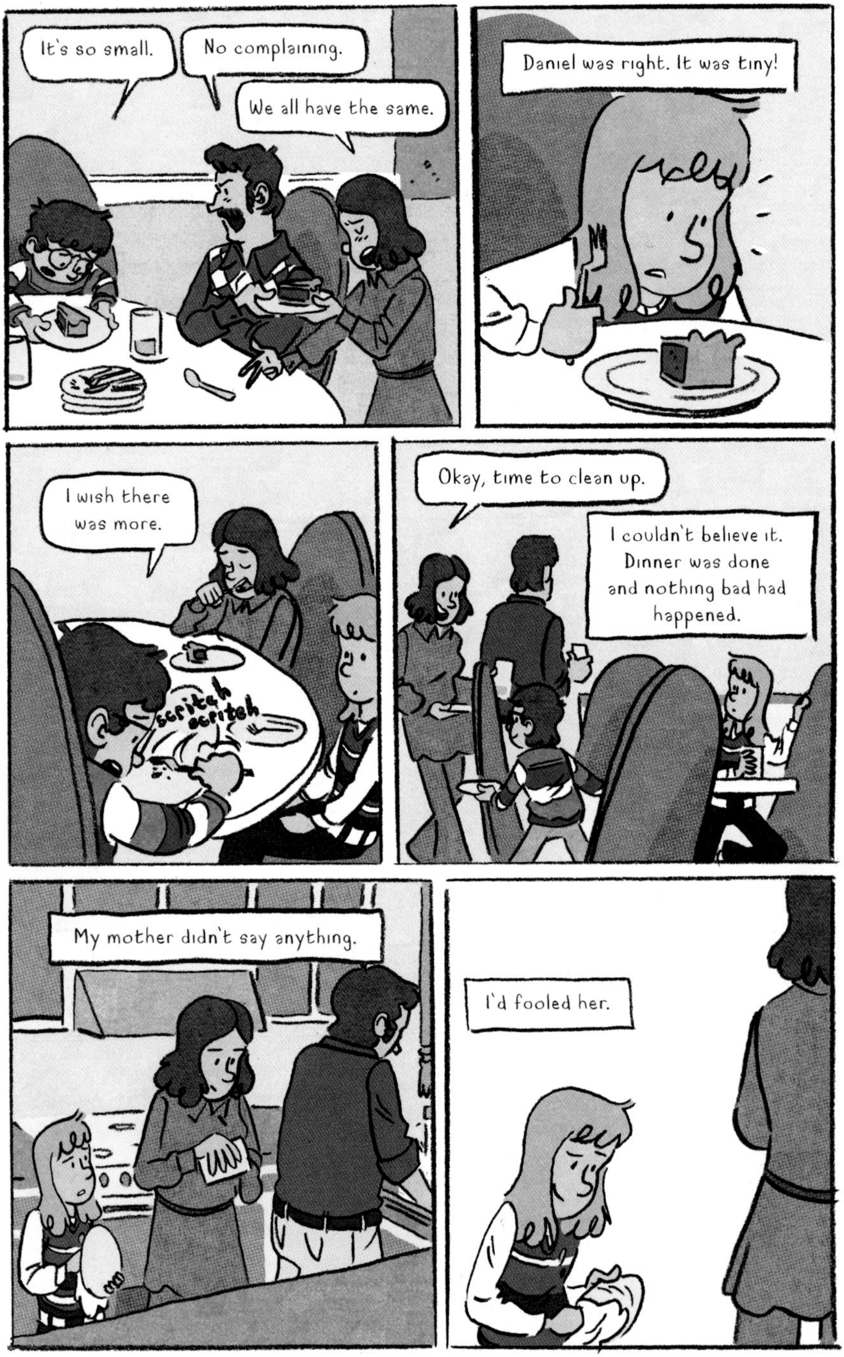
It's so small.
No complaining.
We all have the same.
Daniel was right. It was tiny!
I wish there was more.
scritch scritch
Okay, time to clean up.
I couldn't believe it. Dinner was done and nothing bad had happened.
My mother didn't say anything.
I'd fooled her.

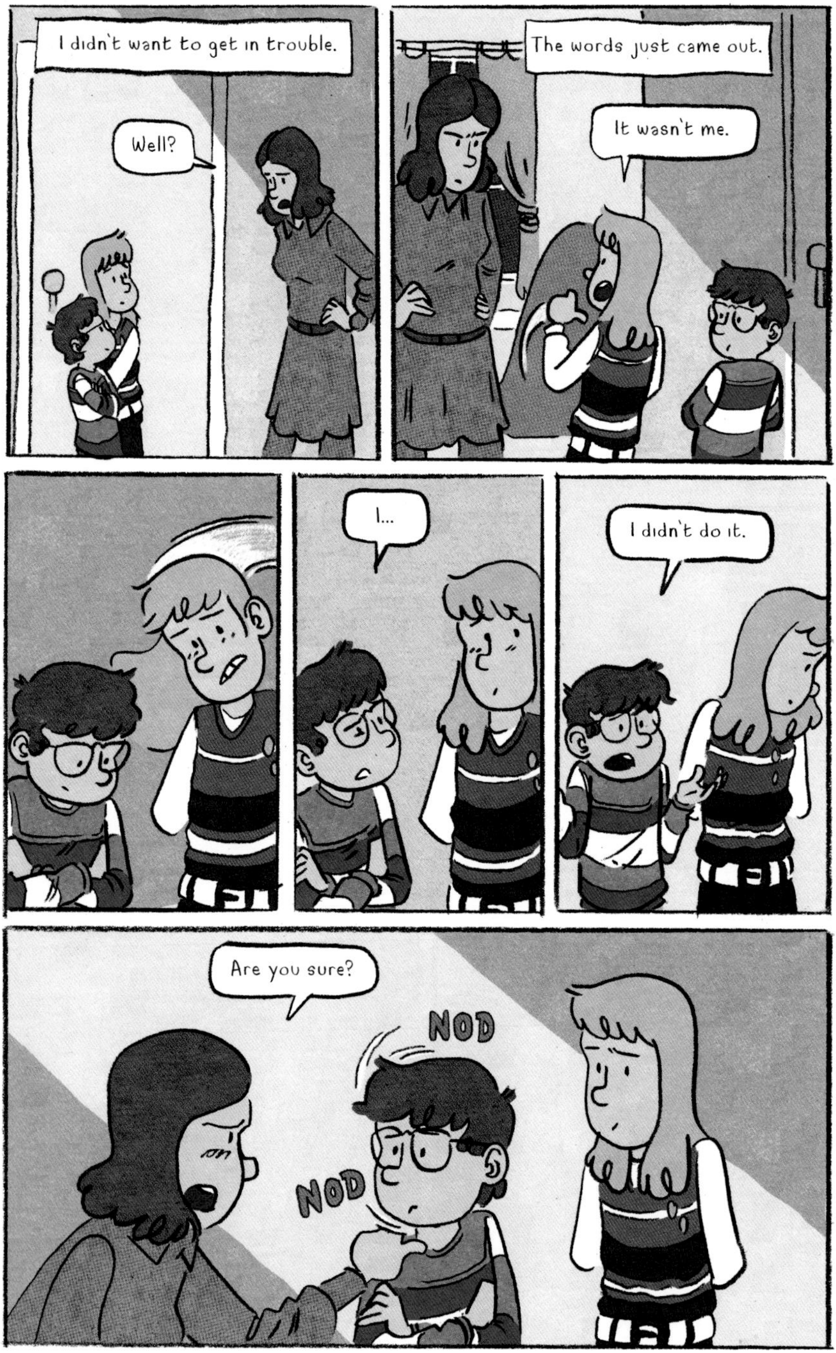
I didn't want to get in trouble.
Well?
The words just came out.
It wasn't me.
I...
I didn't do it.
Are you sure?
NOD
NOD

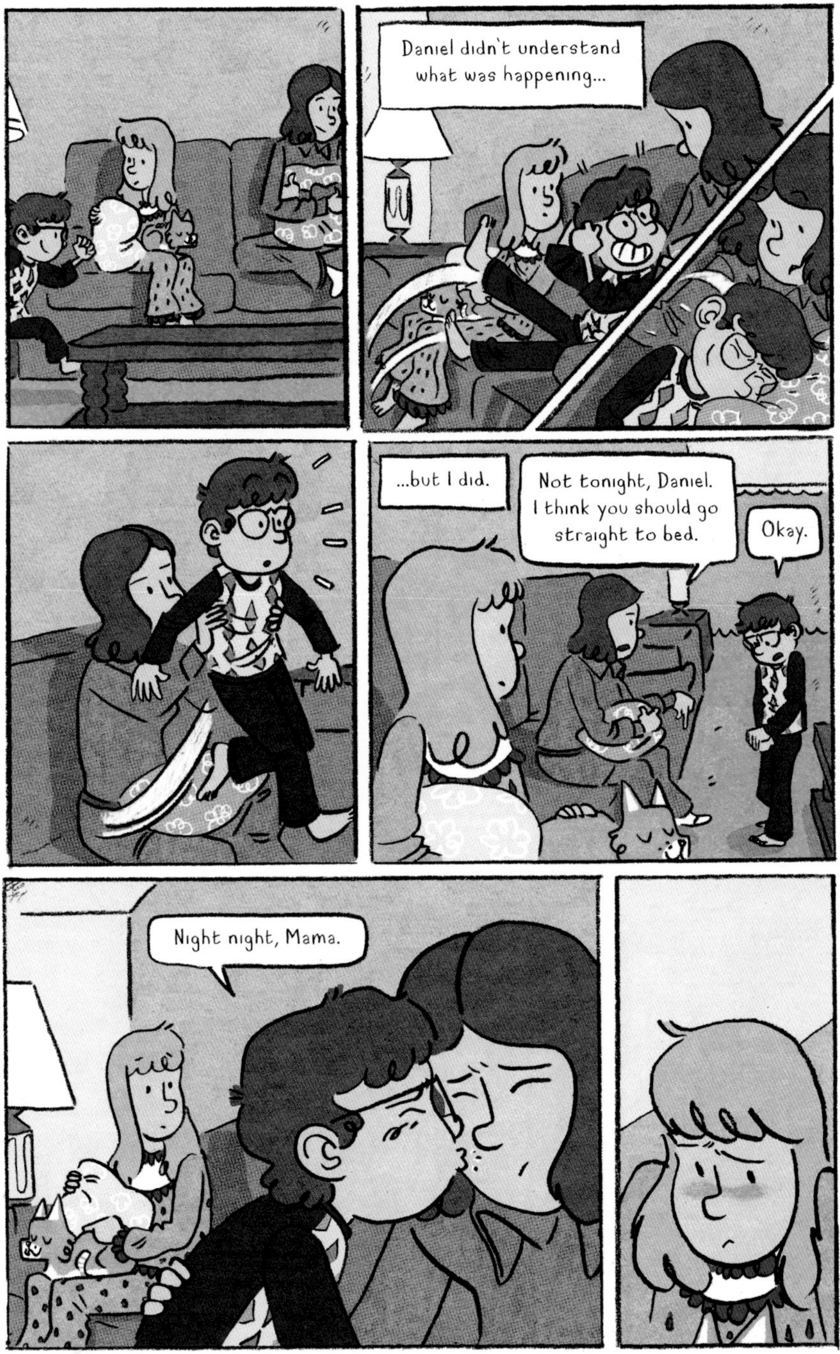
Daniel didn't understand what was happening...
...but I did.
Not tonight, Daniel. I think you should go straight to bed.
Okay.
Night night, Mama.

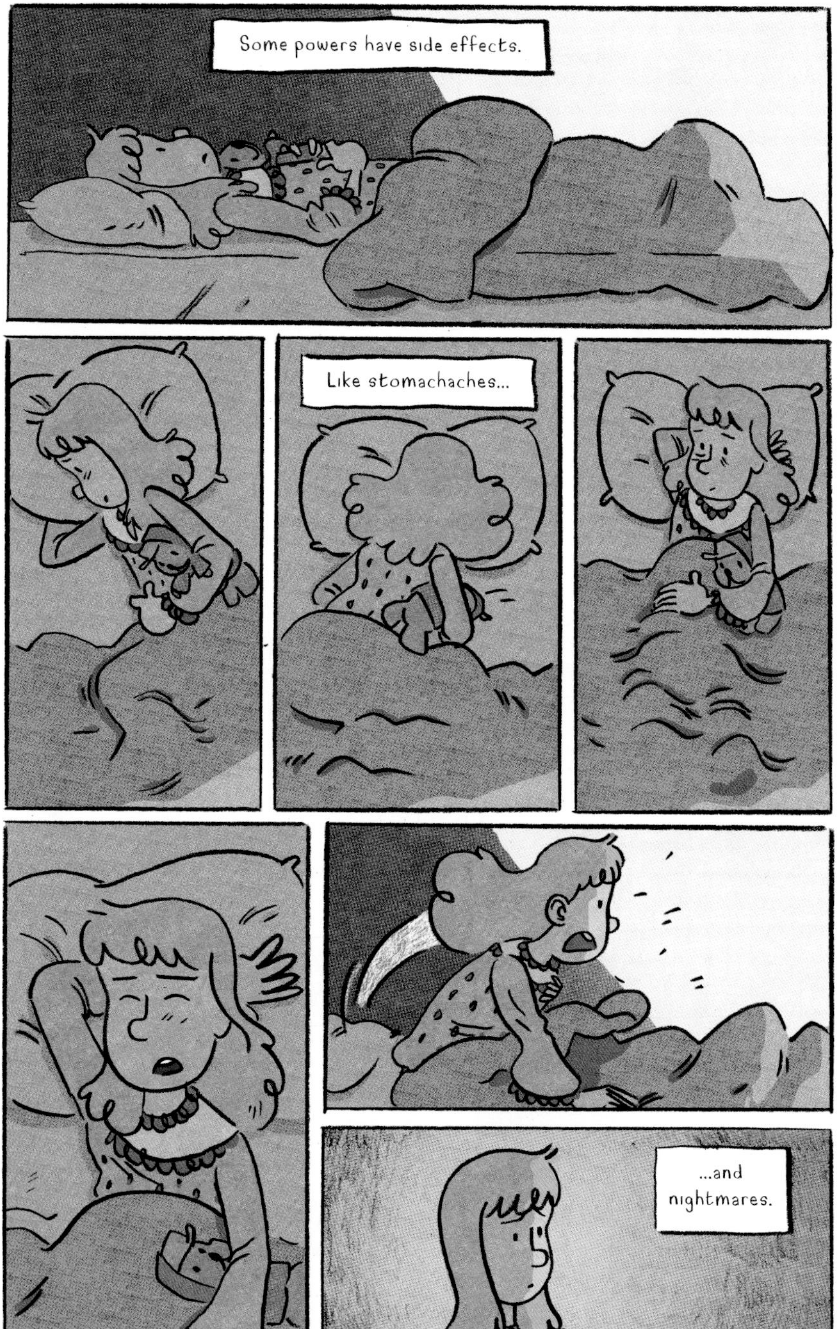

Some powers have side effects.
Like stomachaches...
...and nightmares.

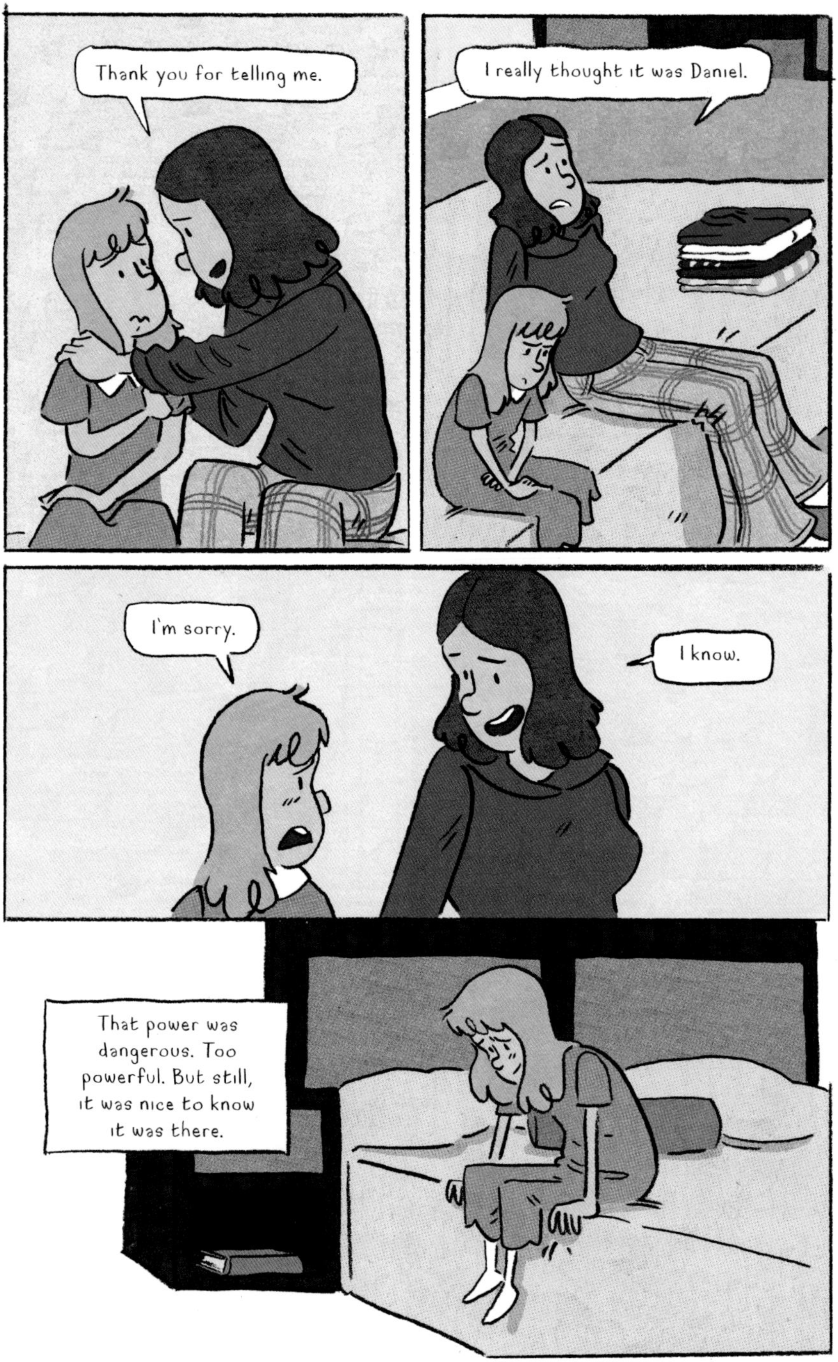
Thank you for telling me.
I really thought it was Daniel.
I'm sorry.
I know.
That power was dangerous. Too powerful. But still, it was nice to know it was there.

5

The Power to Fool

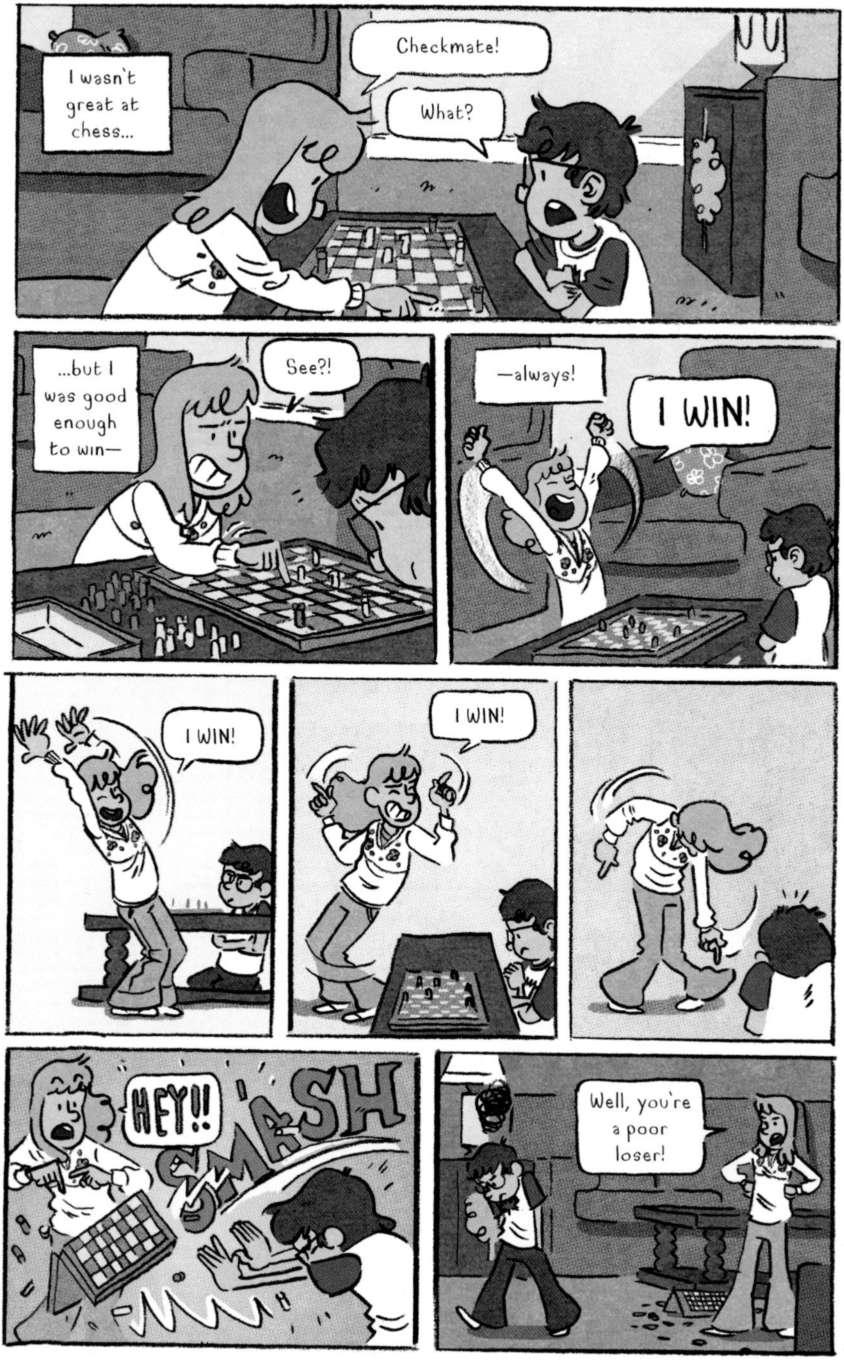
I wasn't great at chess...
Checkmate!
What?
...but I was good enough to win—
See?!
—always!
I WIN!
I WIN!
I WIN!
HEY!!
SMASH
Well, you're a poor loser!

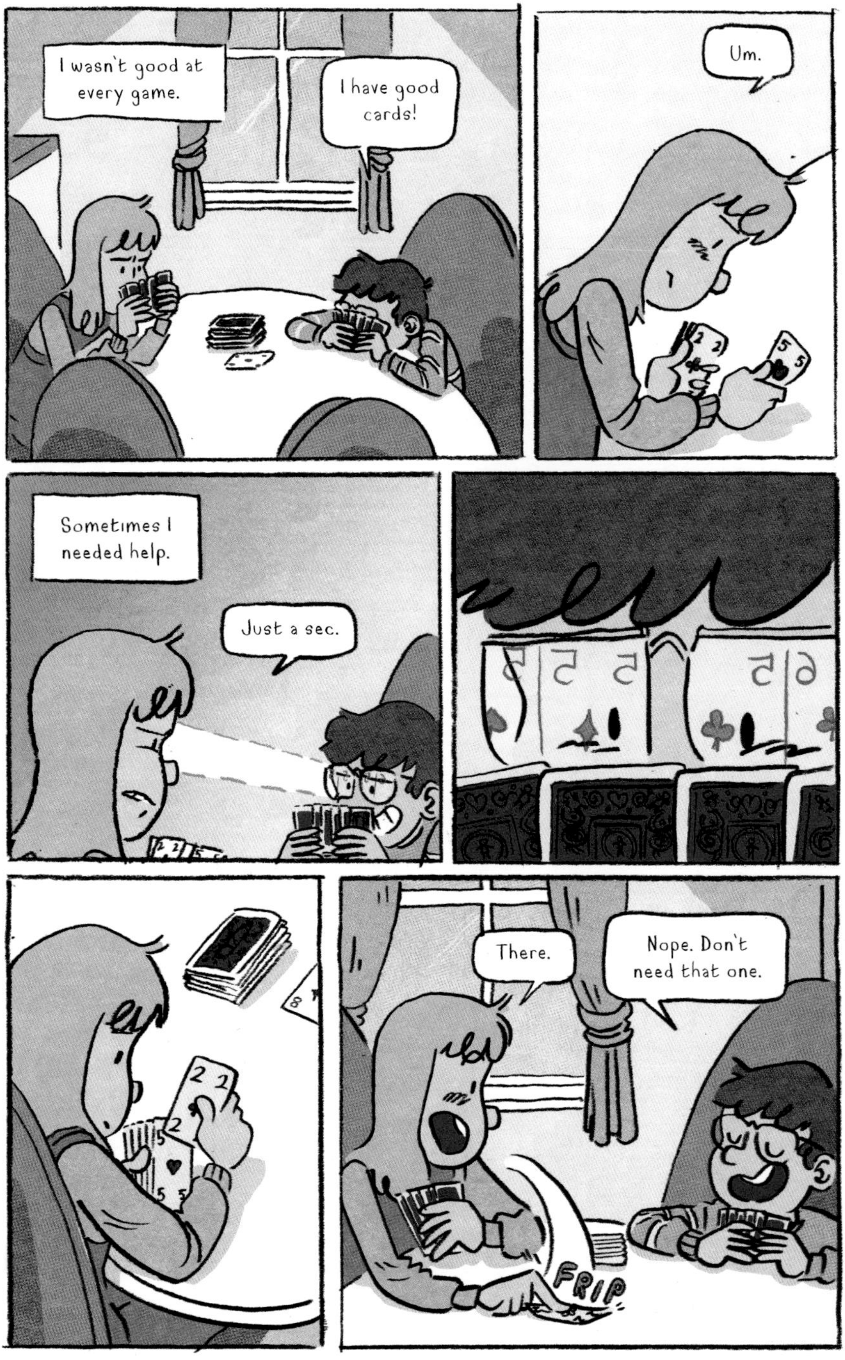
I wasn't good at every game.
I have good cards!
Um.
Sometimes I needed help.
Just a sec.
There.
Nope. Don't need that one.
FRIP

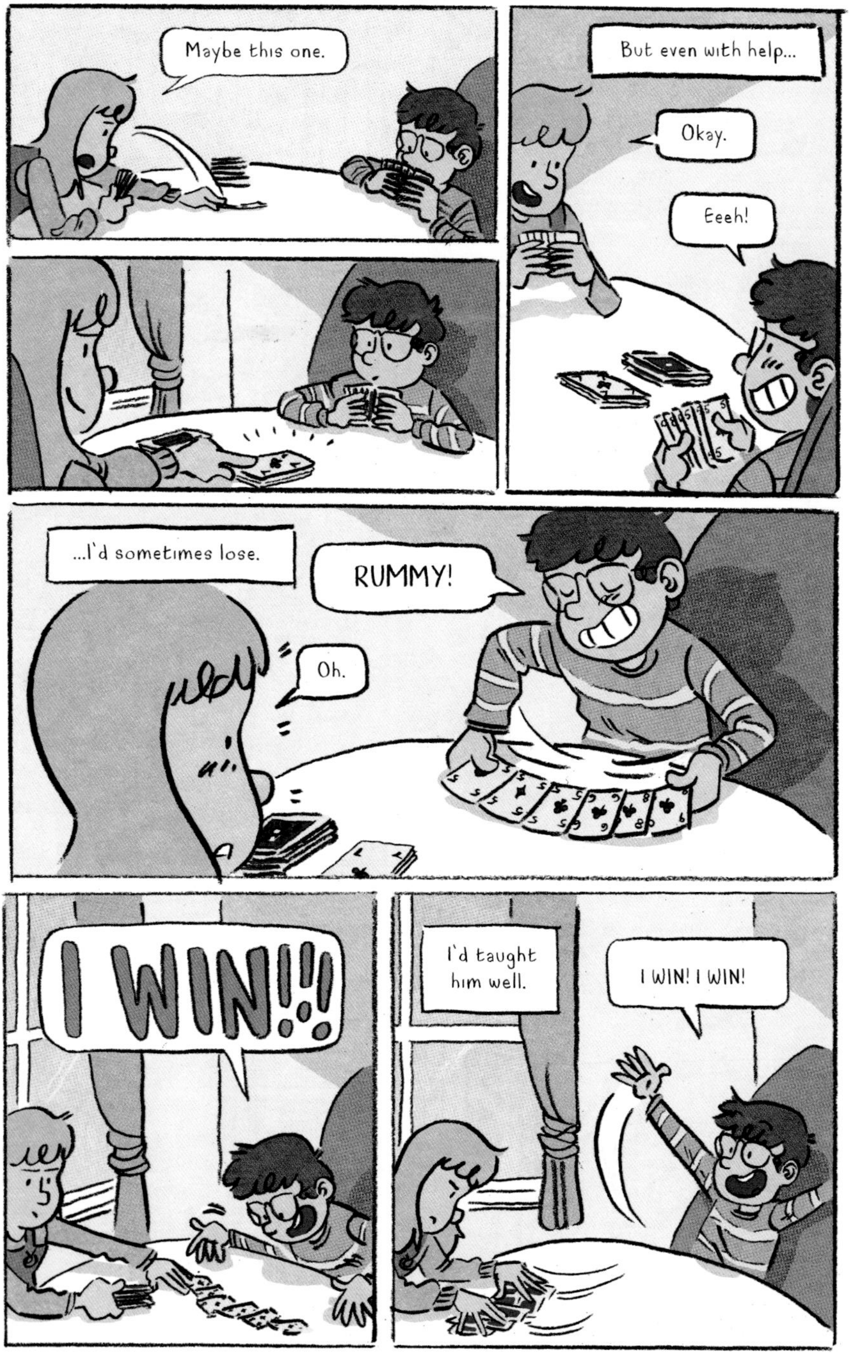
Maybe this one.
But even with help...
Okay.
Eeeh!
...I'd sometimes lose.
RUMMY!
Oh.
I WIN!!!
I'd taught him well.
I WIN! I WIN!

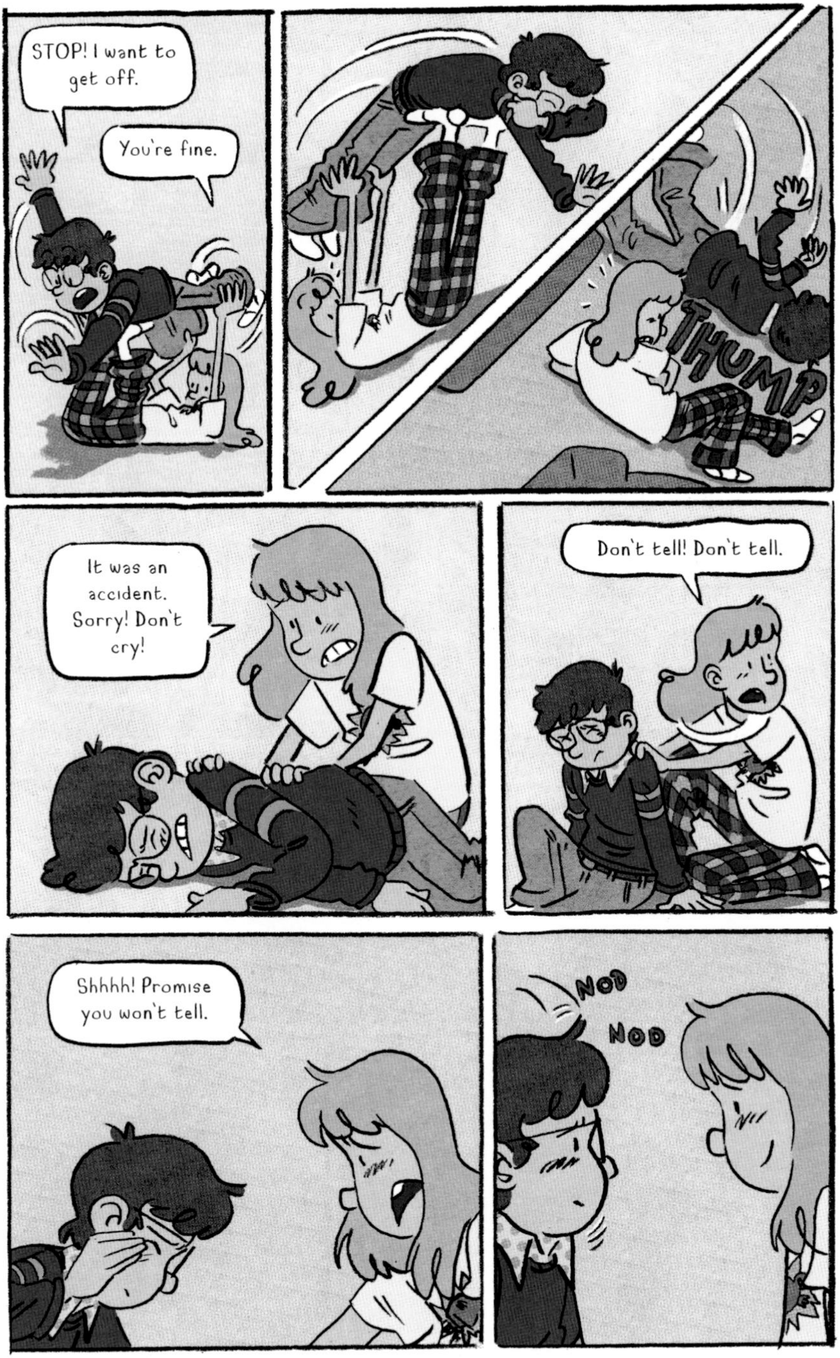
STOP! I want to get off.
You're fine.
THUMP
It was an accident. Sorry! Don't cry!
Don't tell! Don't tell.
Shhhh! Promise you won't tell.
NOD
NOD

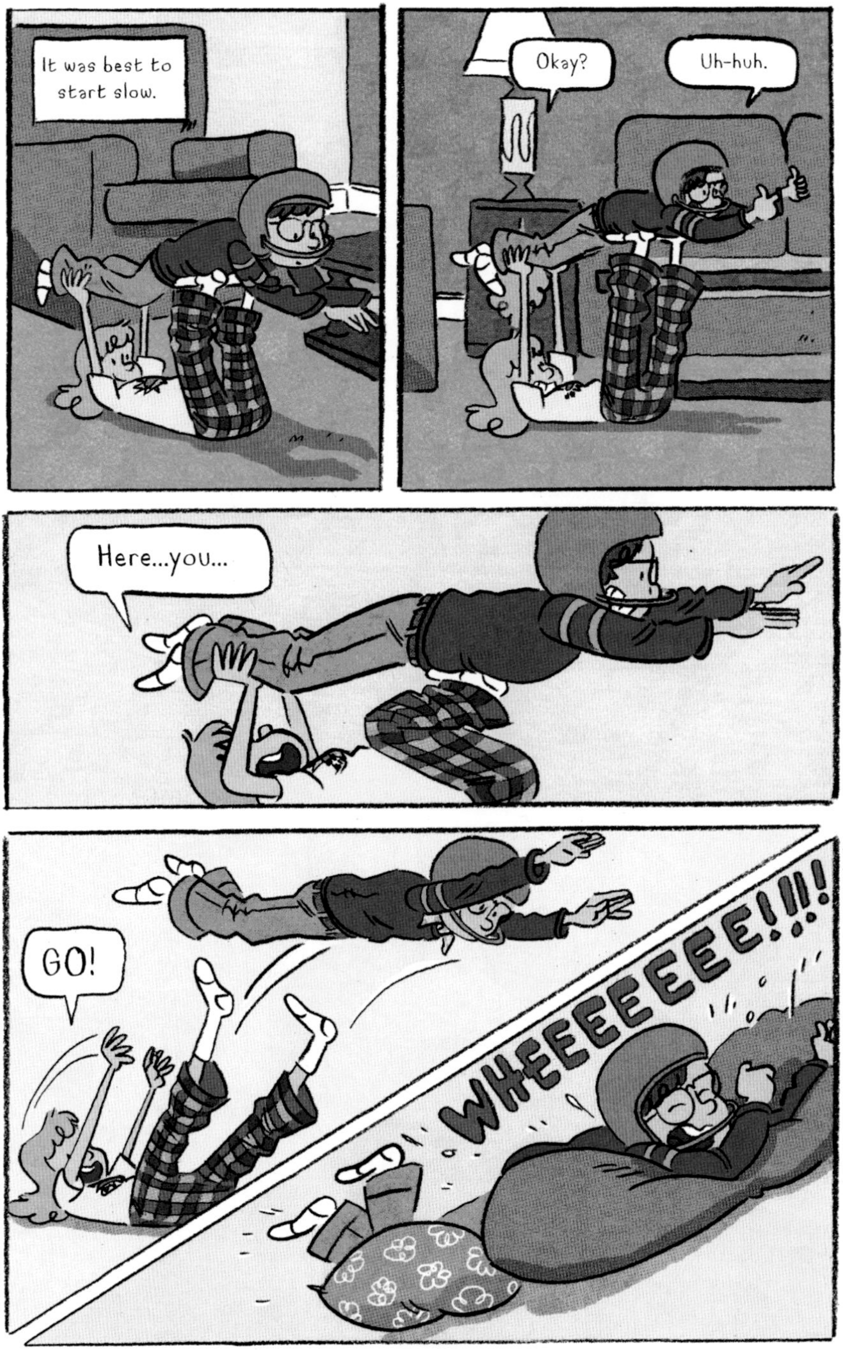

It was best to start slow.
Okay?
Uh-huh.
Here...you...
GO!
WHEEEEEEEE!!!!

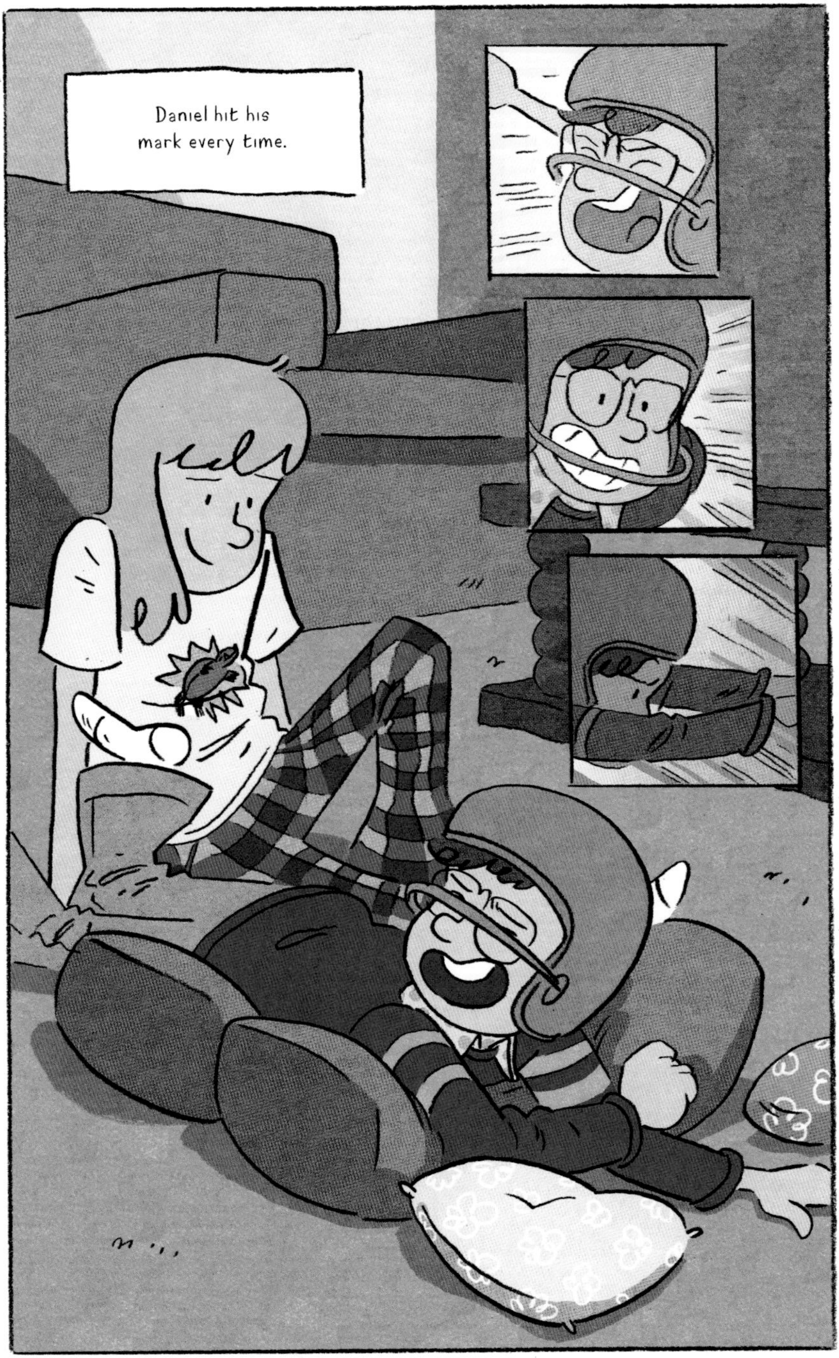
Daniel hit his mark every time.

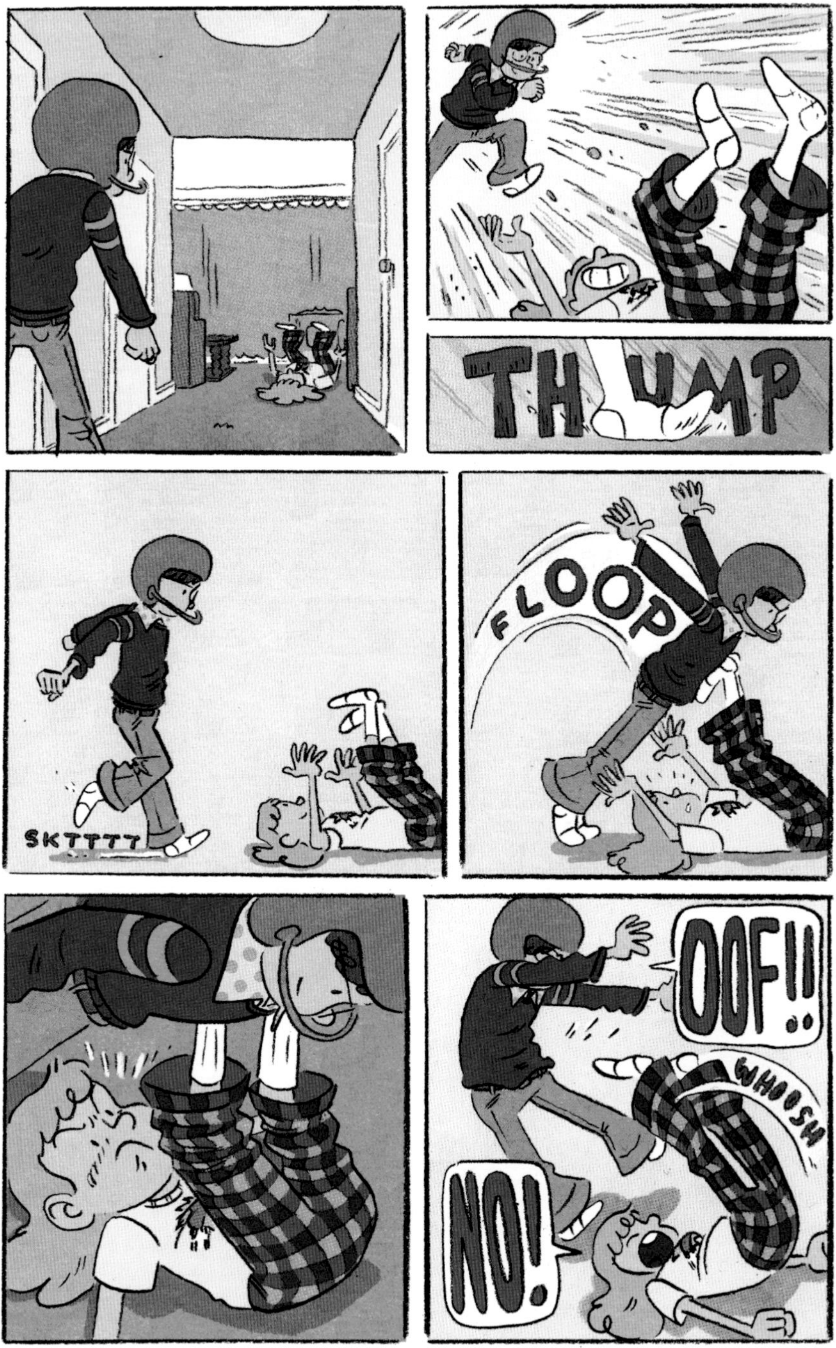
THUMP
SKTTTT
FLOOP
OOF!!
WHOOSH
NO!

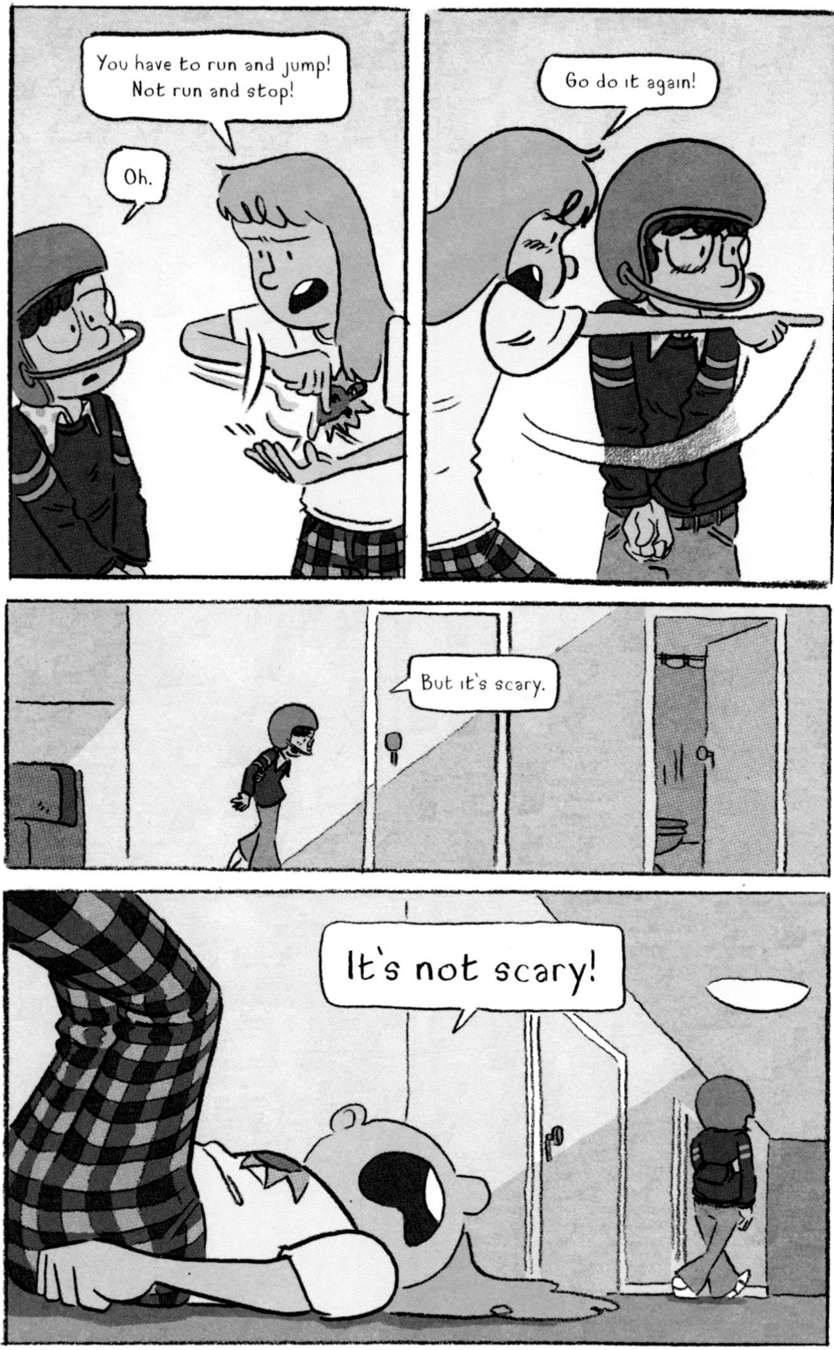
You have to run and jump!
Not run and stop!
Oh.
Go do it again!
But it's scary.
It's not scary!

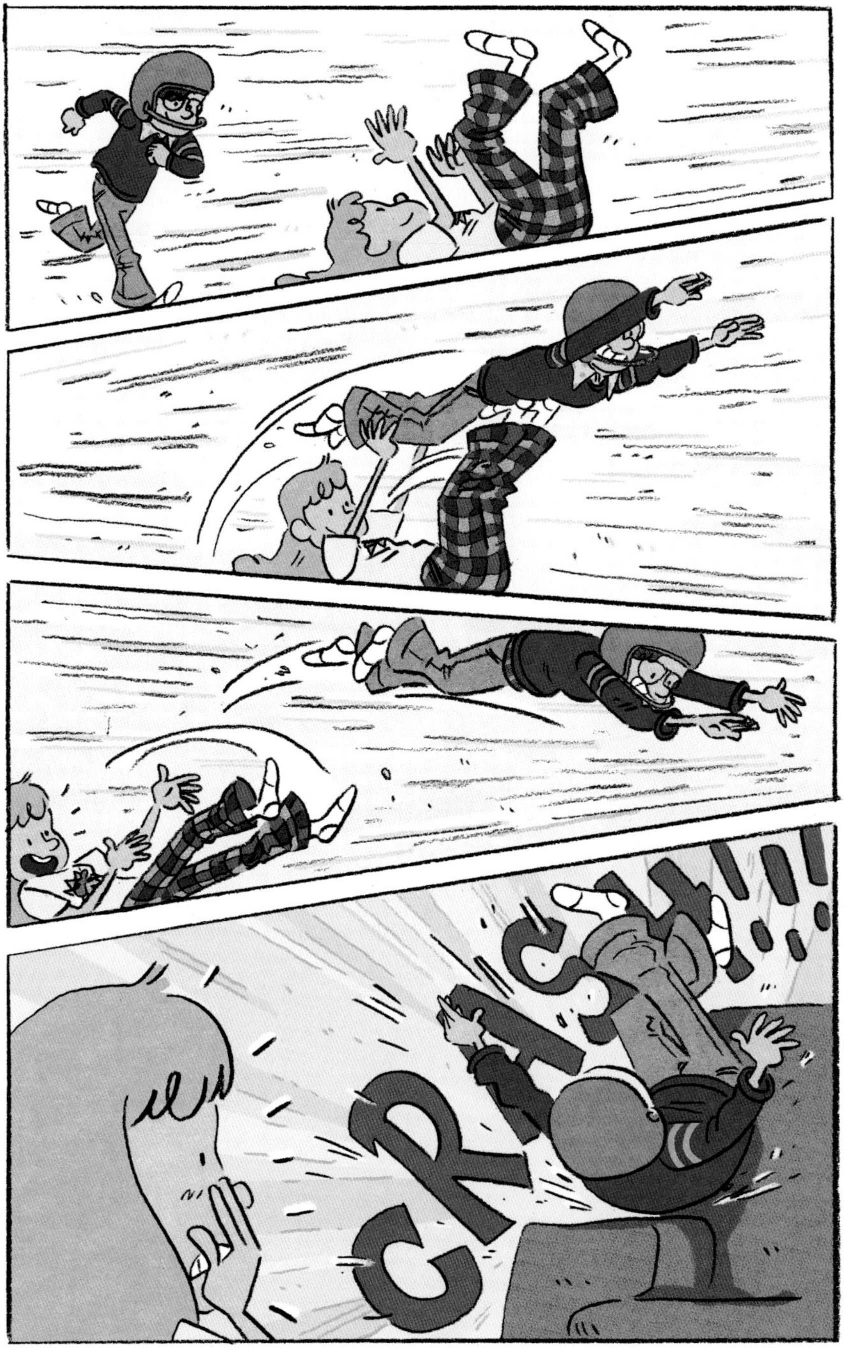
CRASH!!!

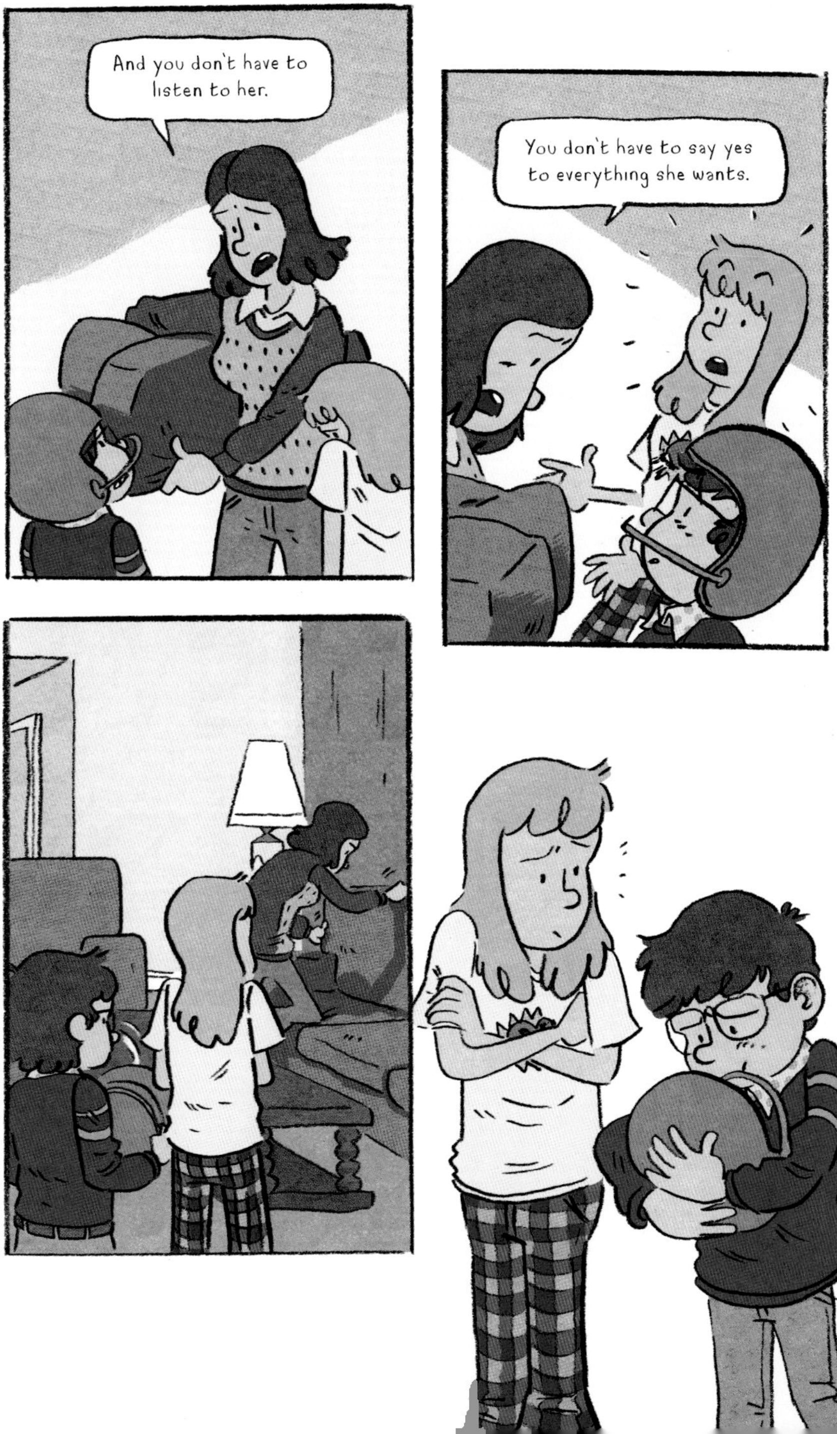
And you don't have to listen to her.
You don't have to say yes to everything she wants.

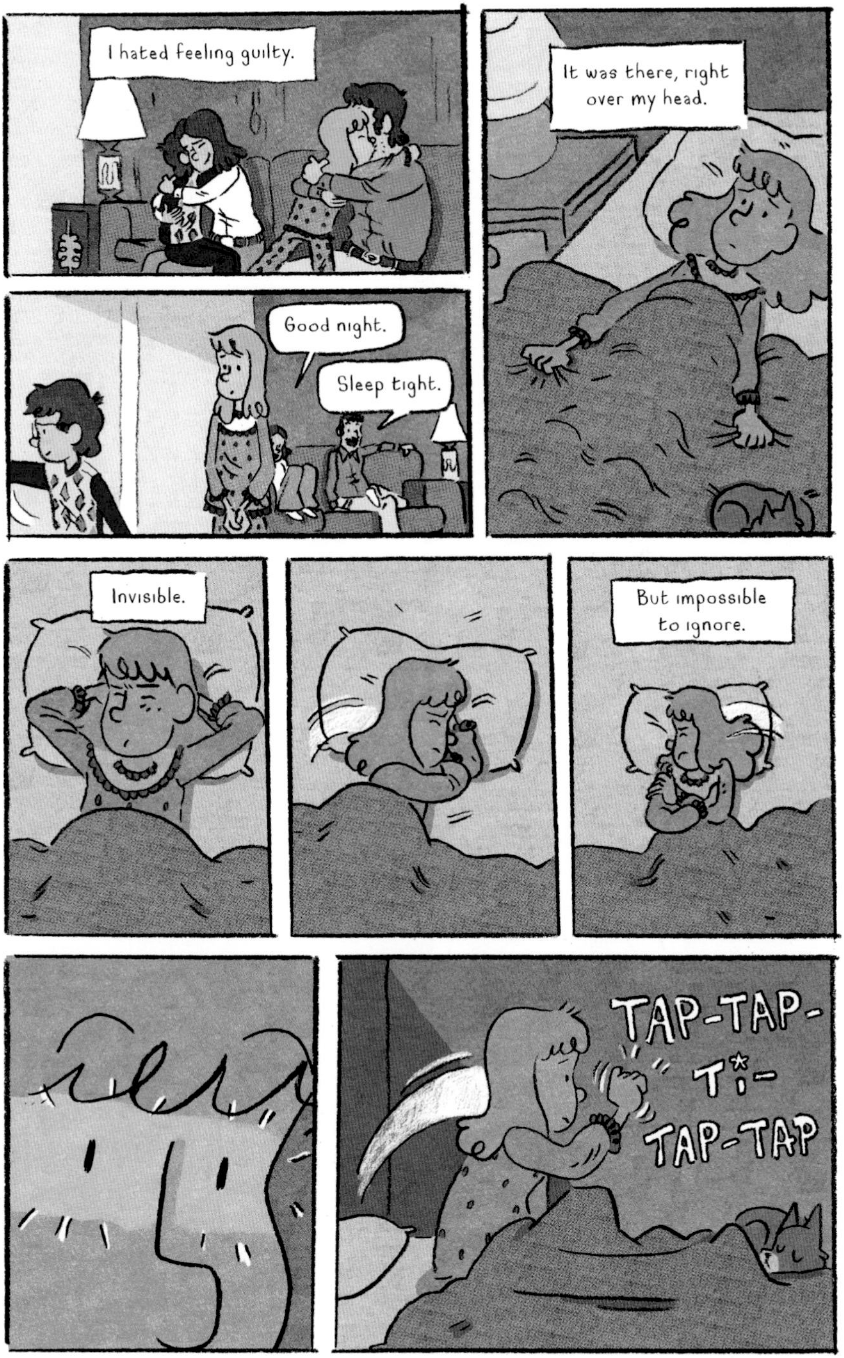
I hated feeling guilty.
It was there, right over my head.
Good night.
Sleep tight.
Invisible.
But impossible to ignore.
TAP-TAP-
T*i-
TAP-TAP

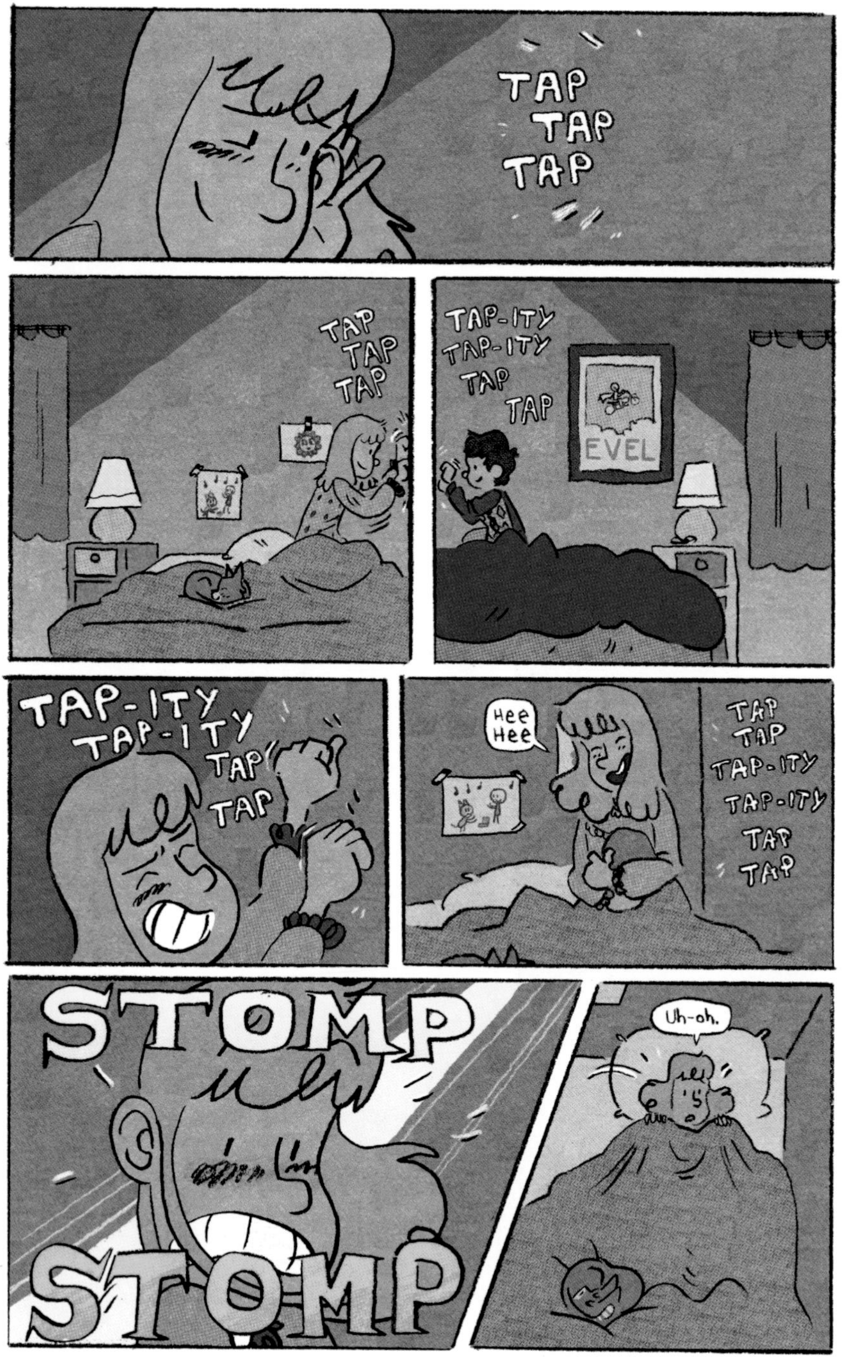
TAP
TAP
TAP
TAP
TAP
TAP
TAP-ITY
TAP-ITY
TAP
TAP
TAP-ITY
TAP-ITY
TAP
TAP
Hee Hee
TAP
TAP
TAP-ITY
TAP-ITY
TAP
TAP
STOMP
STOMP
Uh-oh.

The Power of Blame

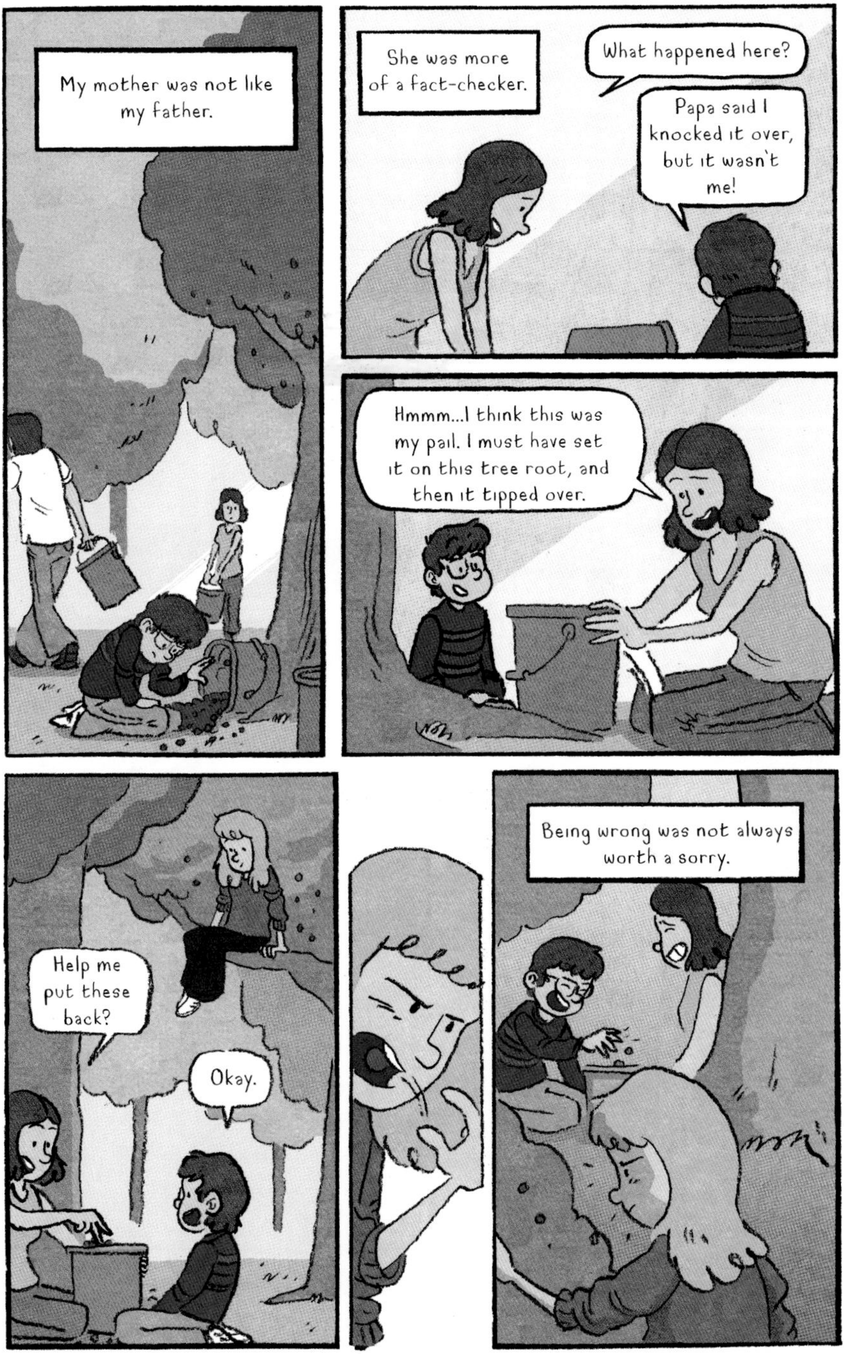
My mother was not like my father.
She was more of a fact-checker.
What happened here?
Papa said I knocked it over, but it wasn't me!
Hmmm...I think this was my pail. I must have set it on this tree root, and then it tipped over.
Help me put these back?
Okay.
Being wrong was not always worth a sorry.

126

128

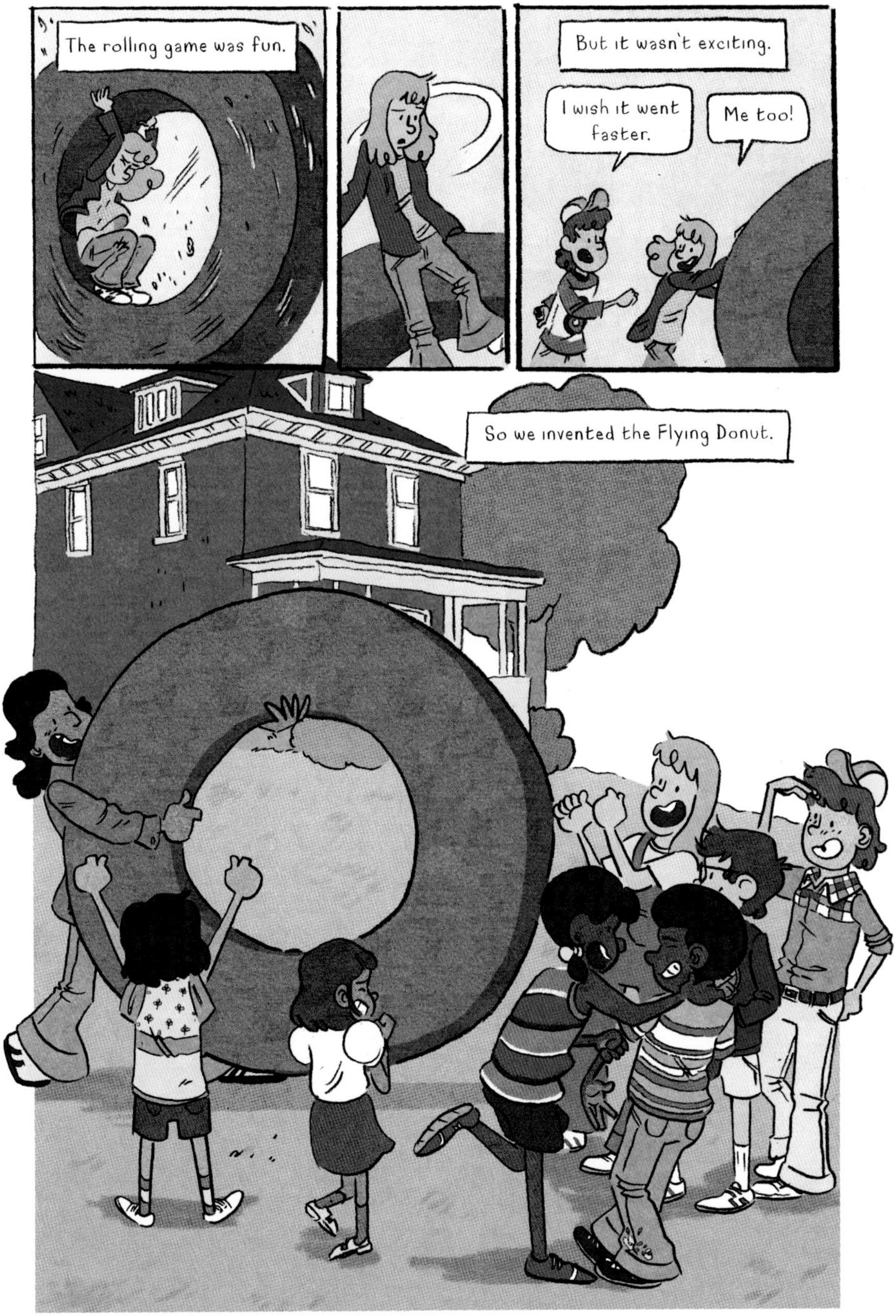
The rolling game was fun.
But it wasn't exciting.
I wish it went faster.
Me too!
So we invented the Flying Donut.

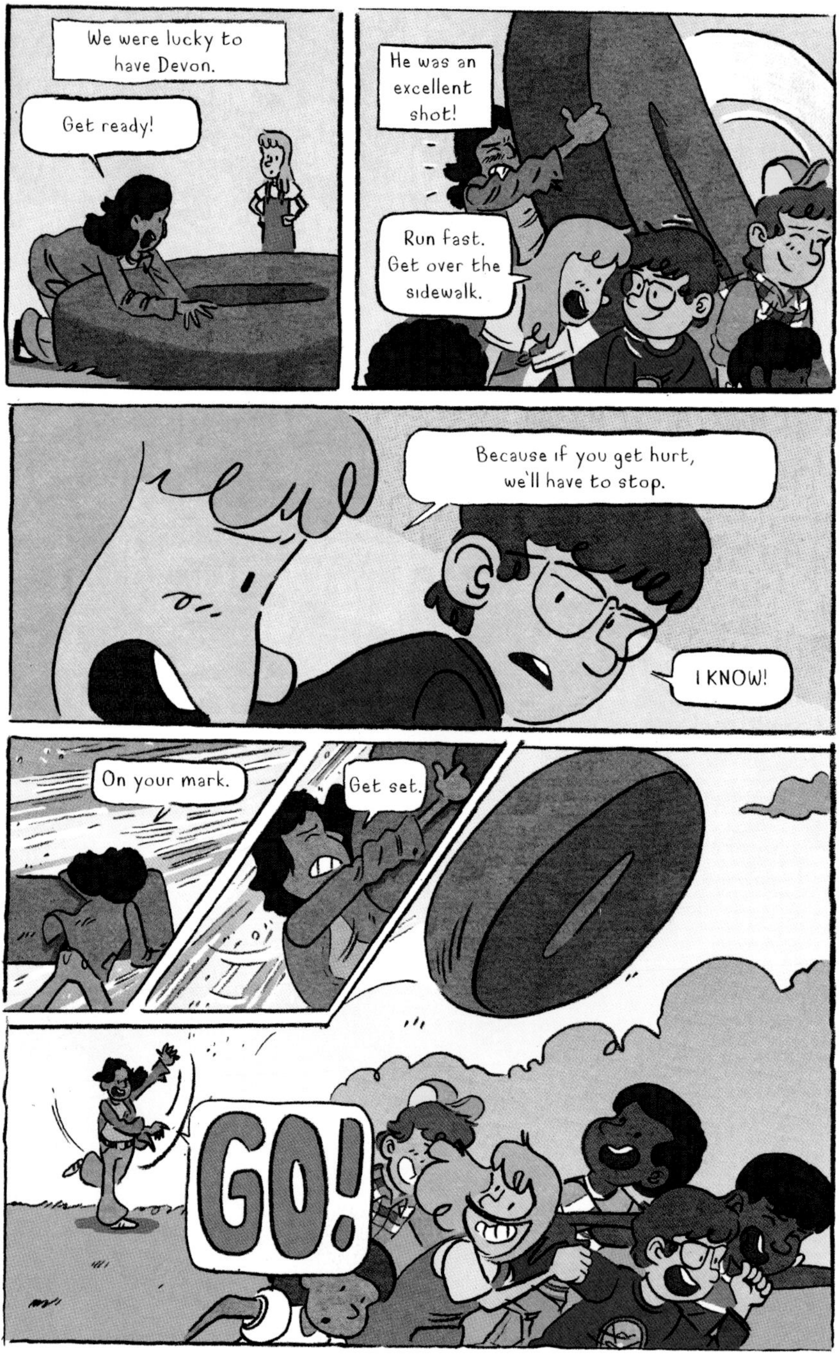

We were lucky to have Devon.
Get ready!
He was an excellent shot!
Run fast. Get over the sidewalk.
Because if you get hurt, we'll have to stop.
I KNOW!
On your mark.
Get set.
GO!

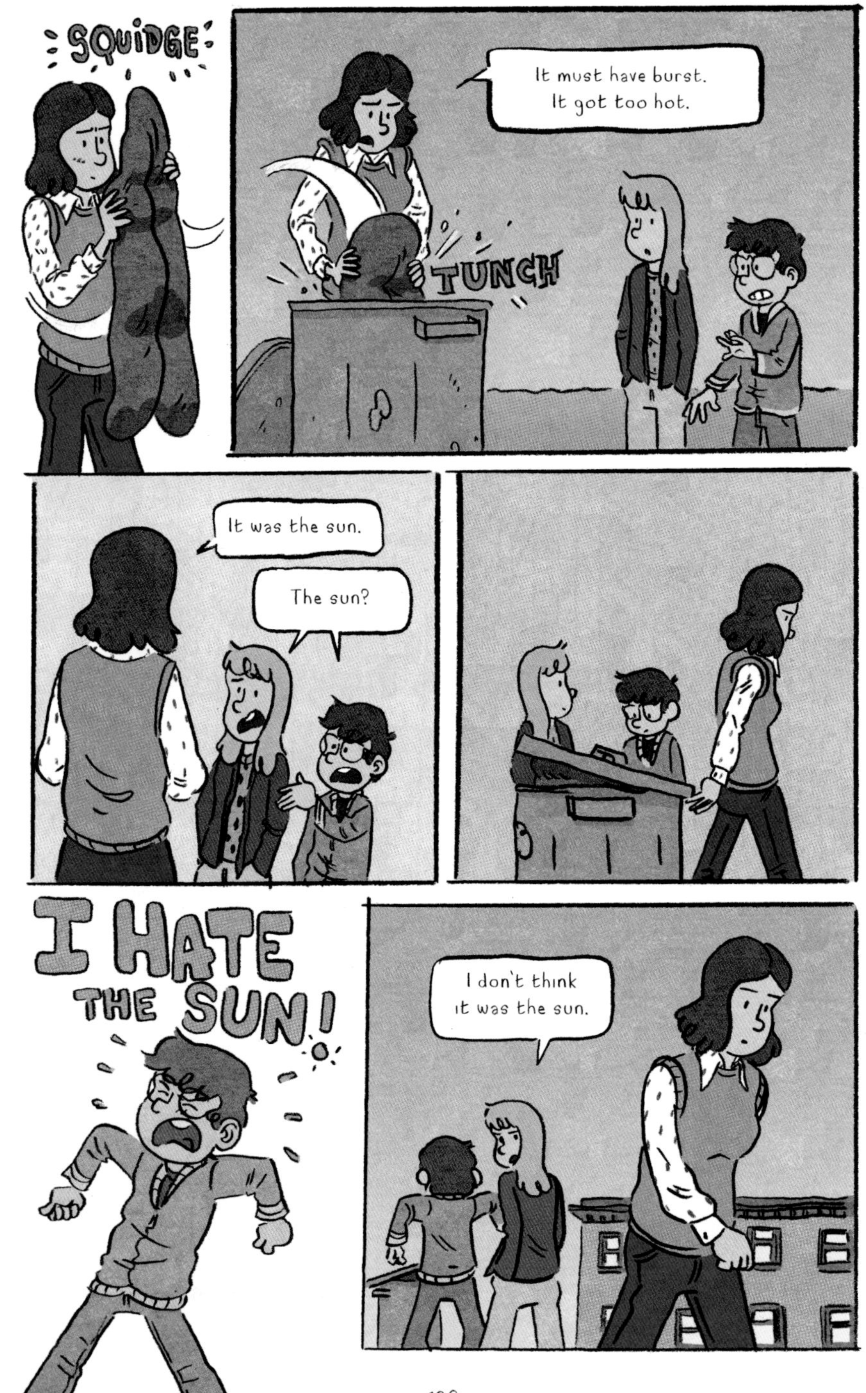
SQUIDGE
It must have burst.
It got too hot.
TUNCH
It was the sun.
The sun?
I HATE THE SUN!
I don't think it was the sun.

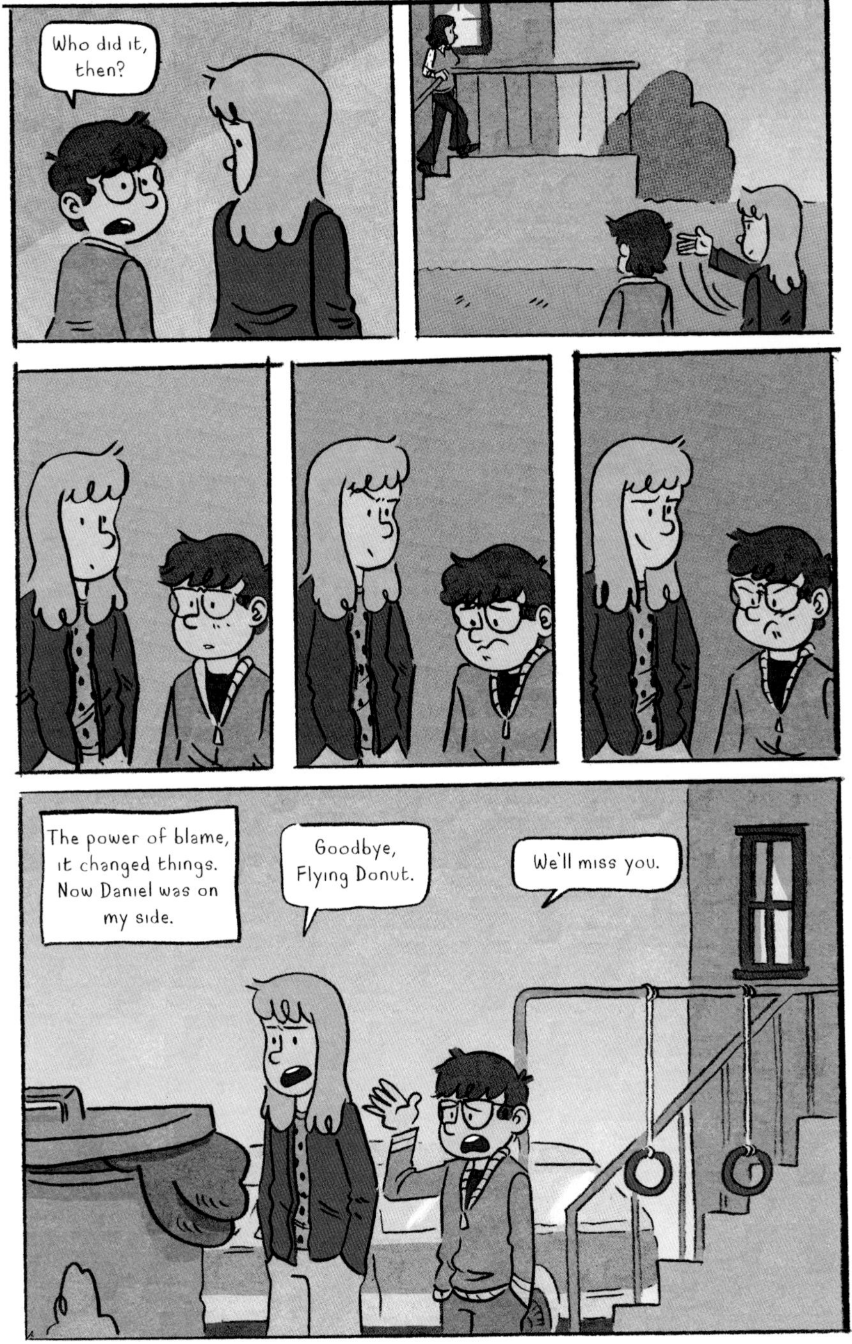

Who did it, then?
The power of blame, it changed things. Now Daniel was on my side.
Goodbye, Flying Donut.
We'll miss you.

The Power of the Boss

142

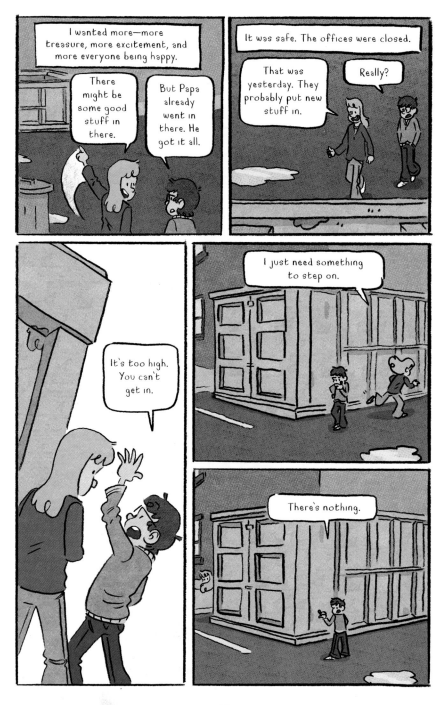

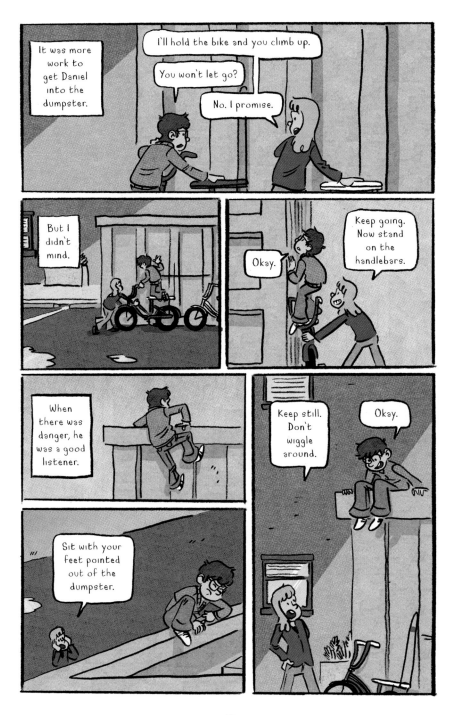

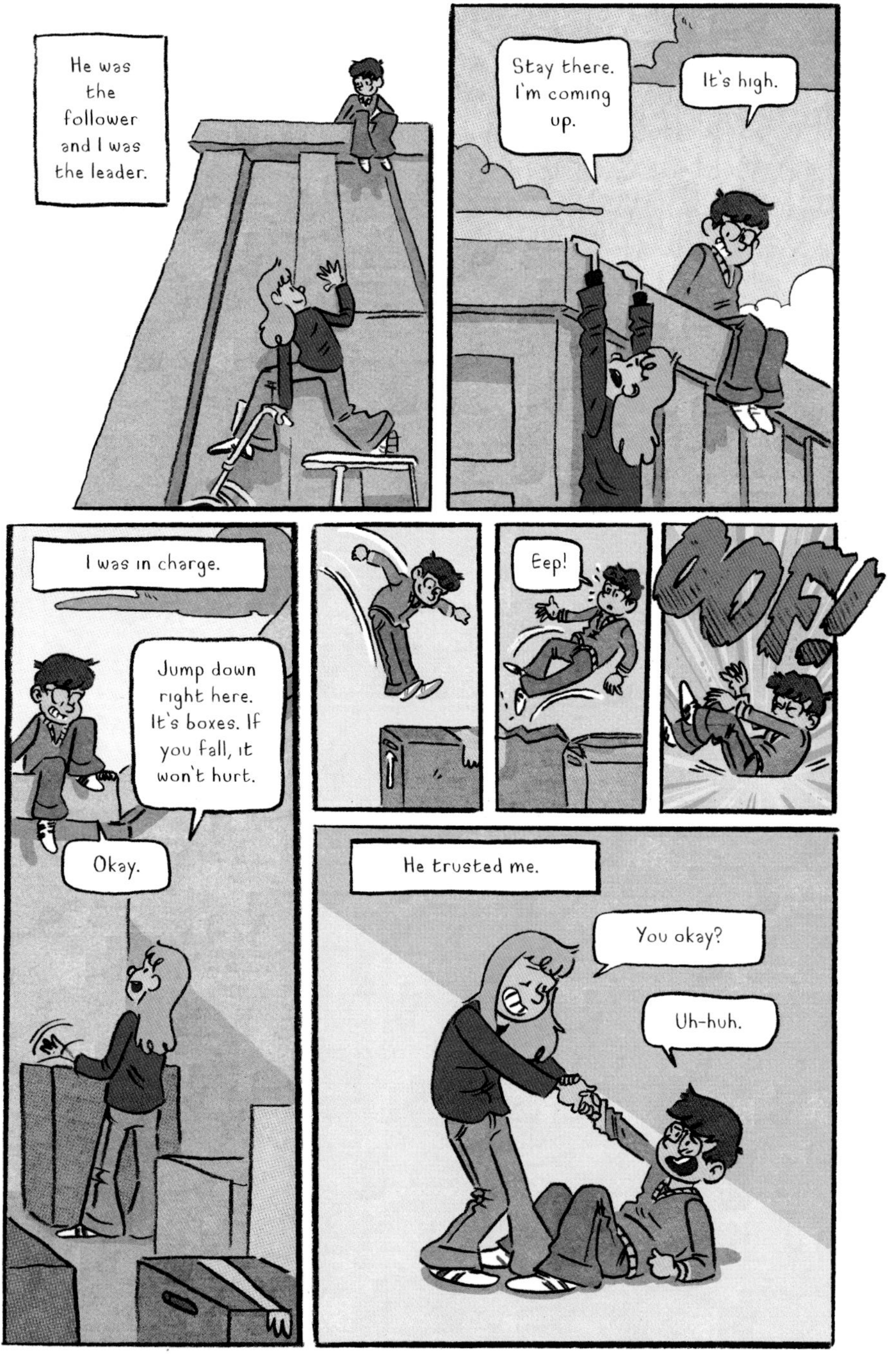

He was the follower and I was the leader.
Stay there. I'm coming up.
It's high.
I was in charge.
Jump down right here. It's boxes. If you fall, it won't hurt.
Okay.
Eep!
OOF!
He trusted me.
You okay?
Uh-huh.

156

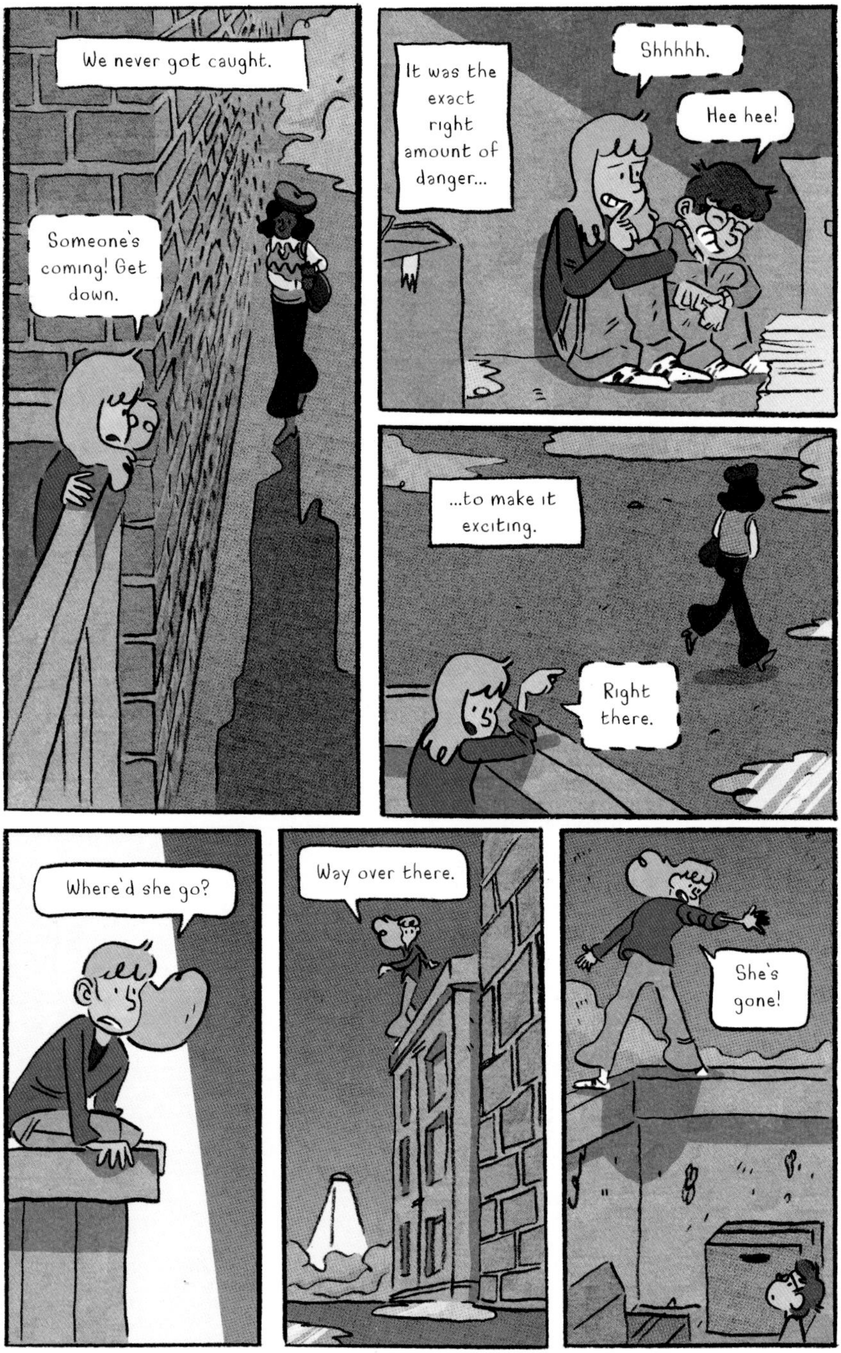

We never got caught.
Someone's coming! Get down.
It was the exact right amount of danger...
Shhhhh.
Hee hee!
...to make it exciting.
Right there.
Where'd she go?
Way over there.
She's gone!

8

The Power to Dare

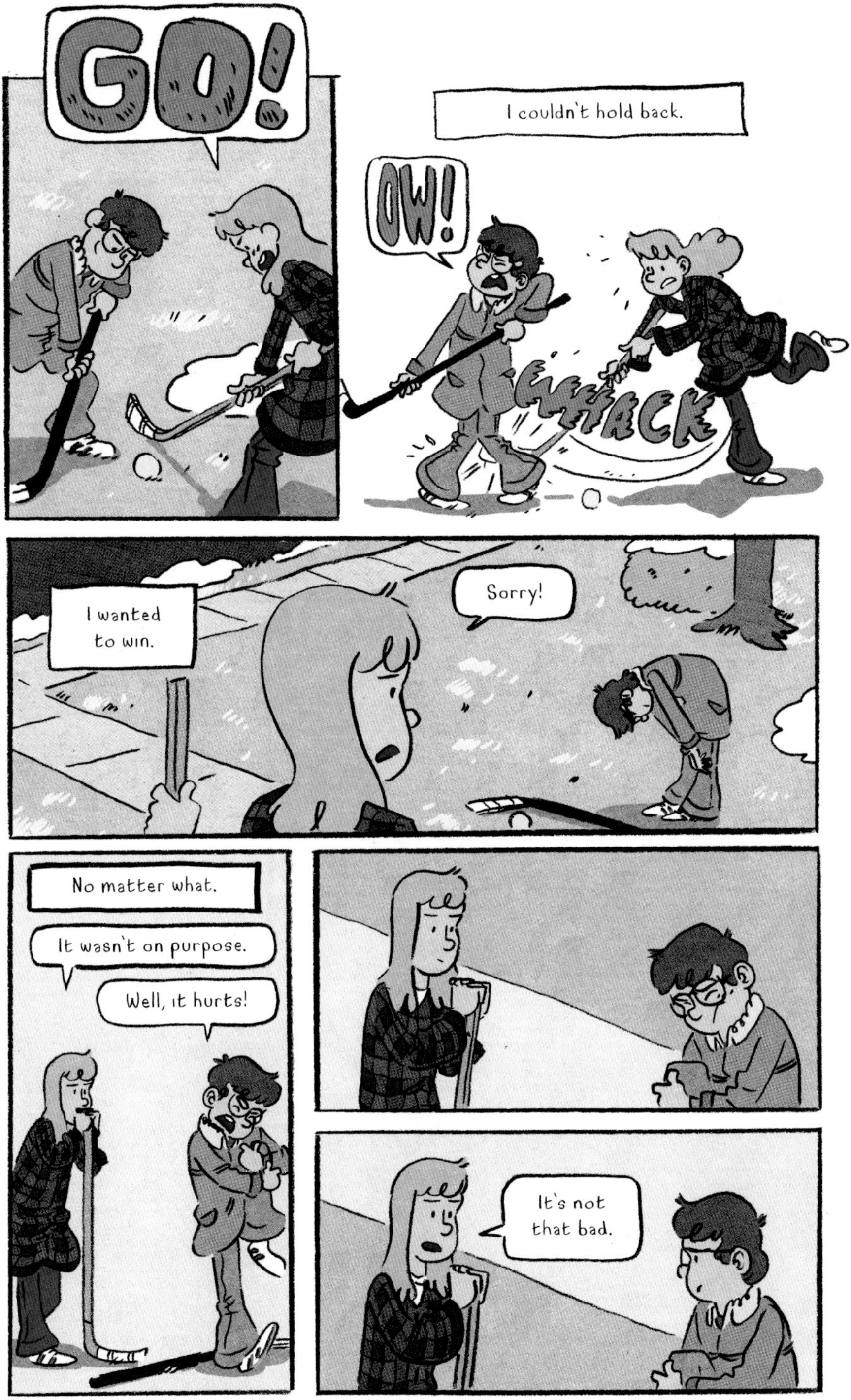
GO!
I couldn't hold back.
OW!
WHACK
I wanted to win.
Sorry!
No matter what.
It wasn't on purpose.
Well, it hurts!
It's not that bad.

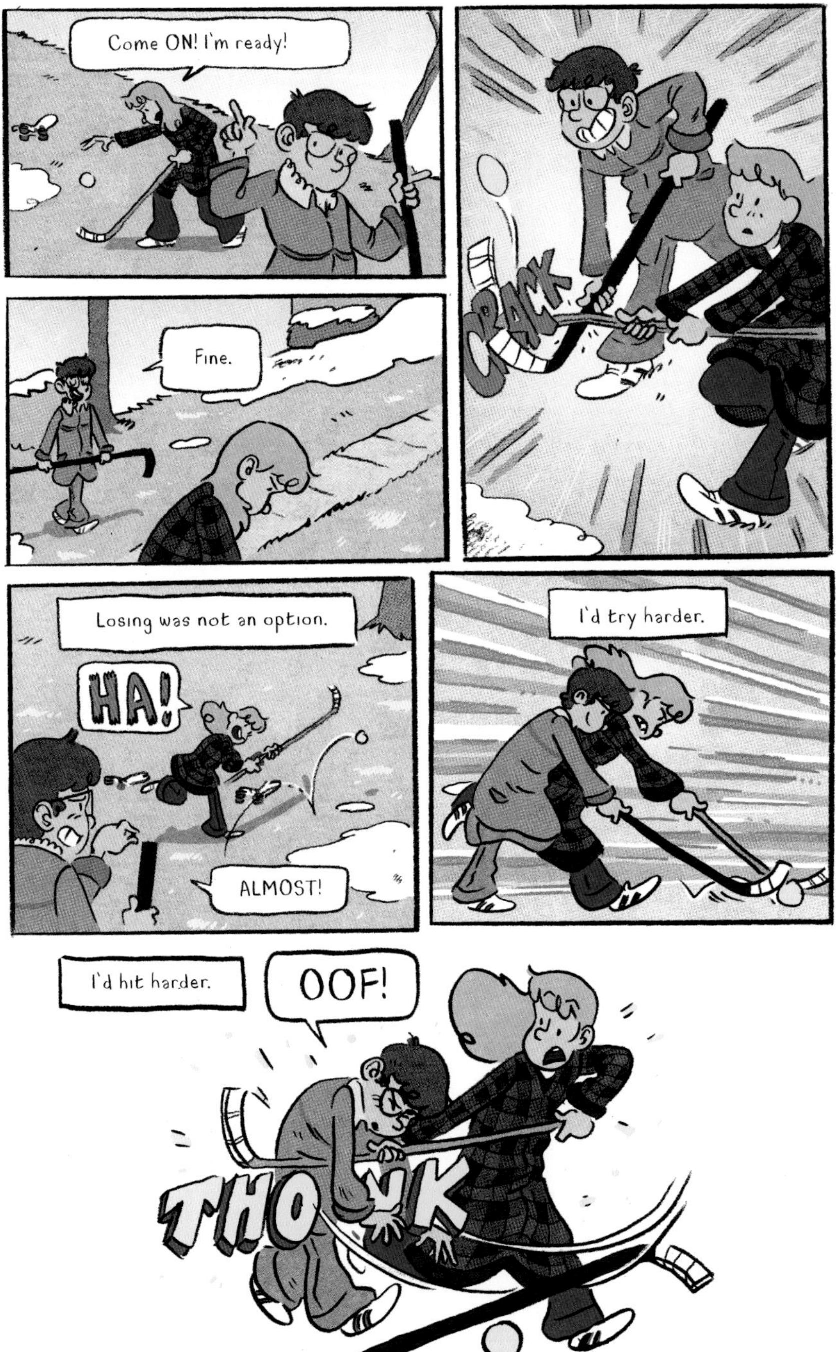
Come ON! I'm ready!
Fine.
CRACK
Losing was not an option.
HA!
ALMOST!
I'd try harder.
I'd hit harder.
OOF!
THONK

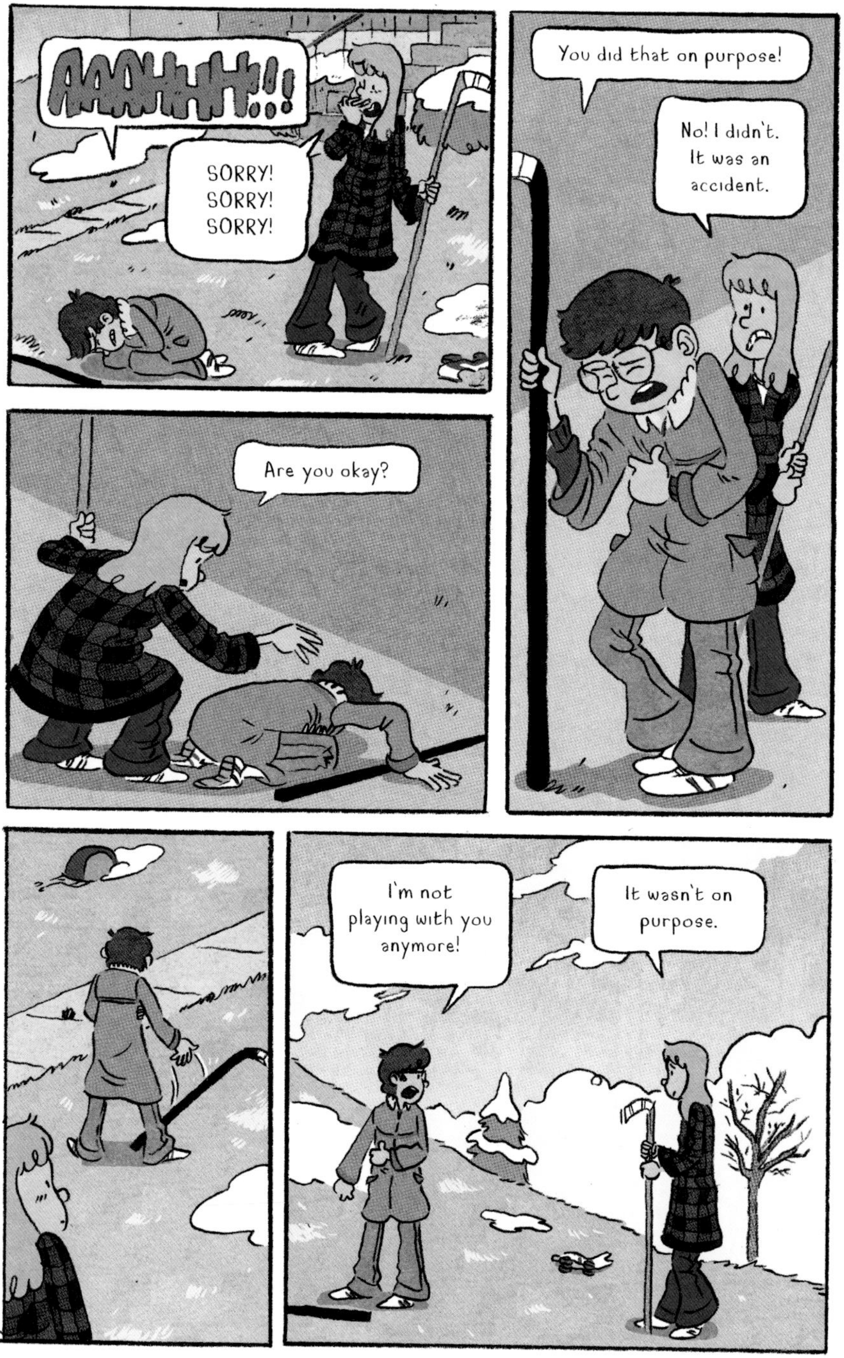
AAAHHH!!!
SORRY! SORRY! SORRY!
You did that on purpose!
No! I didn't. It was an accident.
Are you okay?
I'm not playing with you anymore!
It wasn't on purpose.

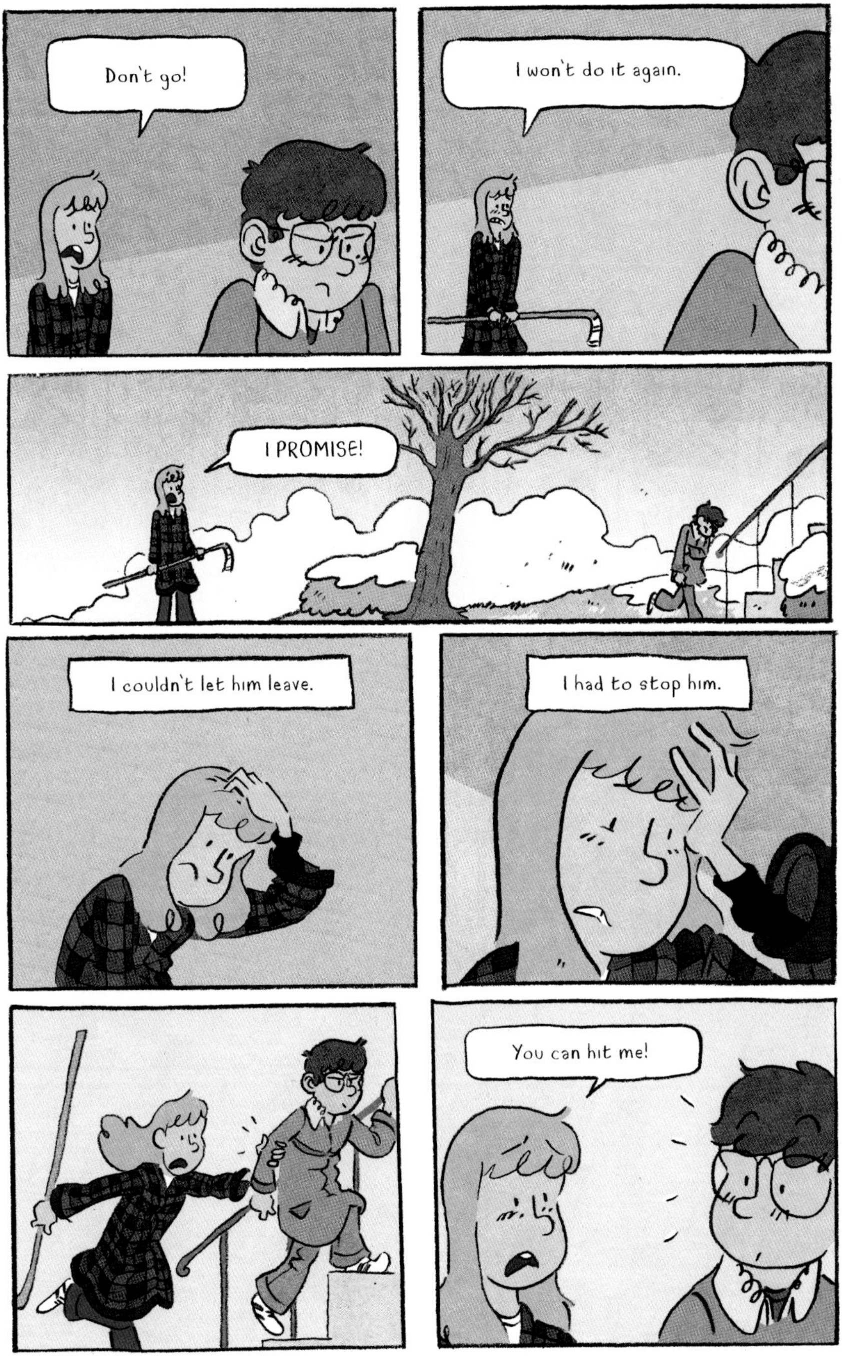
Don't go!
I won't do it again.
I PROMISE!
I couldn't let him leave.
I had to stop him.
You can hit me!

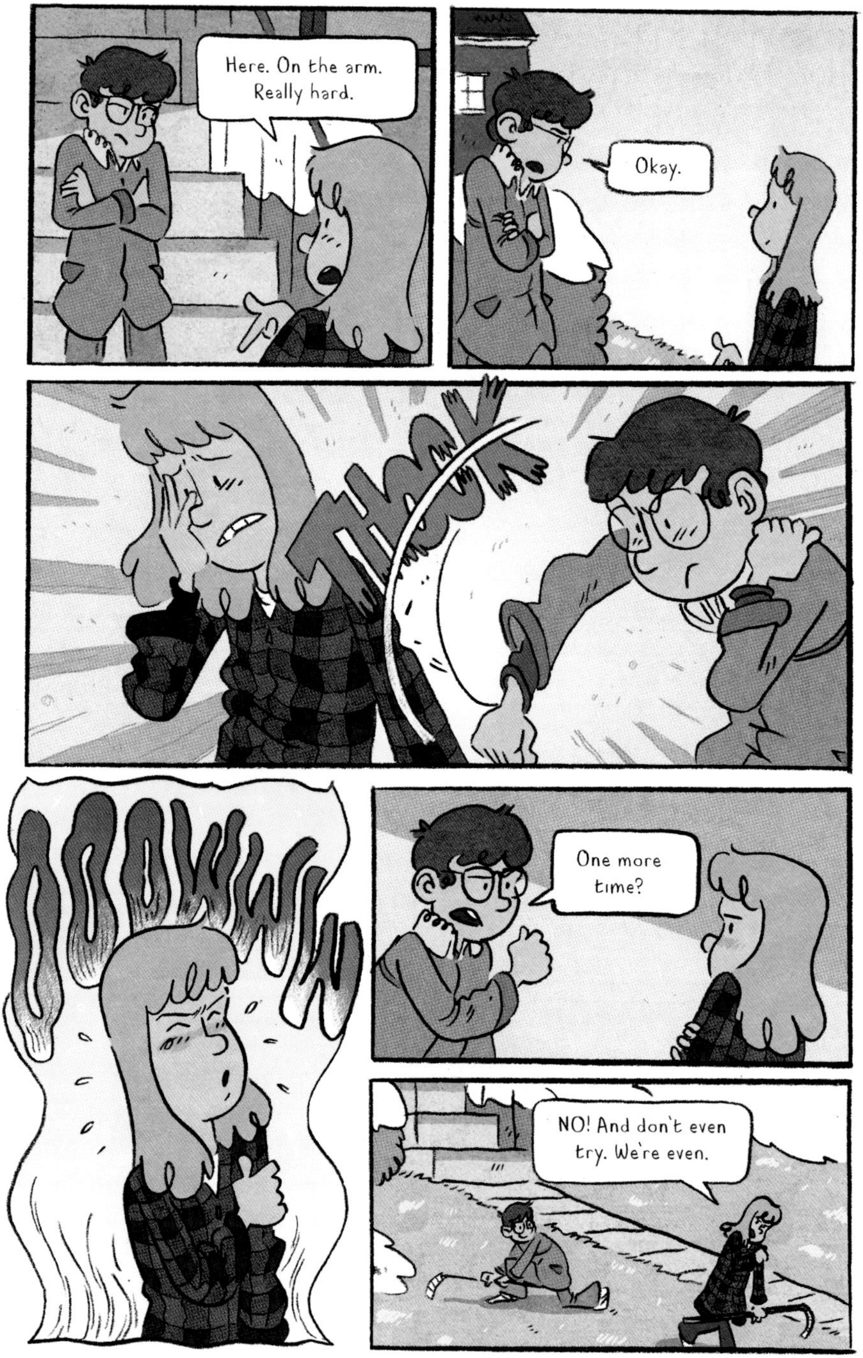
Here. On the arm. Really hard.
Okay.
One more time?
NO! And don't even try. We're even.

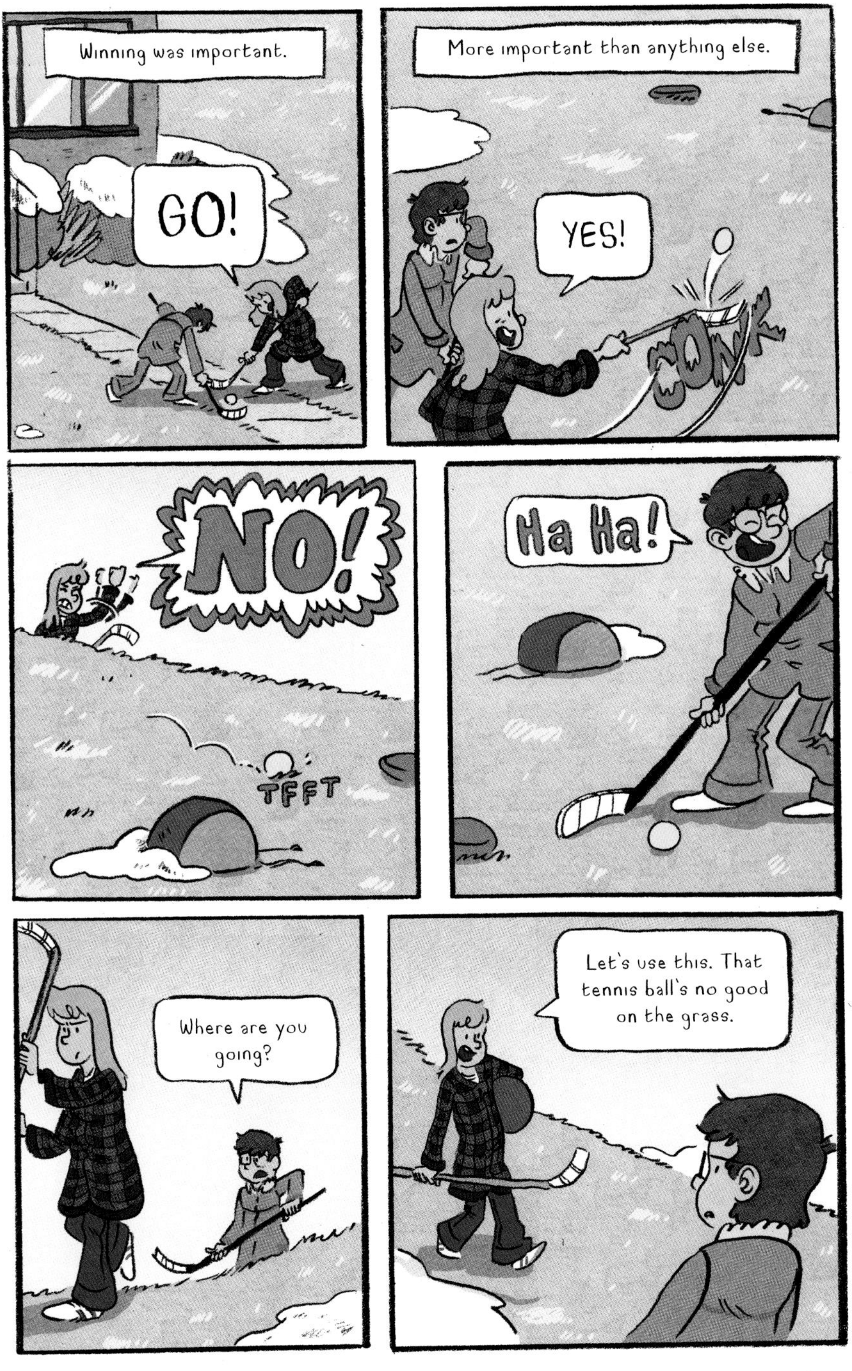

Winning was important.
GO!
More important than anything else.
YES!
CONK
NO!
TFFT
Ha Ha!
Where are you going?
Let's use this. That tennis ball's no good on the grass.

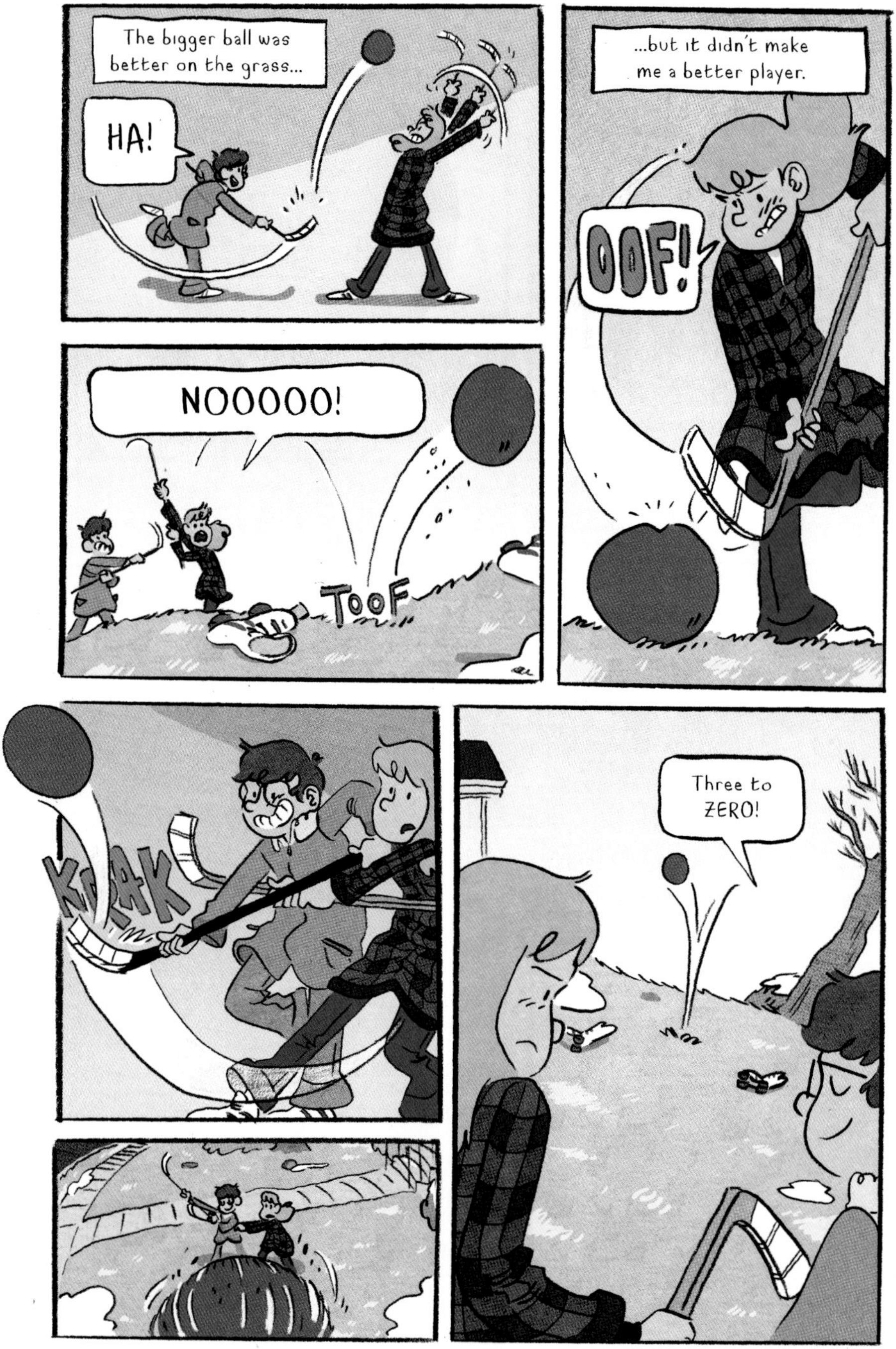
The bigger ball was better on the grass...
HA!
...but it didn't make me a better player.
OOF!
NOOOOO!
TOOF
KRAK
Three to ZERO!

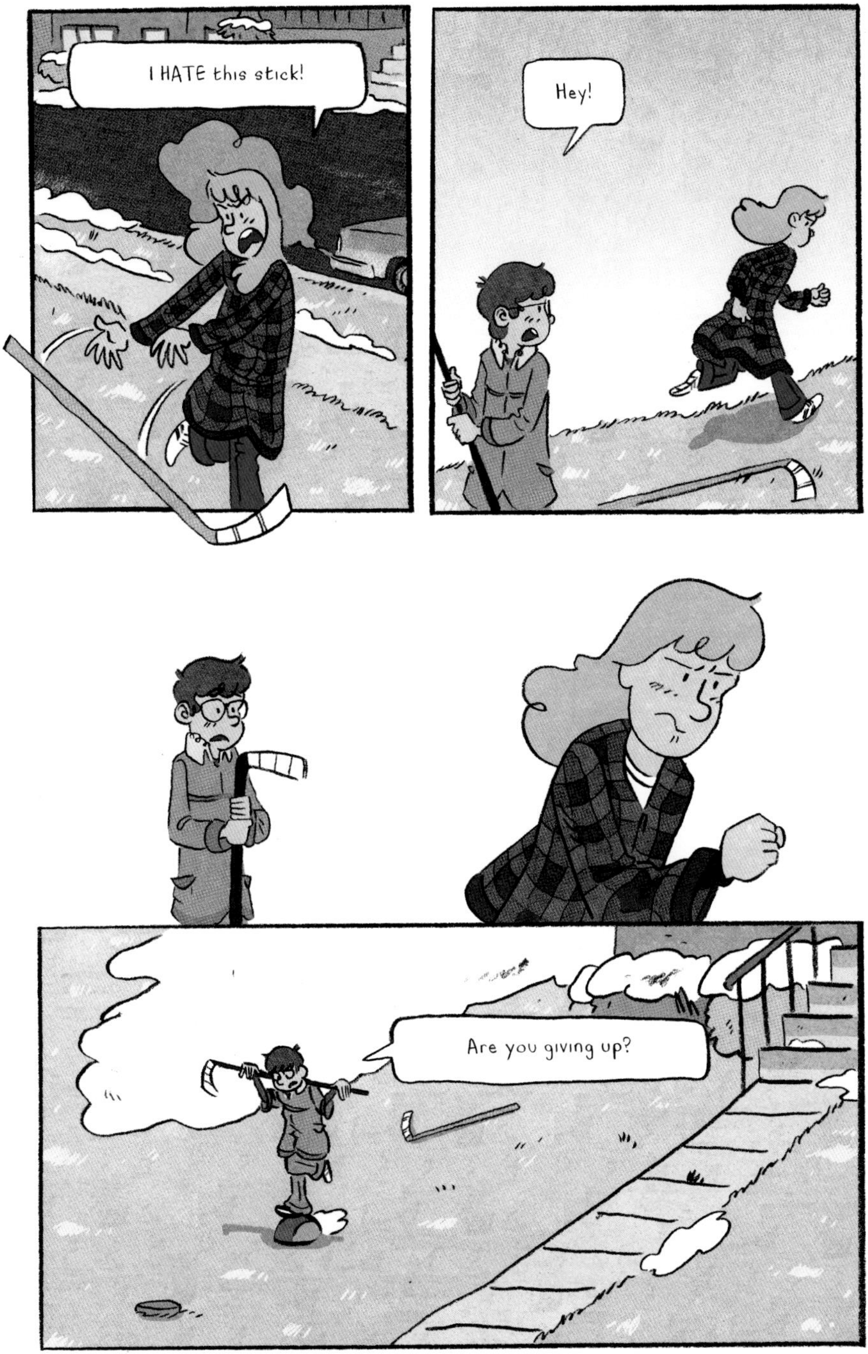
I HATE this stick!
Hey!
Are you giving up?

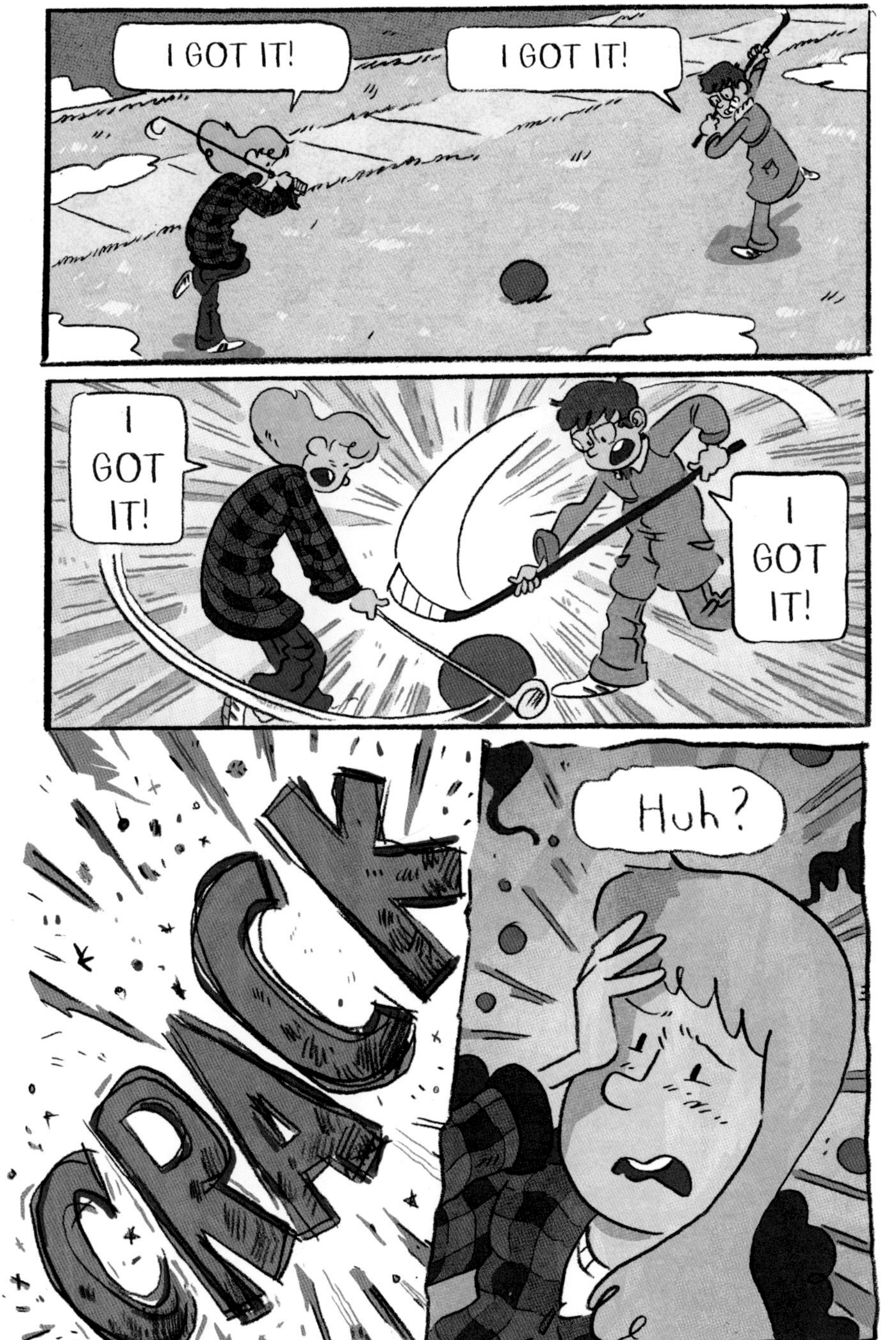
I GOT IT!
I GOT IT!
I GOT IT!
I GOT IT!
CRACK
Huh?

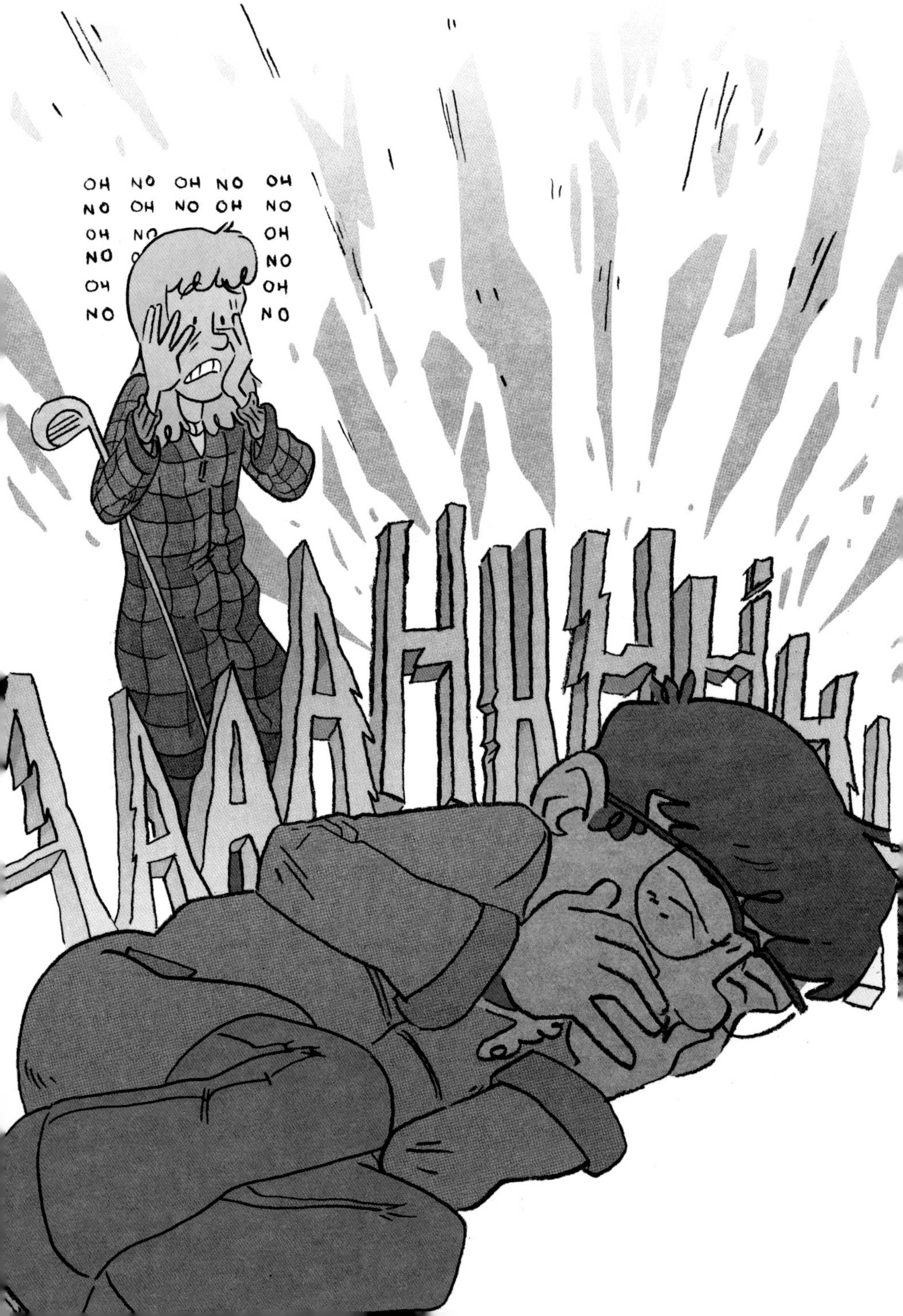
OH NO OH NO OH
NO OH NO OH NO
AAAAHHHHH

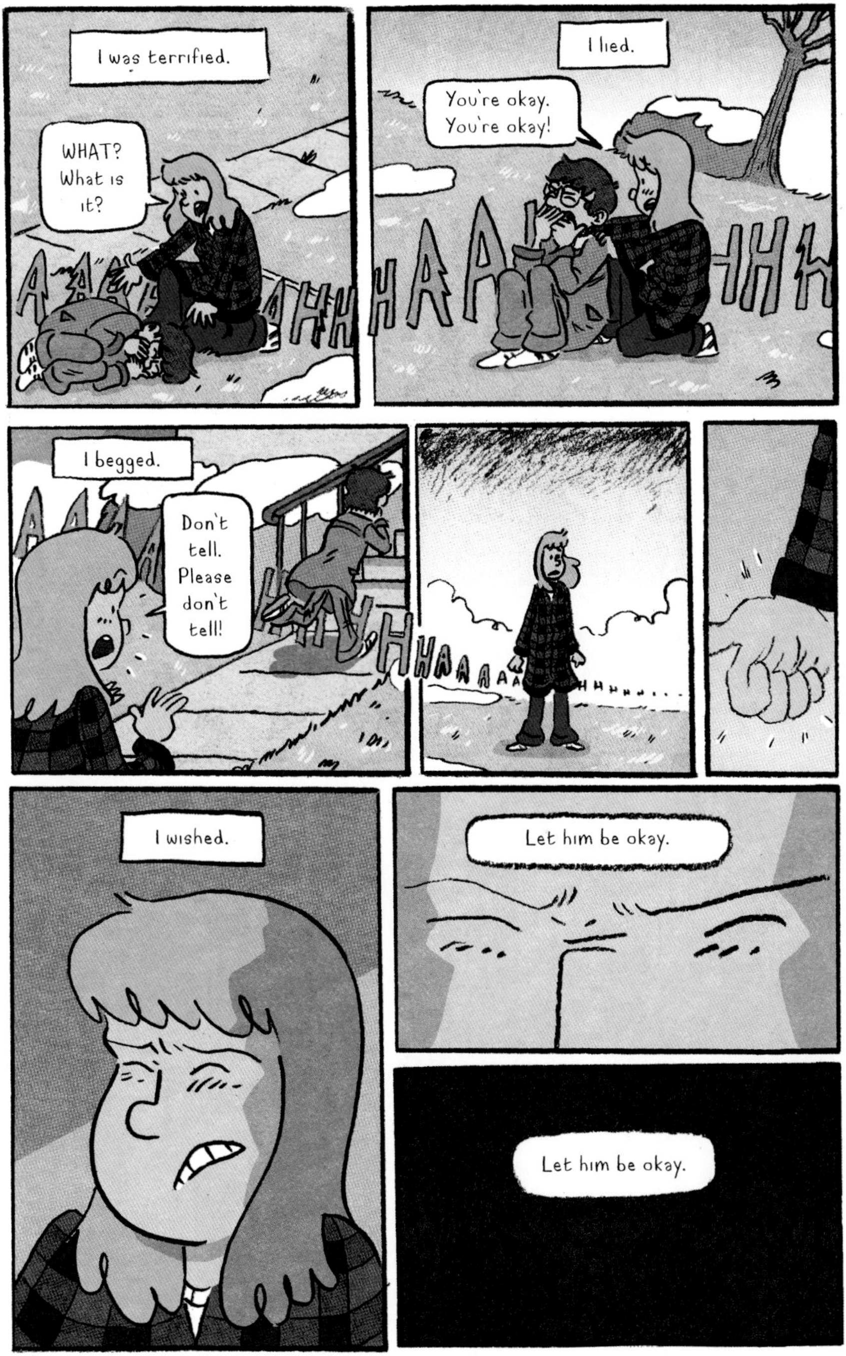
I was terrified.
WHAT? What is it?
AAAHHH
I lied.
You're okay. You're okay!
HAAAHHH
I begged.
Don't tell. Please don't tell!
AAAHHHAAAAAAHHHH...
I wished.
Let him be okay.
Let him be okay.

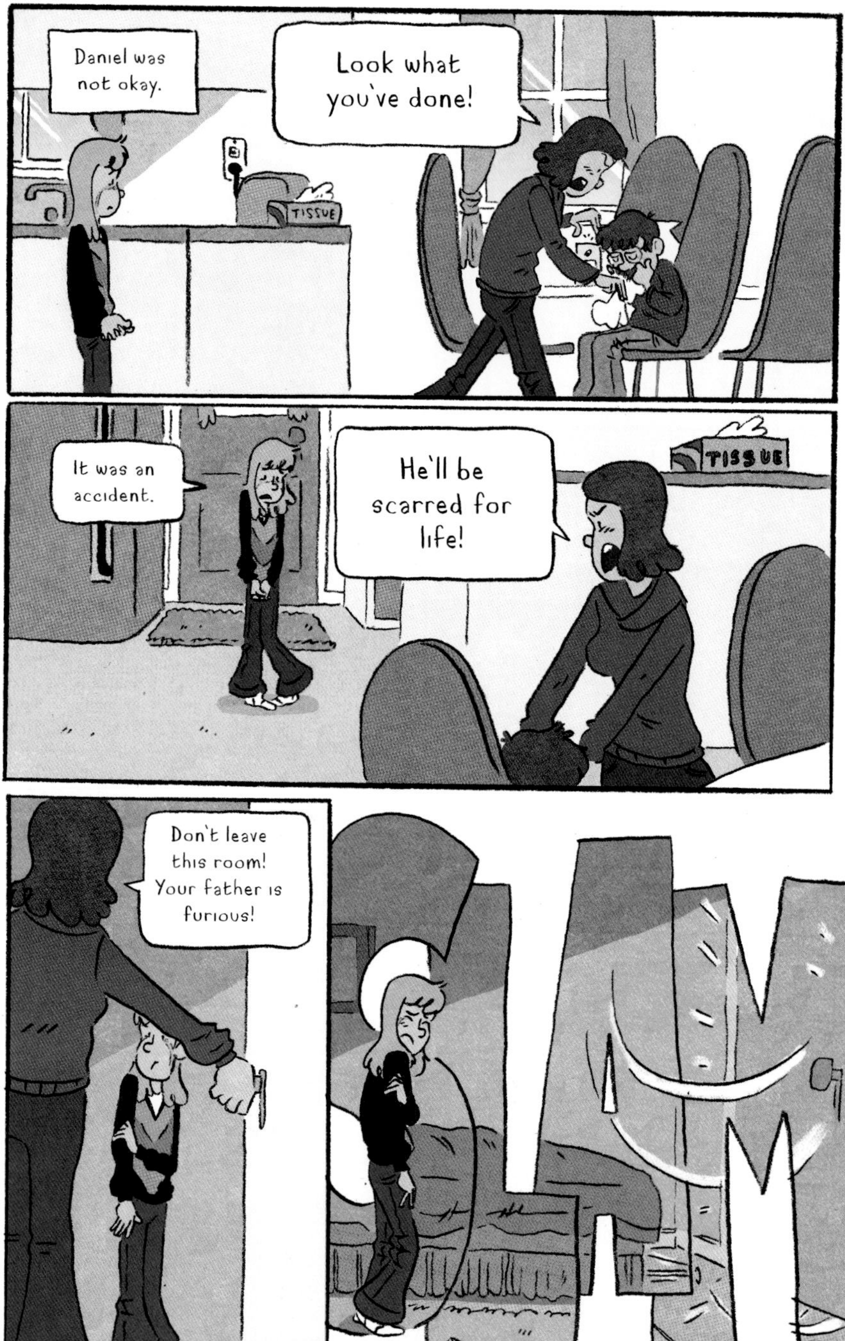
Daniel was not okay.
Look what you've done!
It was an accident.
He'll be scarred for life!
Don't leave this room! Your father is furious!
SLAM

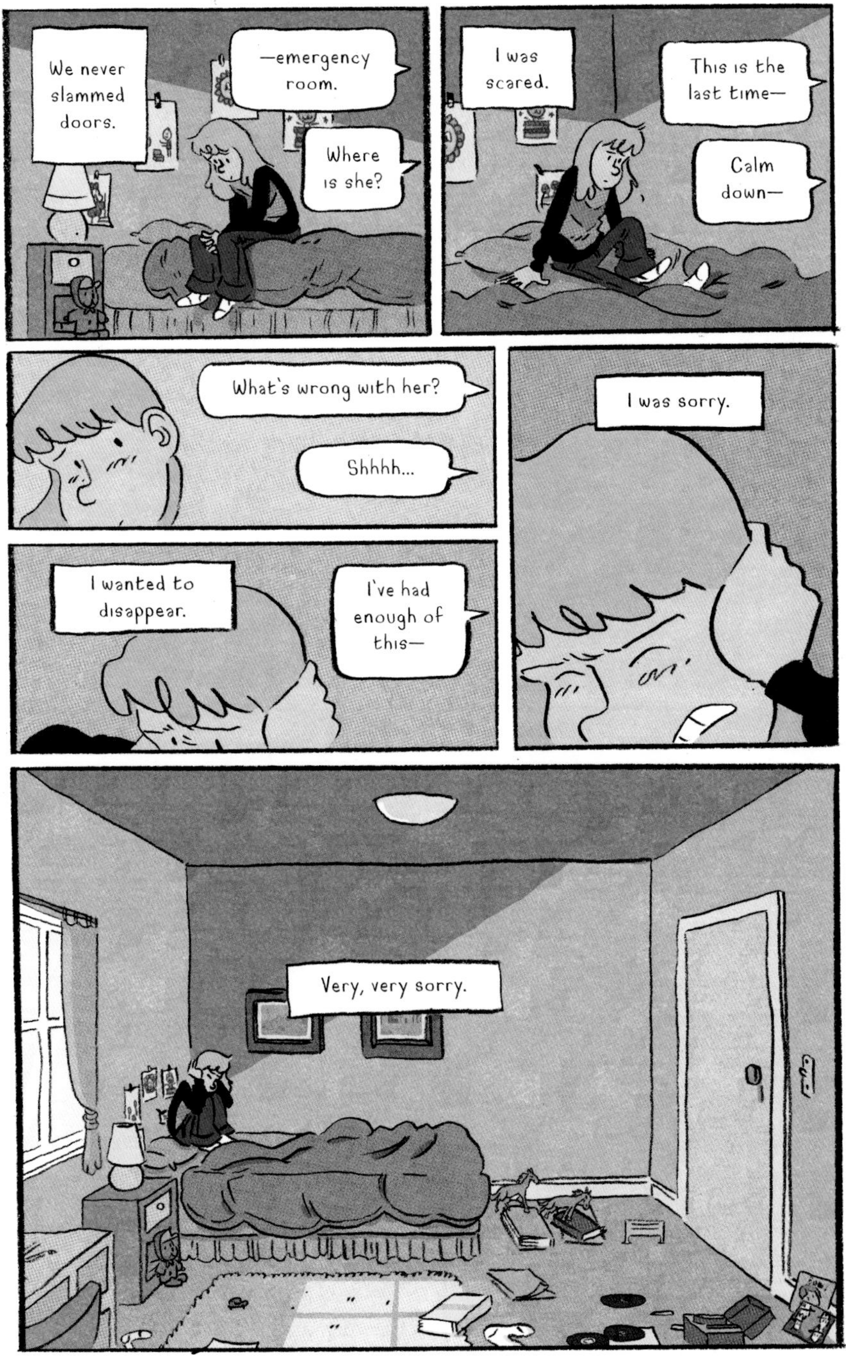
We never slammed doors.
—emergency room.
Where is she?
I was scared.
This is the last time—
Calm down—
What's wrong with her?
Shhhh...
I wanted to disappear.
I've had enough of this—
I was sorry.
Very, very sorry.

184

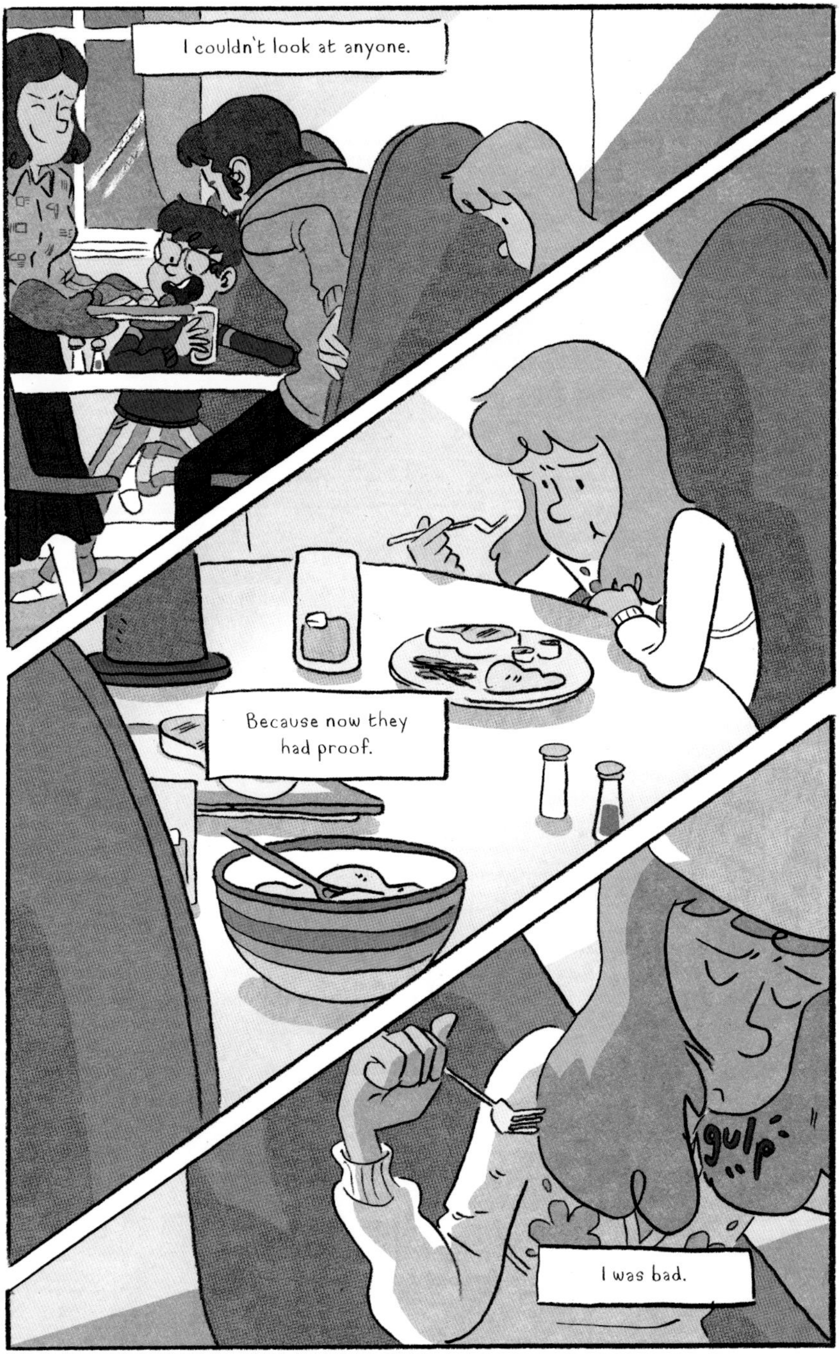
I couldn't look at anyone.
Because now they had proof.
gulp
I was bad.

9

The Power to Lead

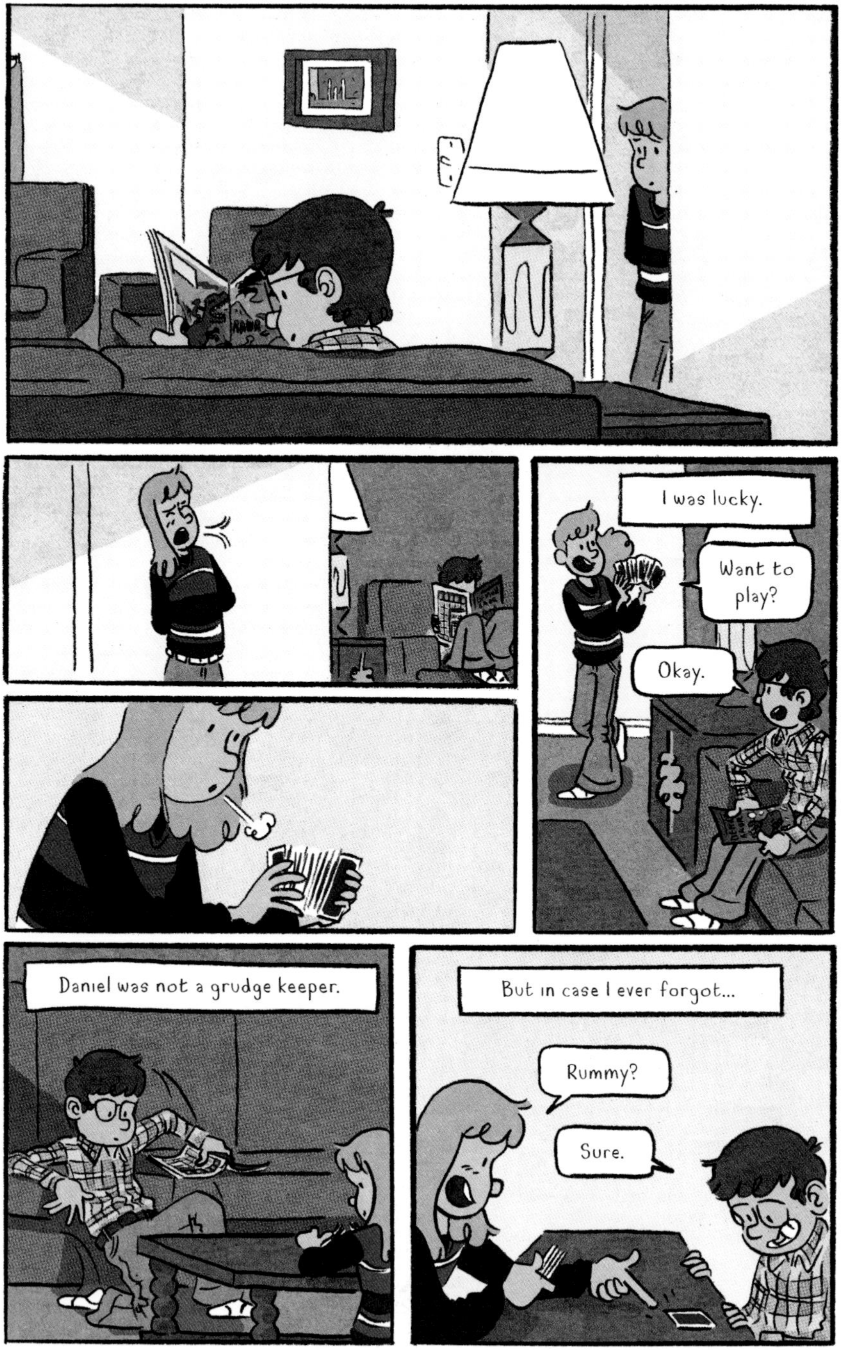
I was lucky.
Want to play?
Okay.
Daniel was not a grudge keeper.
But in case I ever forgot...
Rummy?
Sure.

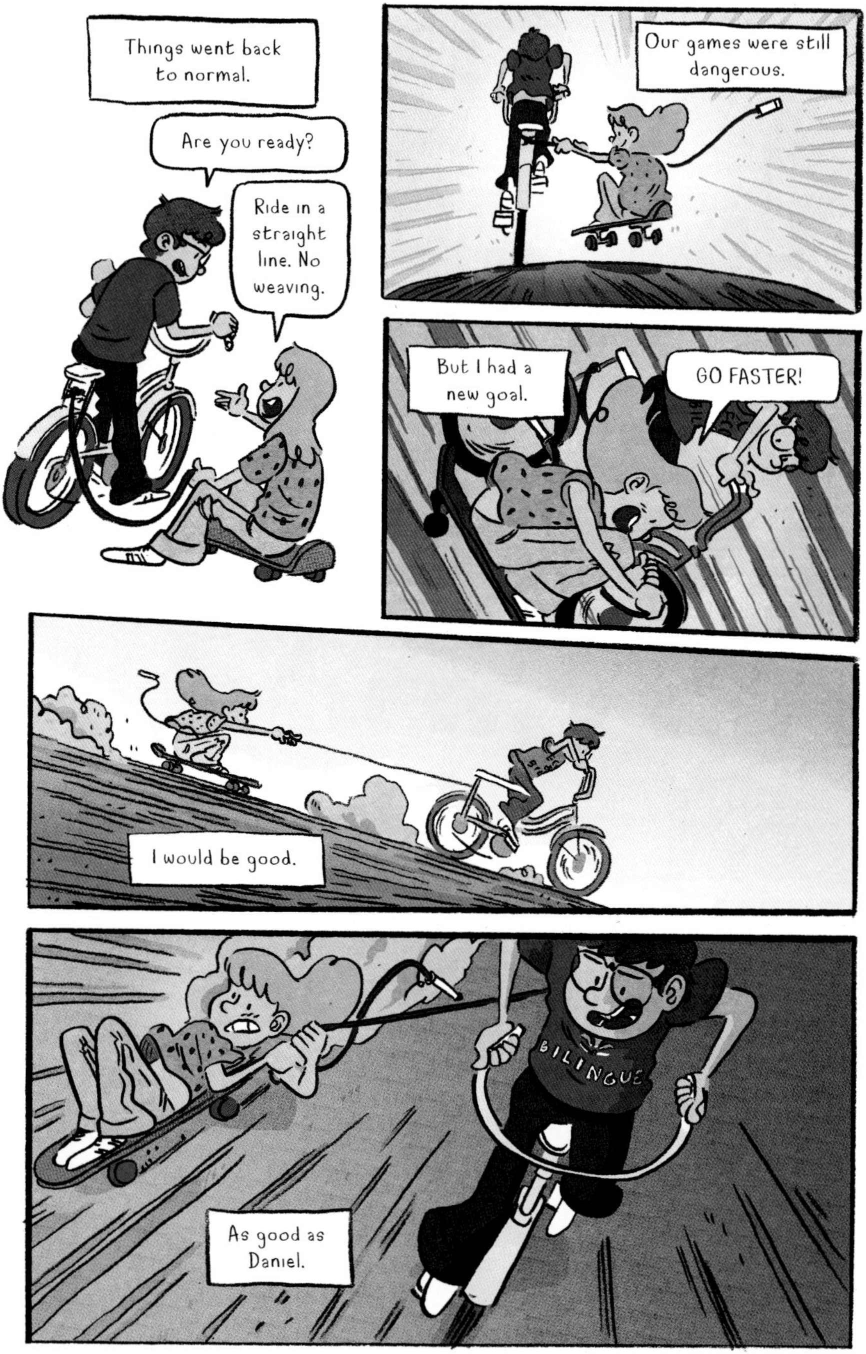
Things went back to normal.
Are you ready?
Ride in a straight line. No weaving.
Our games were still dangerous.
But I had a new goal.
GO FASTER!
I would be good.
BILINGUE
As good as Daniel.

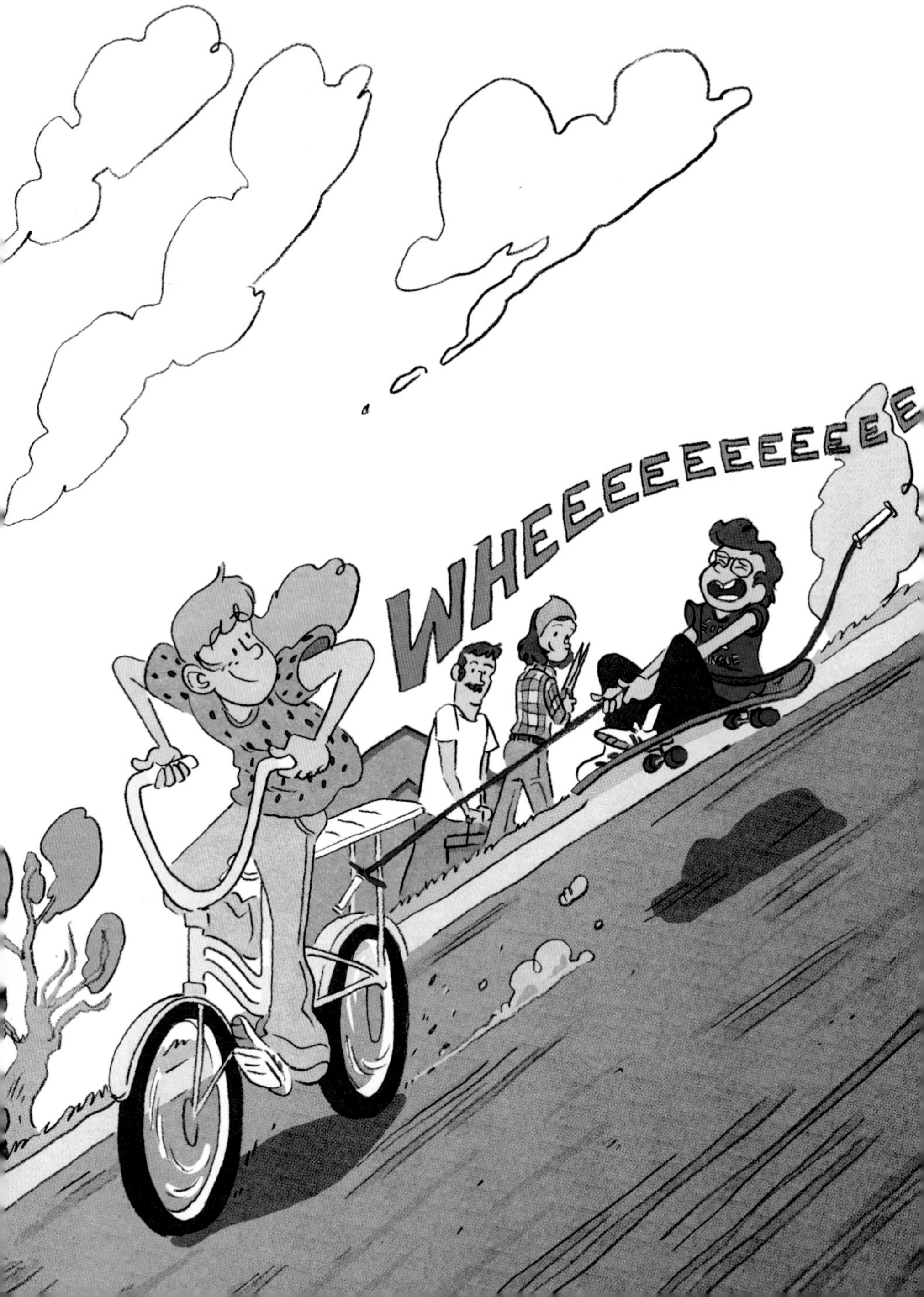
WHEEEEEEEEEEE

200

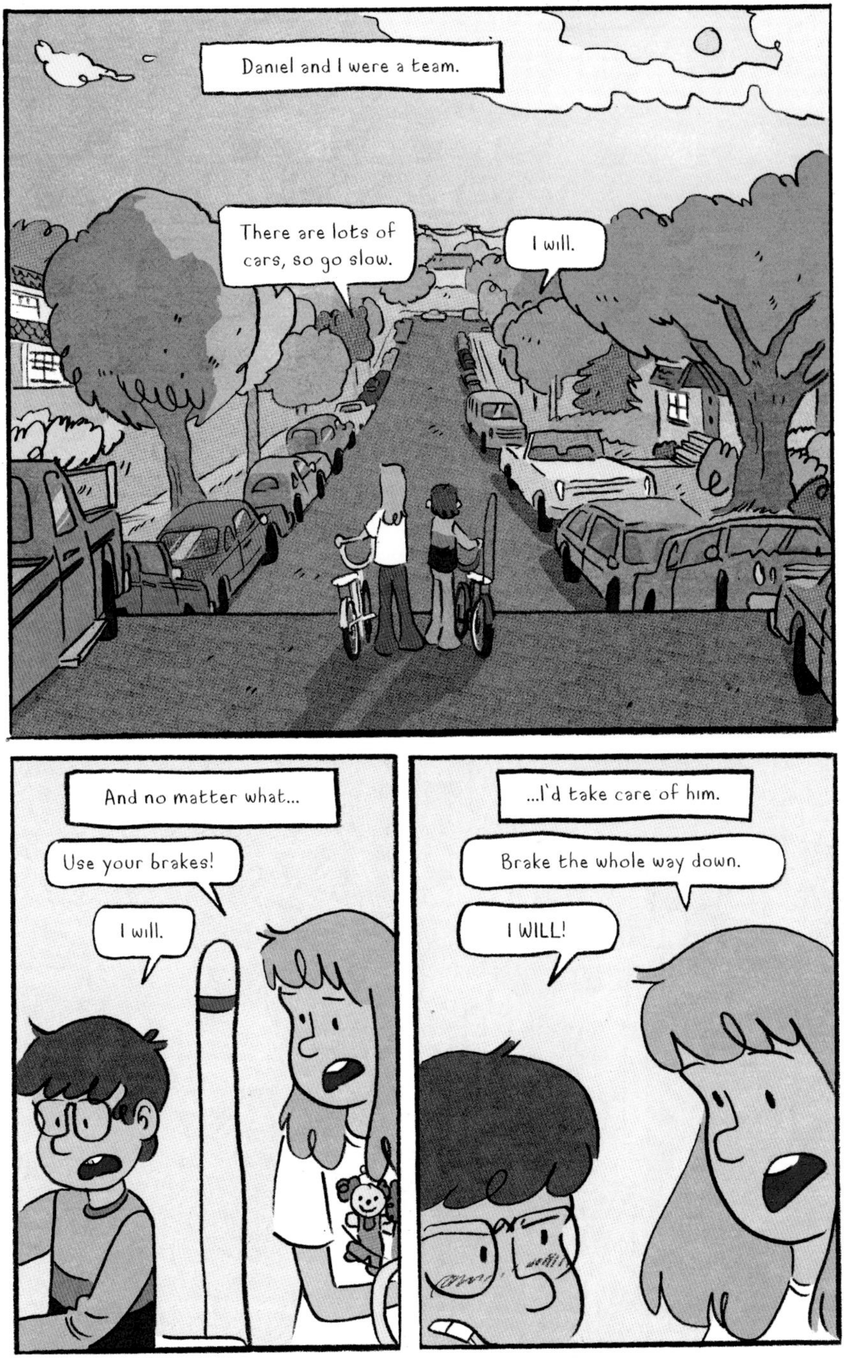

Daniel and I were a team.
There are lots of cars, so go slow.
I will.
And no matter what...
Use your brakes!
I will.
...I'd take care of him.
Brake the whole way down.
I WILL!

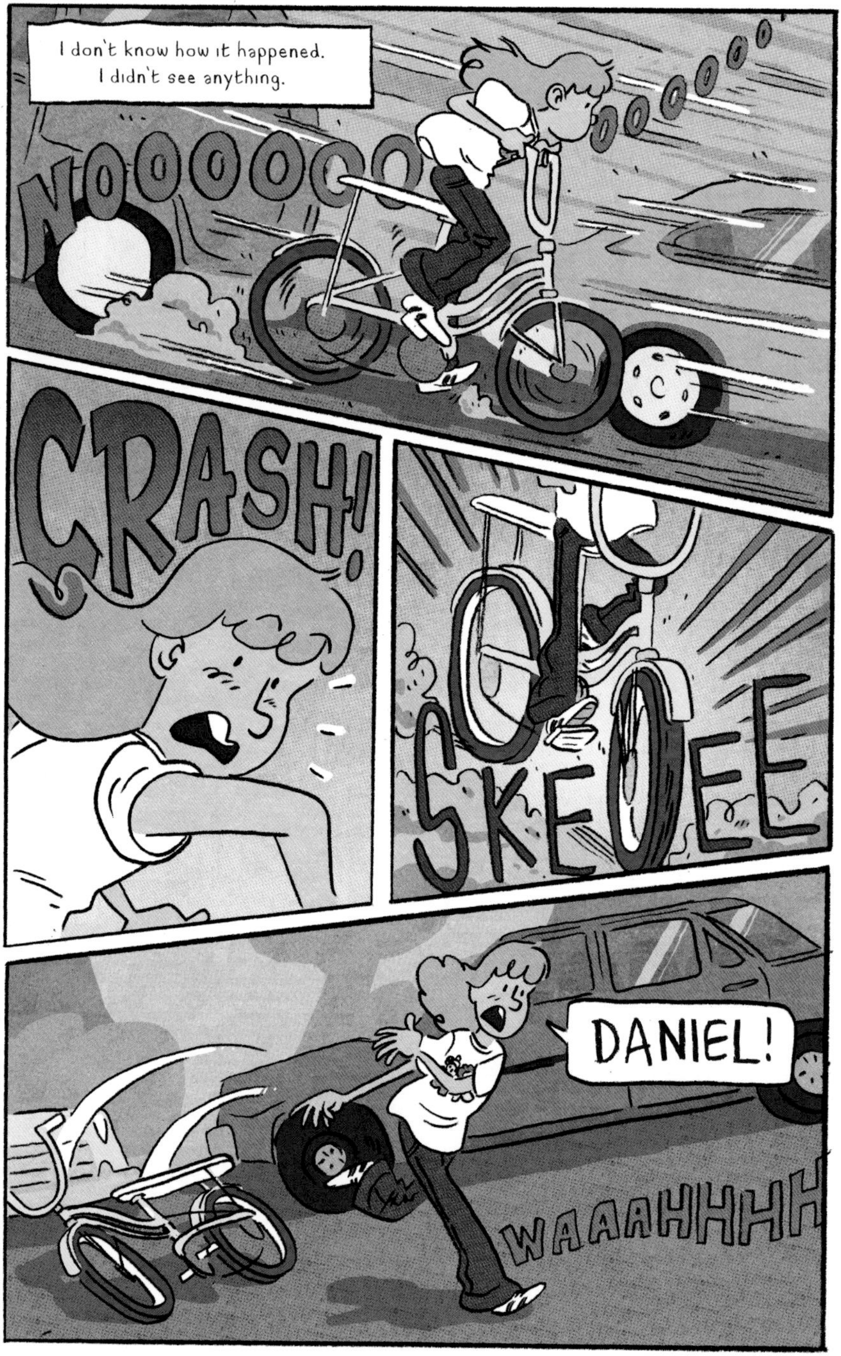
I don't know how it happened.
I didn't see anything.
NOOOOOOOOOOOOOOO
CRASH!
SKEOEE
DANIEL!
WAAAHHHH

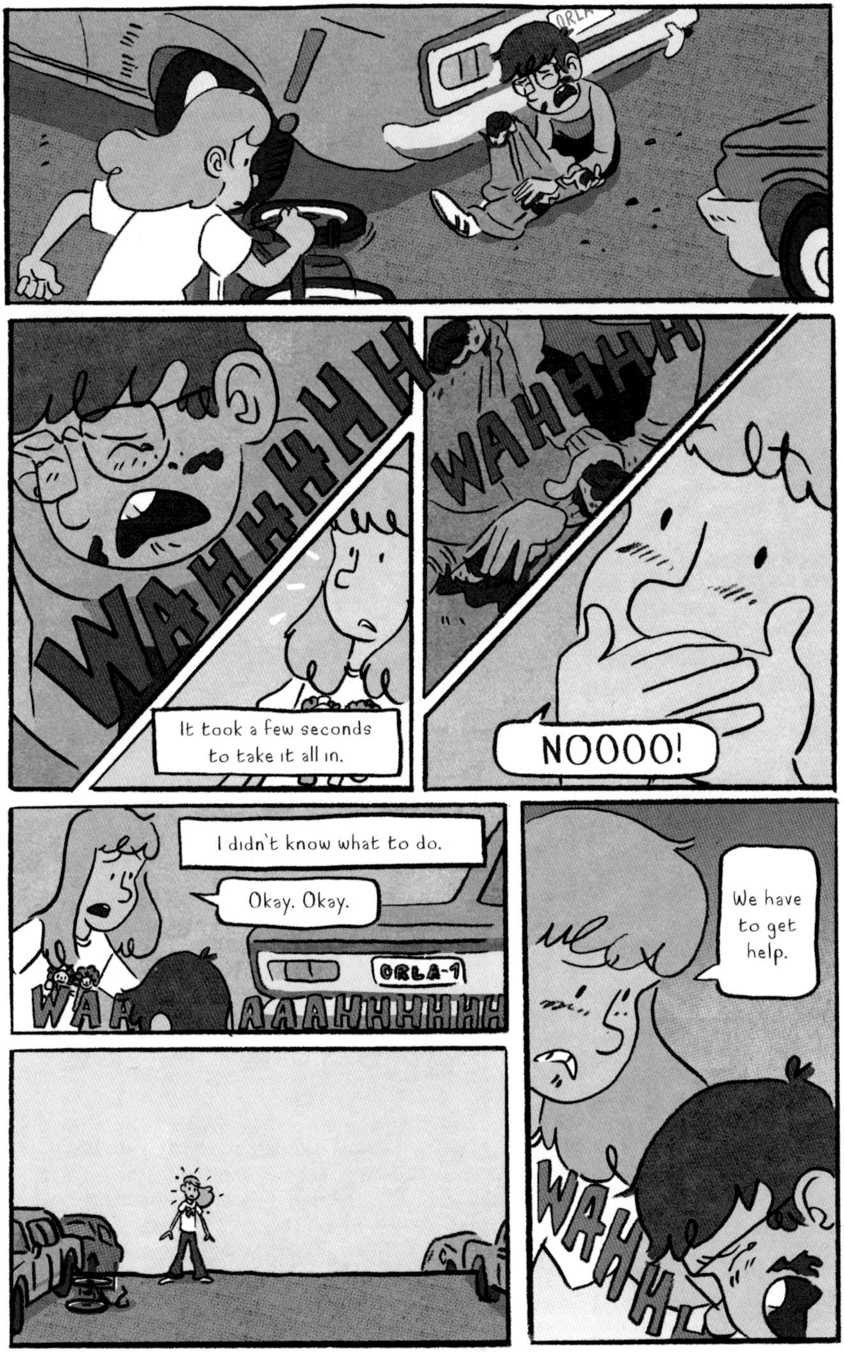
WAHHHHHHH
WAHHHHHH
It took a few seconds to take it all in.
NOOOO!
I didn't know what to do.
Okay. Okay.
ORLA-1
WAAAAAHHHHHHHH
We have to get help.
WAHHH

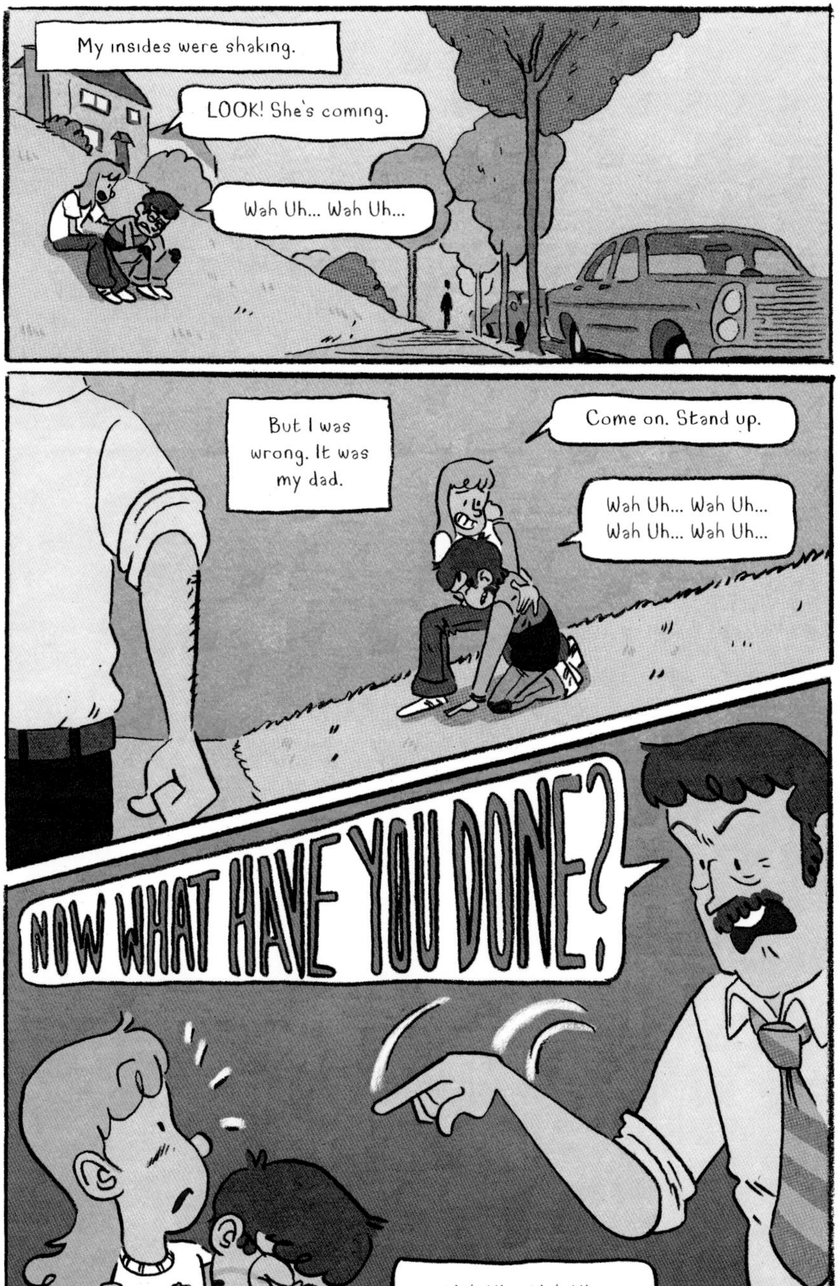
My insides were shaking.
LOOK! She's coming.
Wah Uh... Wah Uh...
But I was wrong. It was my dad.
Come on. Stand up.
Wah Uh... Wah Uh... Wah Uh... Wah Uh...
NOW WHAT HAVE YOU DONE?
Wah Uh... Wah Uh...

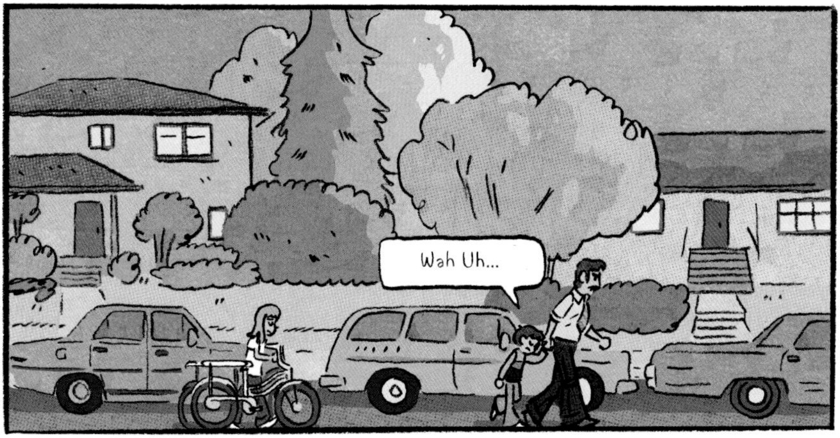
Wah Uh...

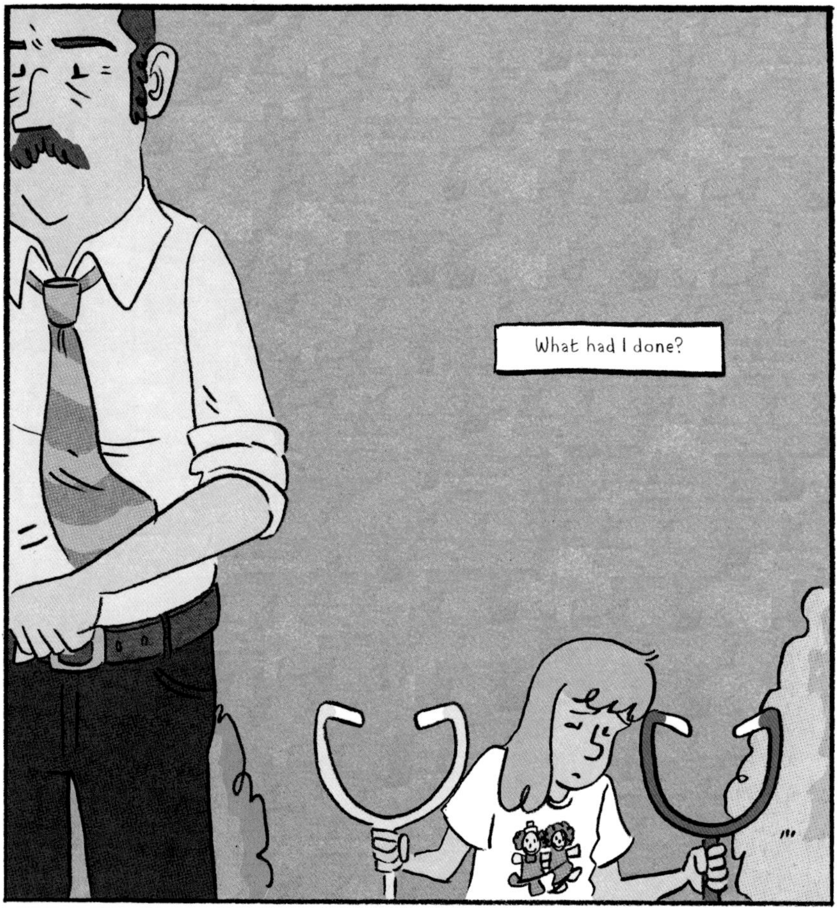
What had I done?

The Biggest Power

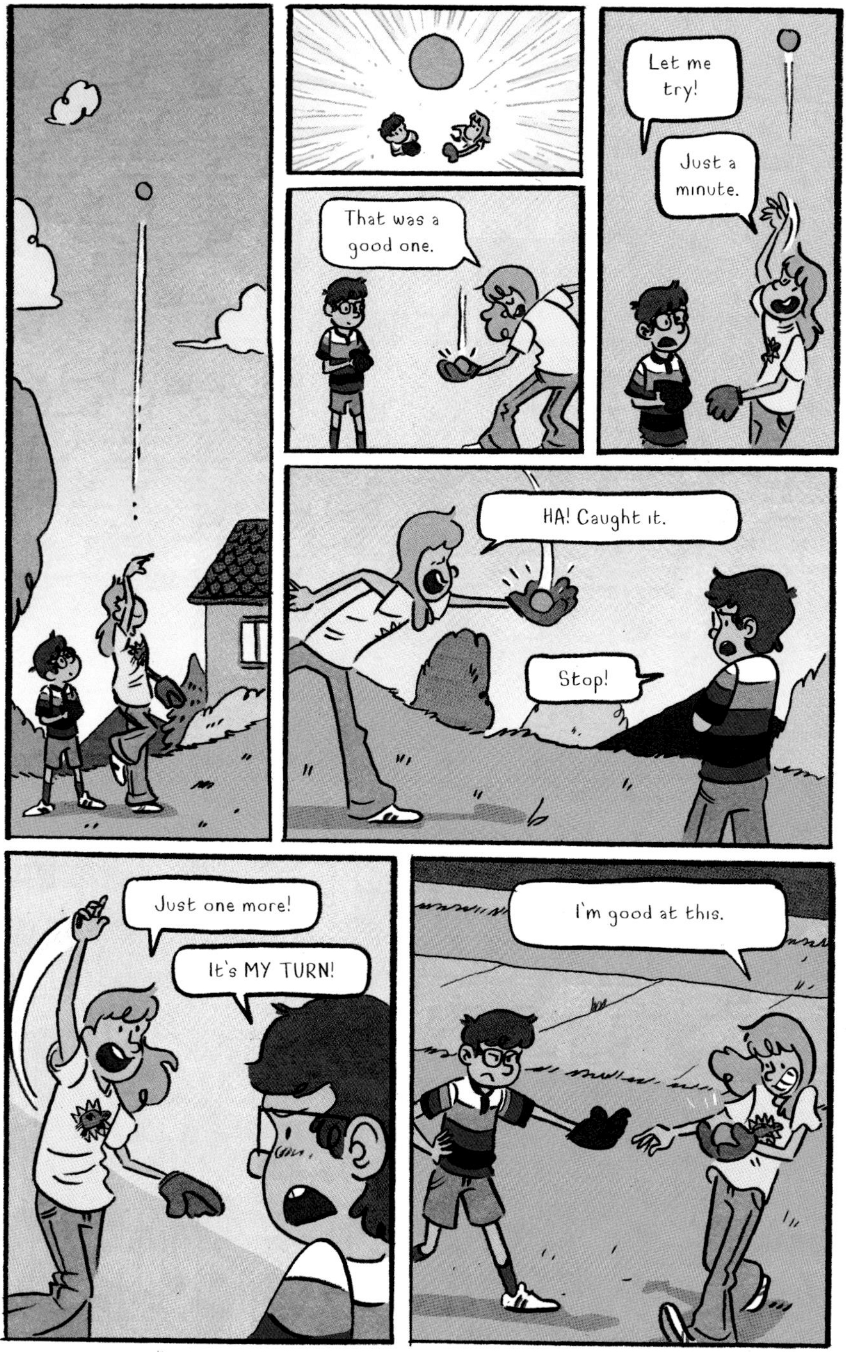

Let me try!
Just a minute.
That was a good one.
HA! Caught it.
Stop!
Just one more!
It's MY TURN!
I'm good at this.

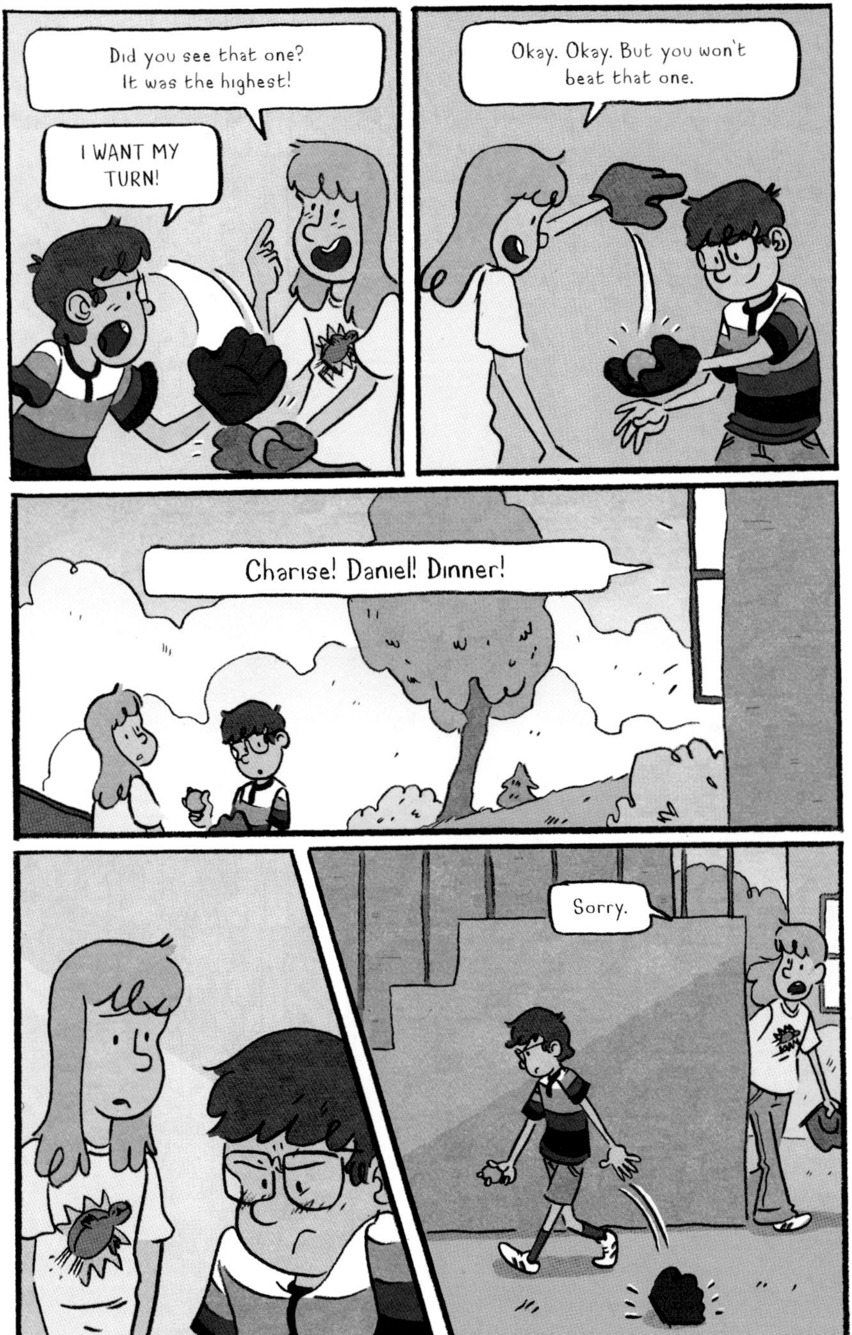
Did you see that one?
It was the highest!
I WANT MY TURN!
Okay. Okay. But you won't beat that one.
Charise! Daniel! Dinner!
Sorry.

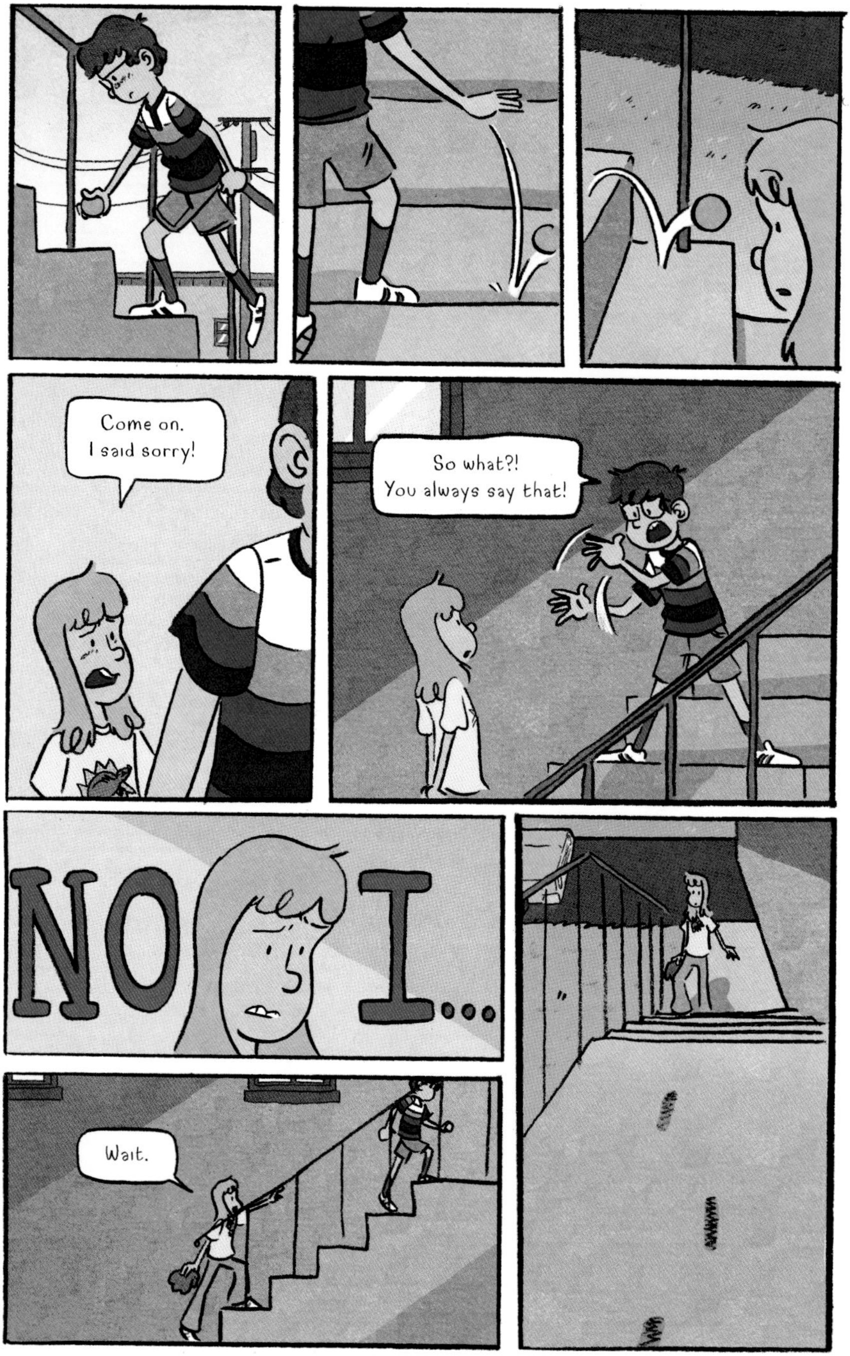
Come on.
I said sorry!
So what?!
You always say that!
NO I...
Wait.

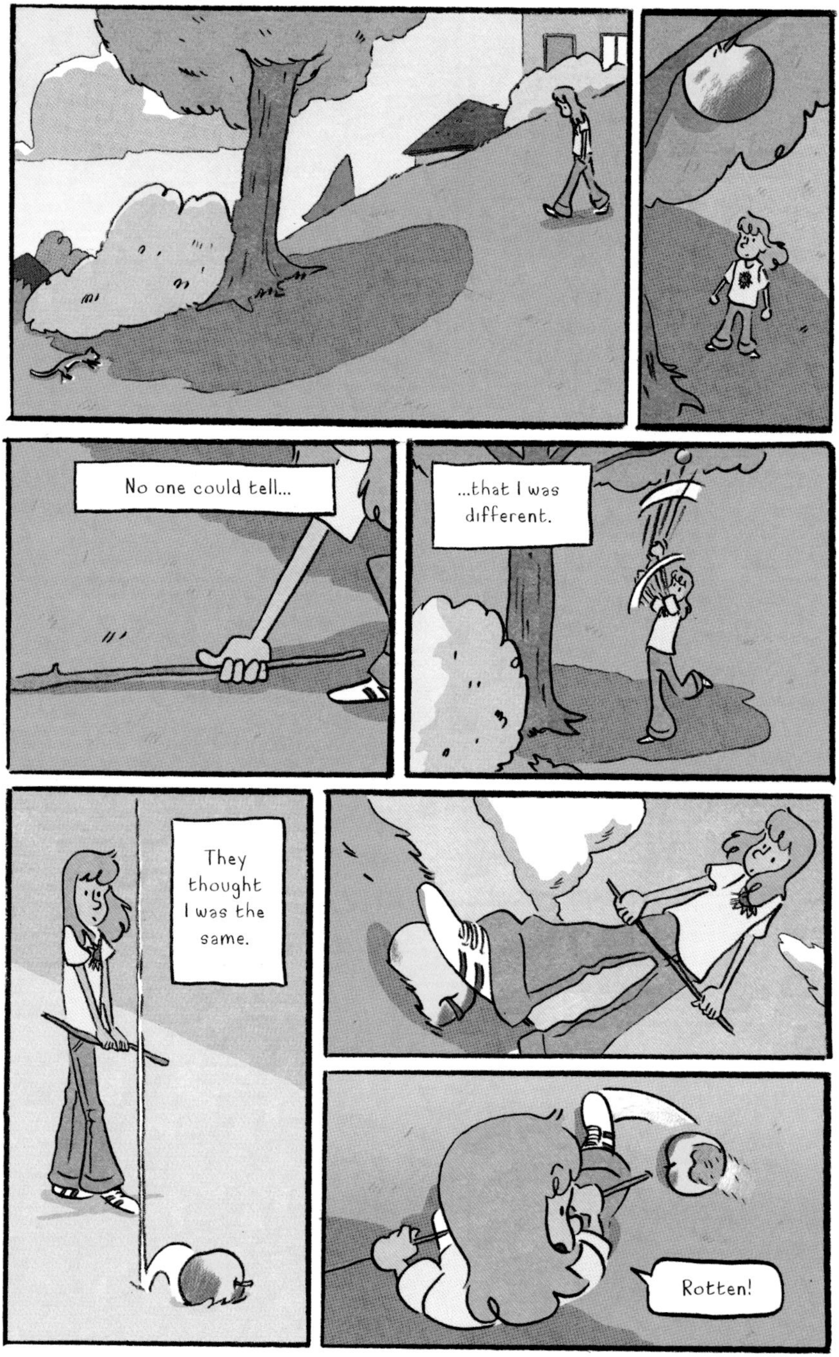
No one could tell...
...that I was different.
They thought I was the same.
Rotten!

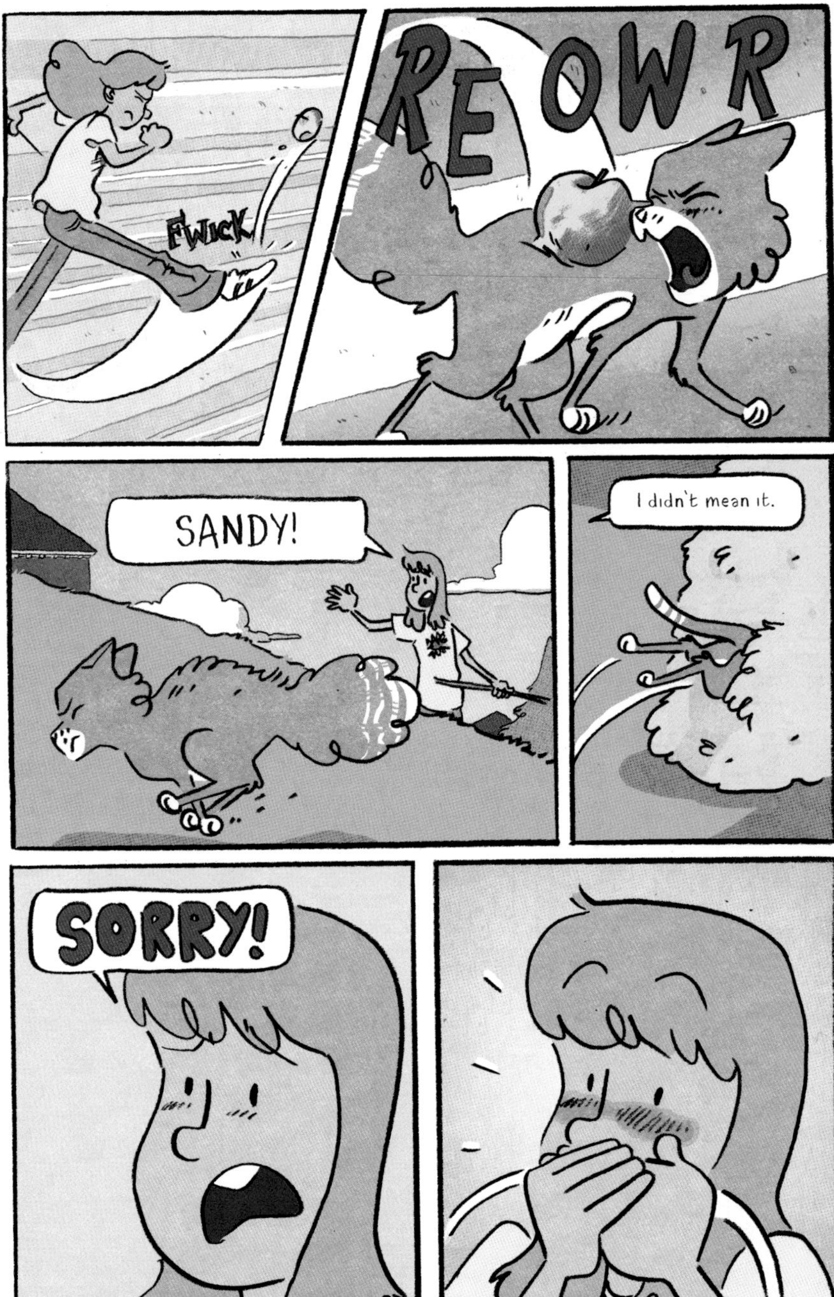
FWICK
REOWR
SANDY!
I didn't mean it.
SORRY!

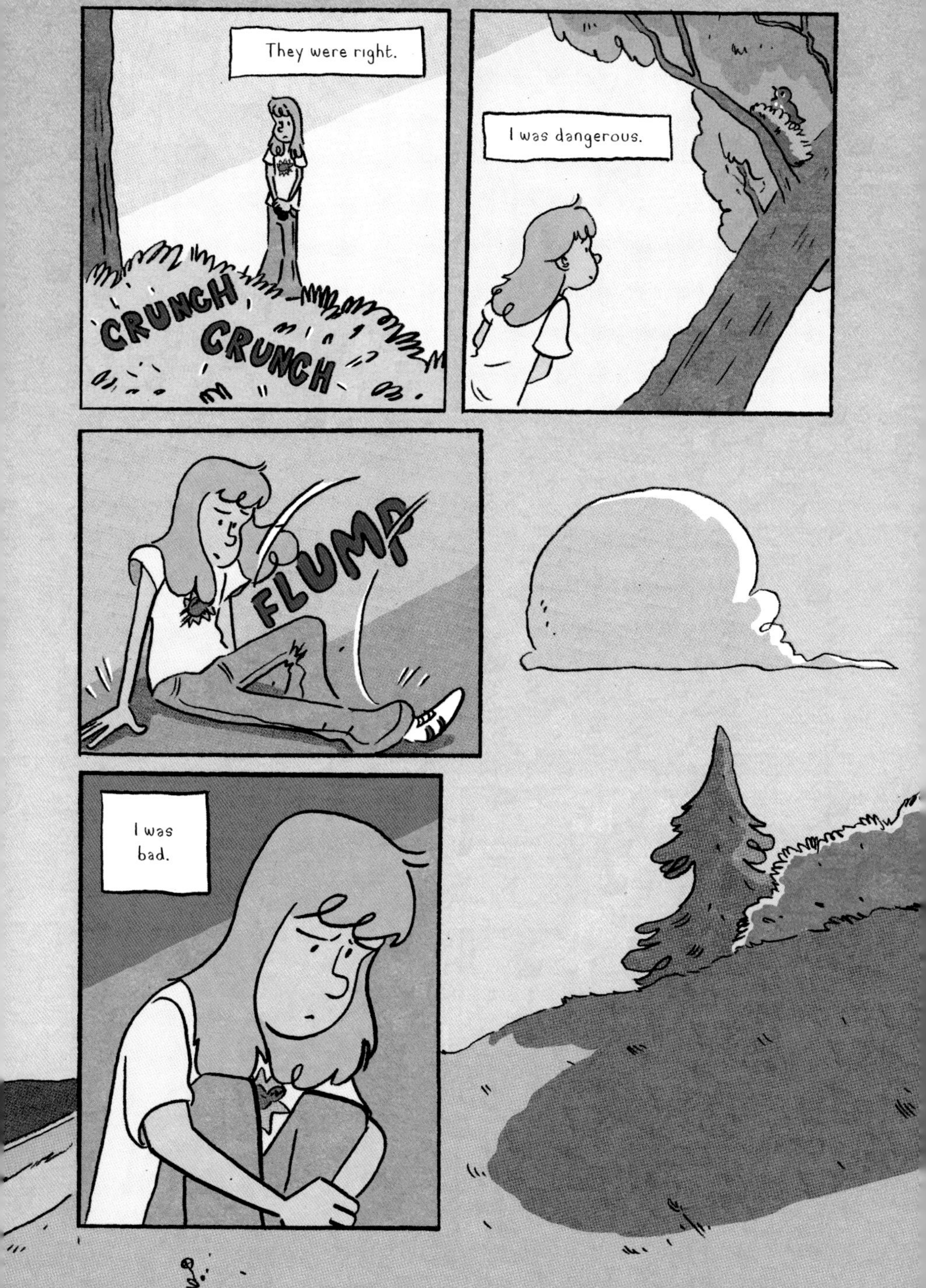

They were right.
CRUNCH
CRUNCH
I was dangerous.
FLUMP
I was bad.

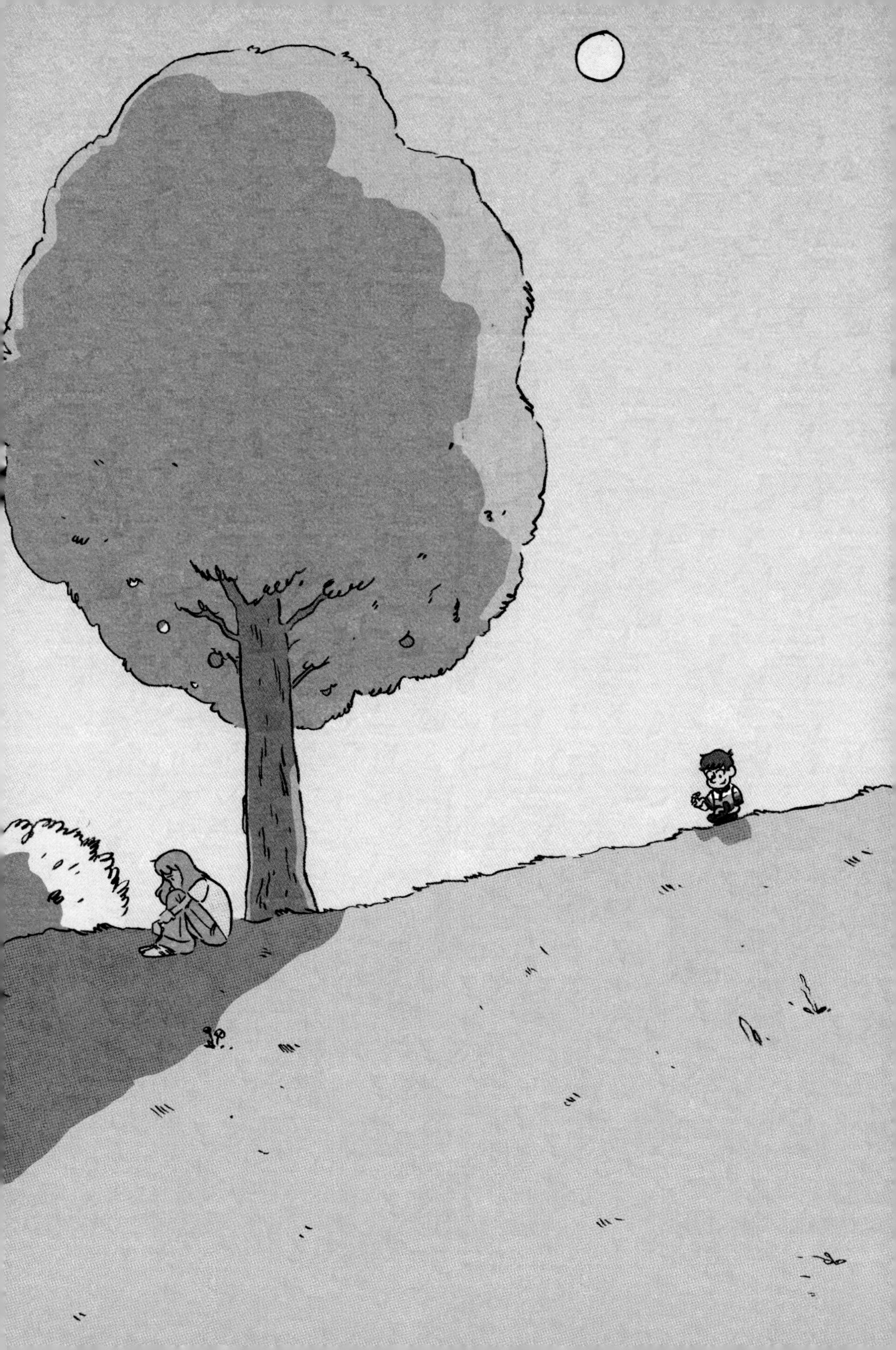

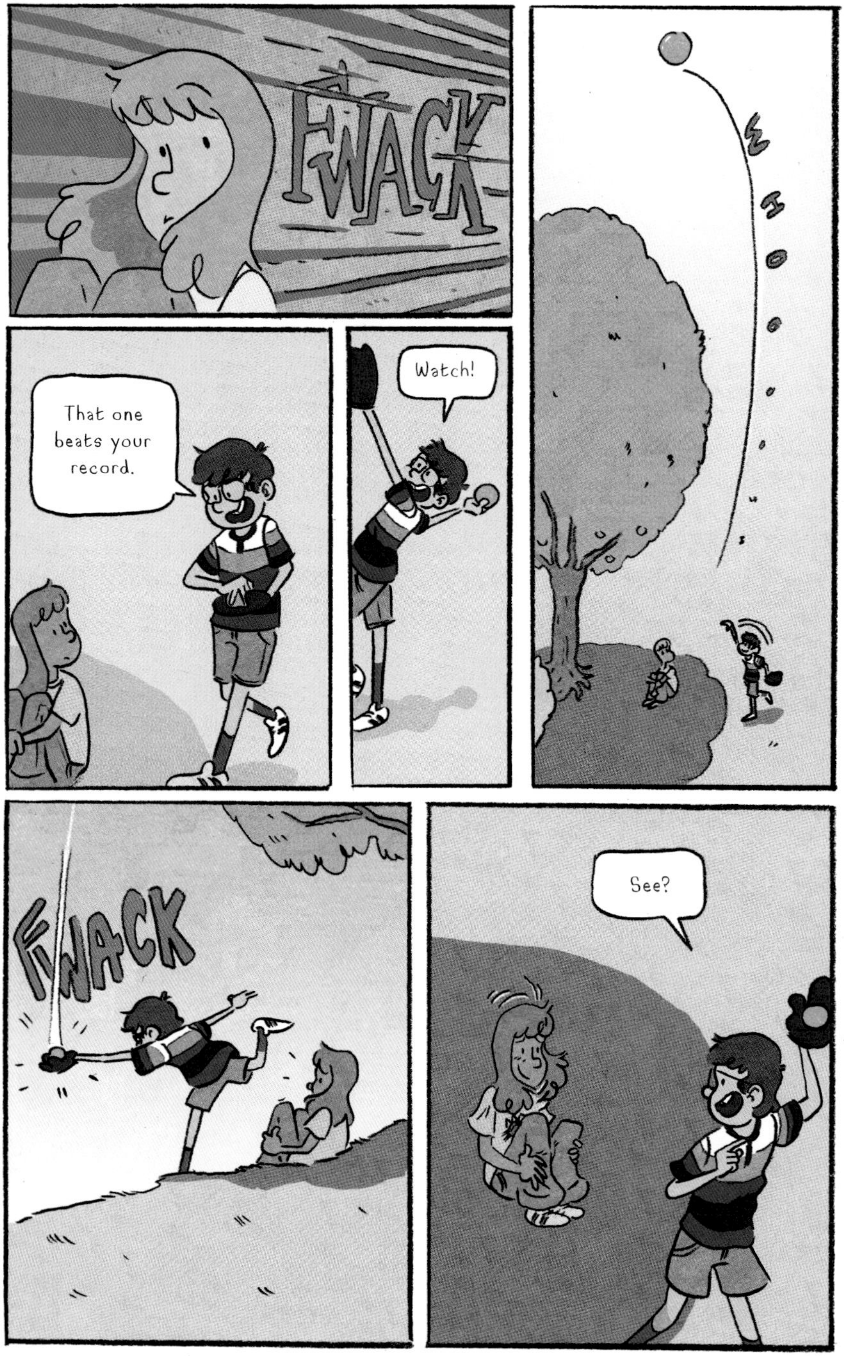
FWACK
WHOOOOOSH
That one beats your record.
Watch!
FWACK
See?

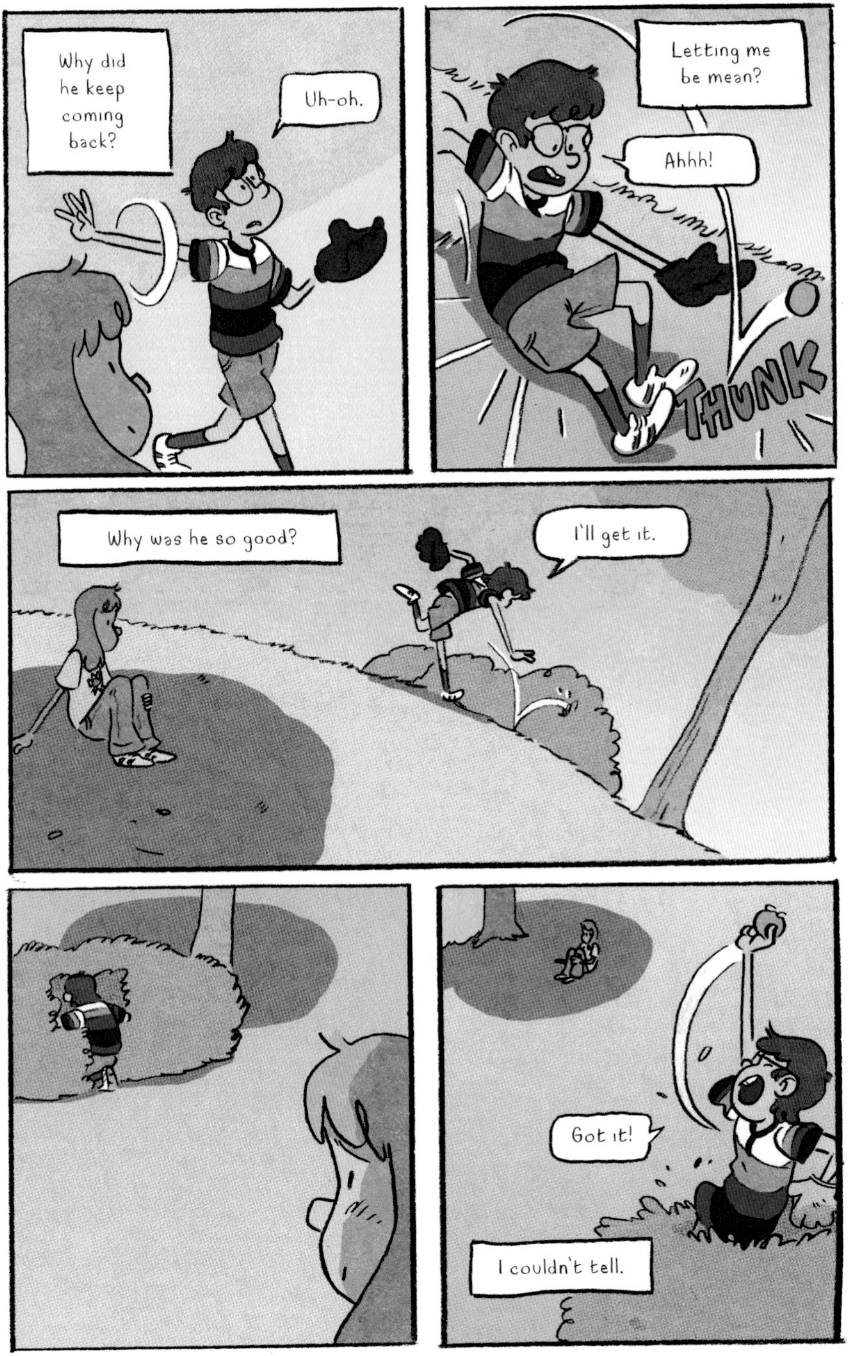
Why did he keep coming back?
Uh-oh.
Letting me be mean?
Ahhh!
THUNK
Why was he so good?
I'll get it.
Got it!
I couldn't tell.

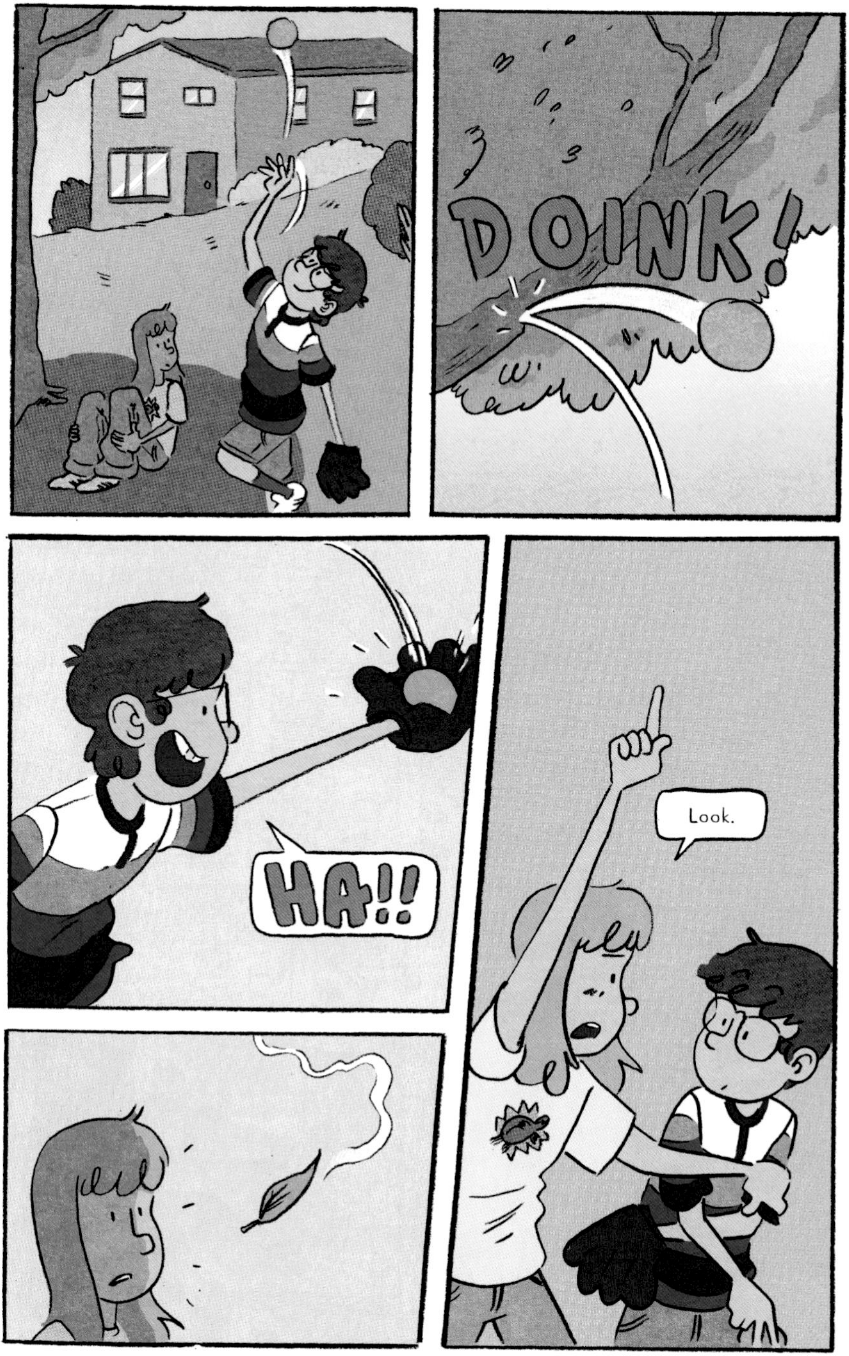
DOINK!
HA!!
Look.

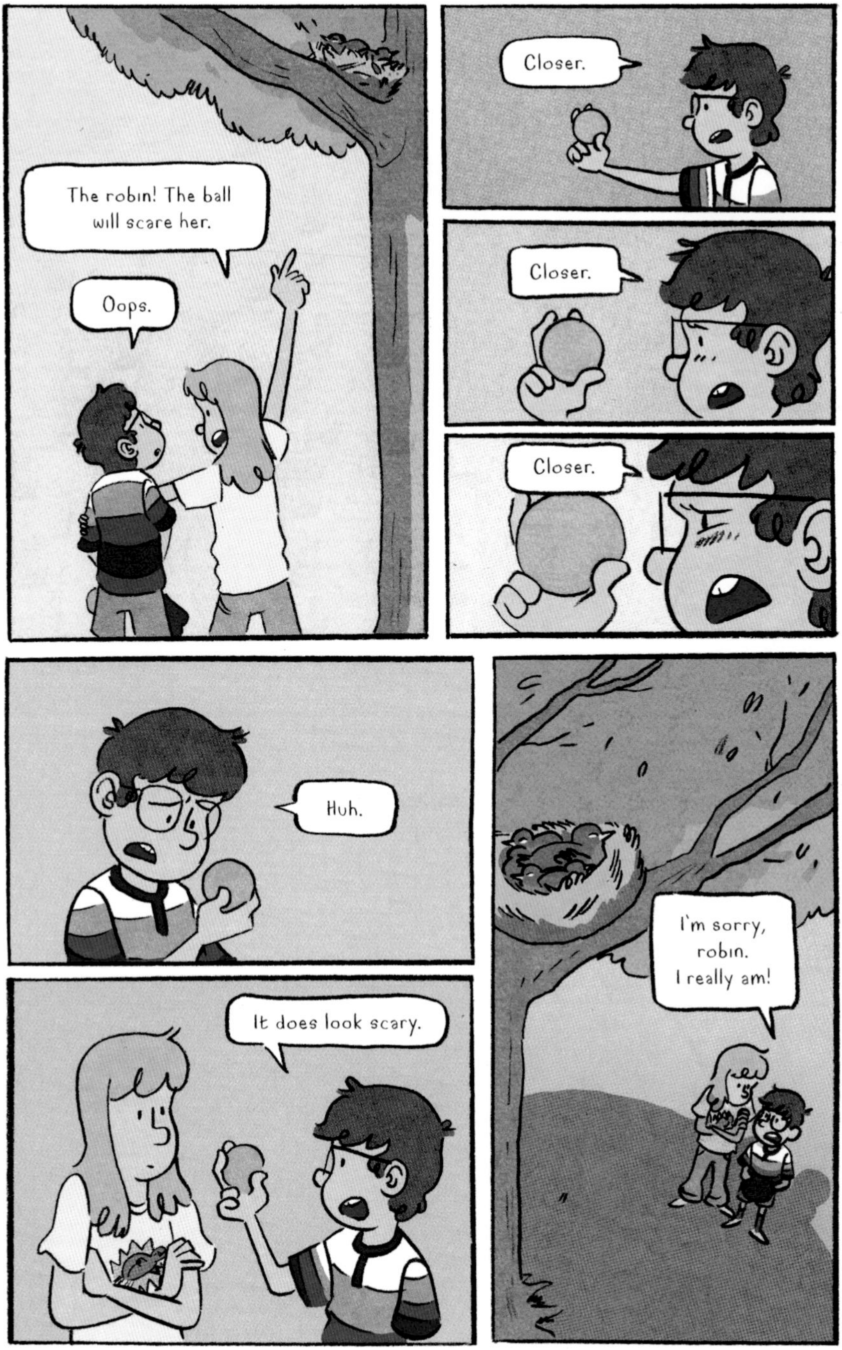
The robin! The ball will scare her.
Oops.
Closer.
Closer.
Closer.
Huh.
It does look scary.
I'm sorry, robin. I really am!

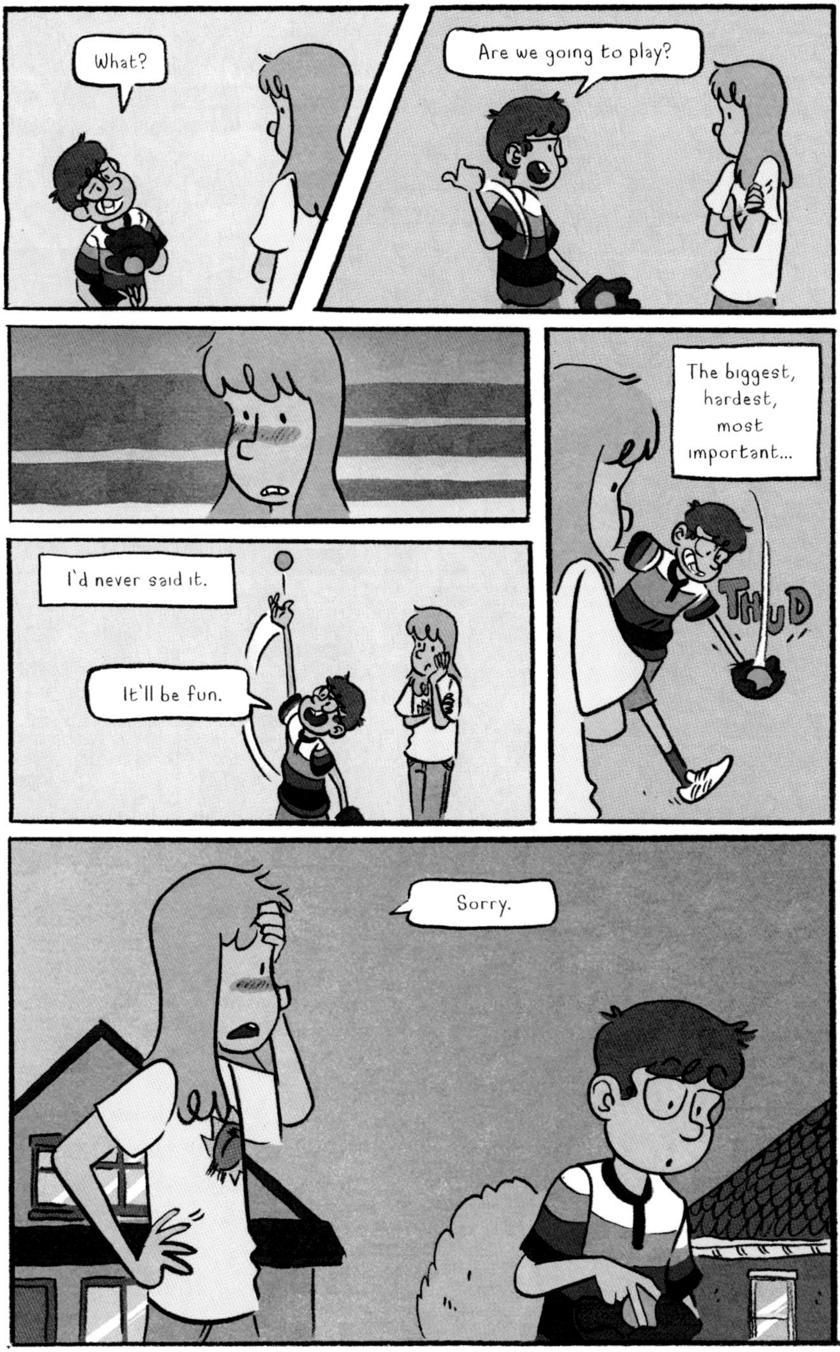
What?
Are we going to play?
The biggest, hardest, most important...
I'd never said it.
It'll be fun.
THUD
Sorry.

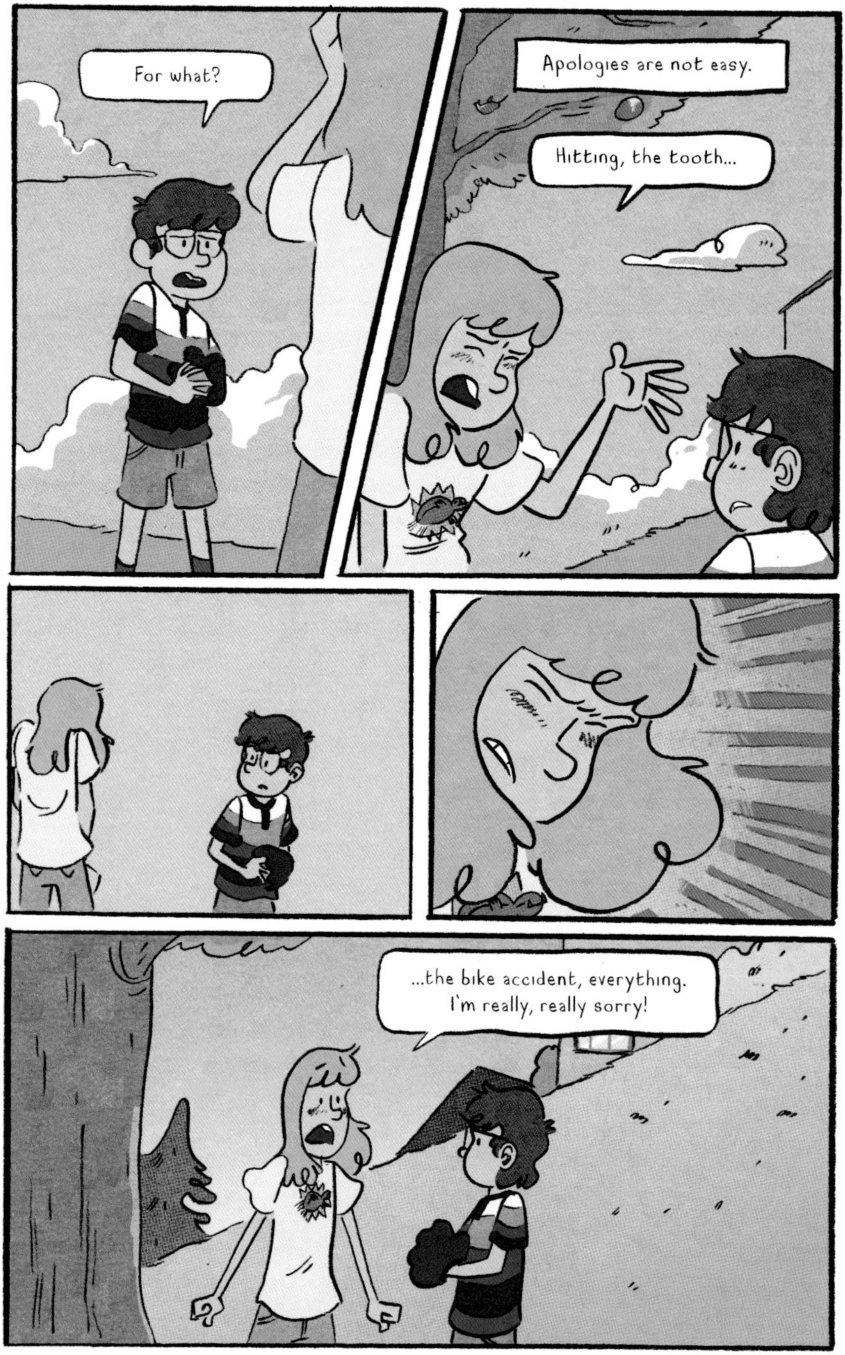
For what?
Apologies are not easy.
Hitting, the tooth...
...the bike accident, everything.
I'm really, really sorry!

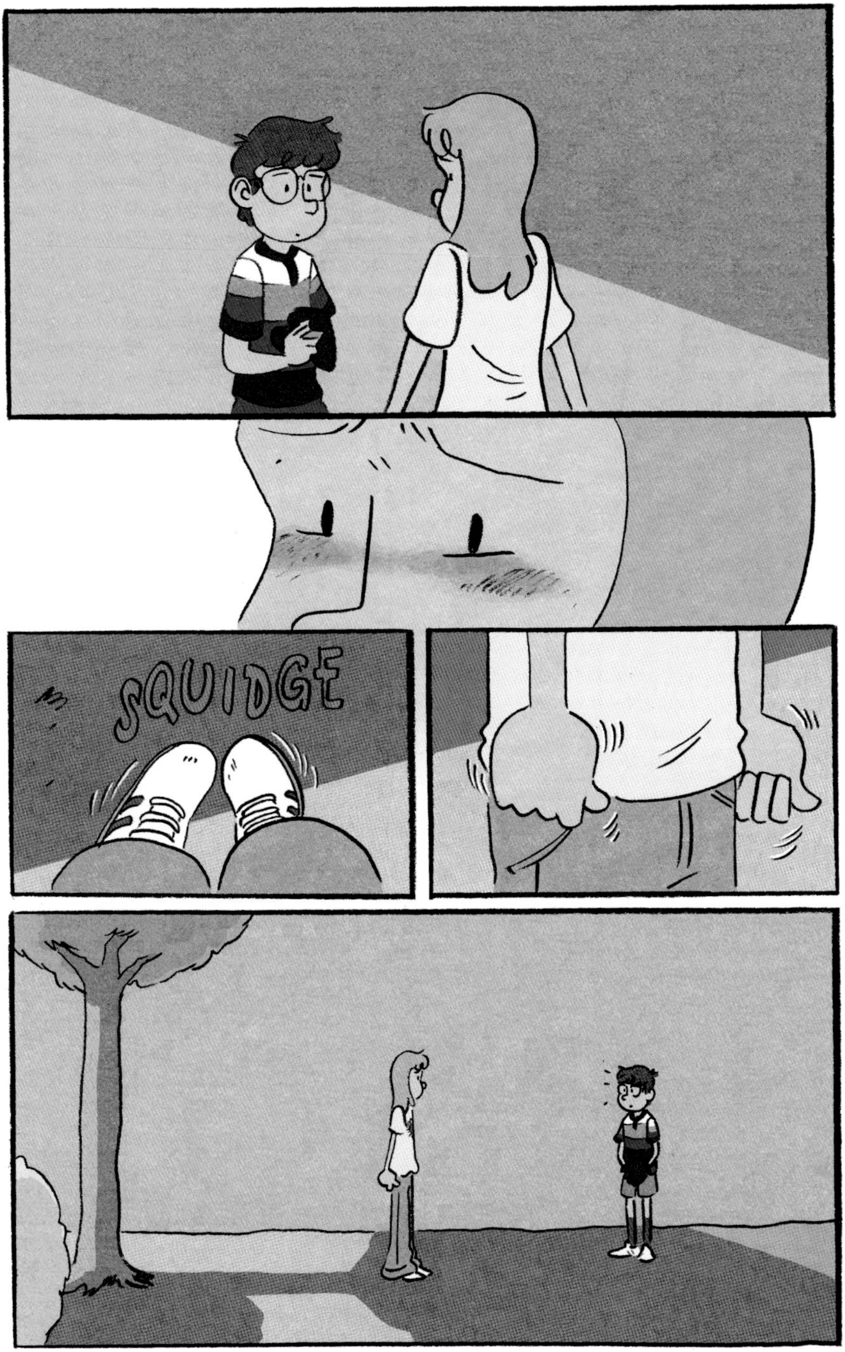
SQUIDGE

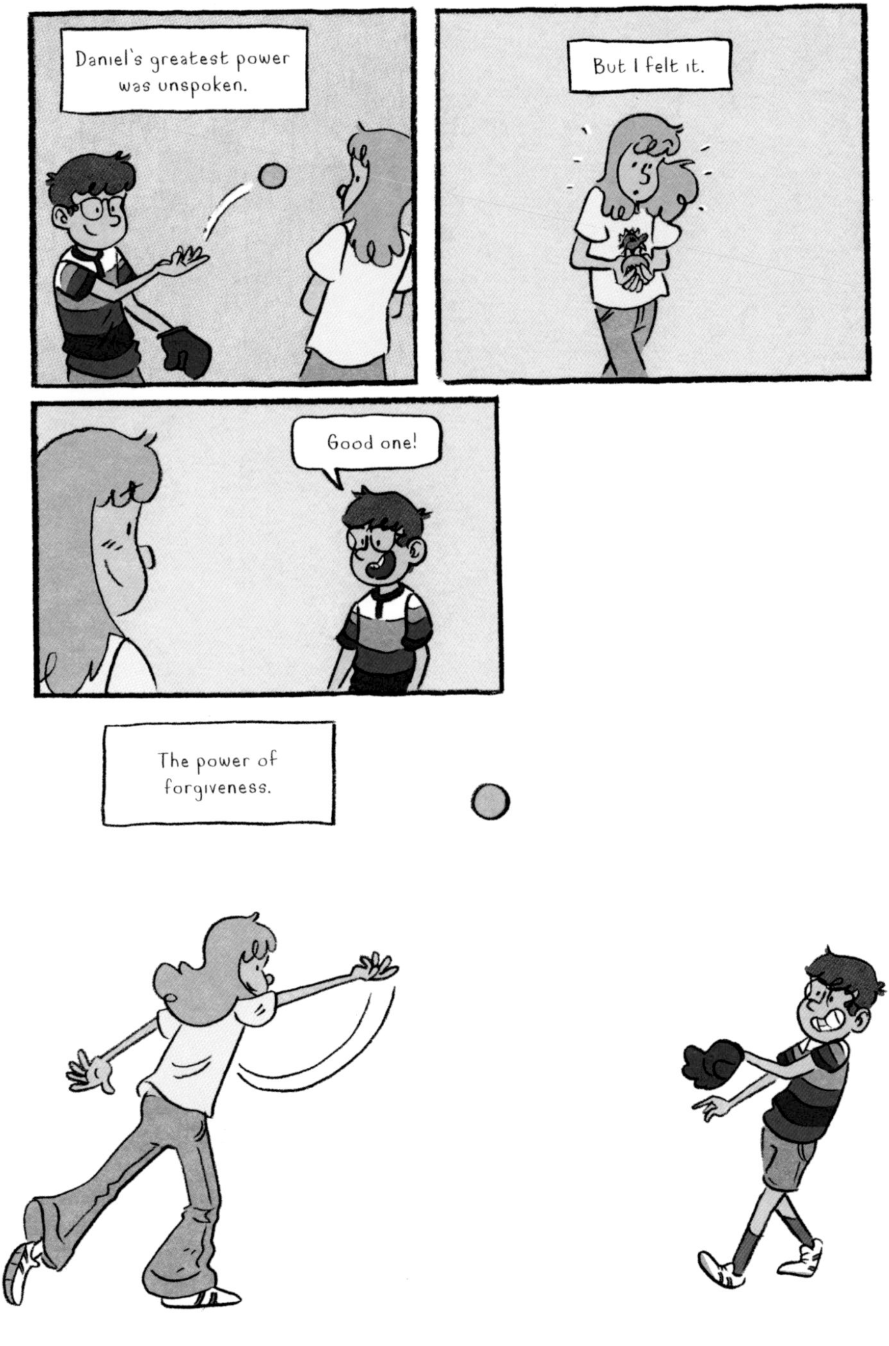

Daniel's greatest power was unspoken.
But I felt it.
Good one!
The power of forgiveness.

Years ago I took my brother's truck.
It still lives in my studio.
He doesn't know.

This book is dedicated to my brother, Daniel.
I wish I could go back in time.
To be more compassionate, patient, supportive,
understanding, and forgiving.
You are a silent teacher—the best kind.
Showing by example.
Thank you.
I love you.

I have to bestow a big parade of thank yous to Calista Brill,
Rachel Stark, and Alex Lu. Your work made this a better book.

And now look across the page—I'm waving a flag for Rory.
Thank you for your hours, your talent, and your vision.
You are awesome!

—Charise

To Charise Harper, thank you for sharing this beautiful story—
I still cannot believe how lucky I am to help tell it.

To everyone from First Second—Calista Brill, Alex Lu,
Kirk Benshoff, and Molly Johanson—as well as Rachel Stark and
Charlie Olsen, thank you for championing this book and
making me a better artist.

To the Haddonfield Friends School community,
thank you for your continued support of my art.

To my family, especially my nieces and nephews—
Cillian, Eleanor, Orla, and Onslow—a special thanks for inspiring me.

And to my wife, Emily. I don't have enough words
to thank you for always supporting me.

—Rory

:01

First Second

Published by First Second
First Second is an imprint of Roaring Brook Press,
a division of Holtzbrinck Publishing Holdings Limited Partnership
120 Broadway, New York, NY 10271
firstsecondbooks.com
mackids.com

Library of Congress Control Number: 2020919298

Our books may be purchased in bulk for promotional, educational, or business use.
Please contact your local bookseller or the Macmillan Corporate and Premium Sales Department
at (800) 221-7945 ext. 5442 or by email at MacmillanSpecialMarkets@macmillan.com.

First edition, 2021
Edited by Calista Brill, Alex Lu, and Rachel Stark
Cover and interior book design by Molly Johanson
Lettering assistance by Rory Lucey
Printed in China by 1010 Printing International Limited, North Point, Hong Kong

The book was penciled digitally in Procreate on an iPad, the final lines were drawn with a Staedtler
Mars Lumograph 6B pencil on Blick Hot Press watercolor paper and colored digitally in Photoshop.

ISBN 978-1-250-21905-3 (paperback)
10 9 8 7 6 5 4 3 2 1

ISBN 978-1-250-21906-0 (hardcover)
10 9 8 7 6 5 4 3 2 1

Don't miss your next favorite book from First Second! For the latest updates go
to firstsecondnewsletter.com and sign up for our enewsletter.

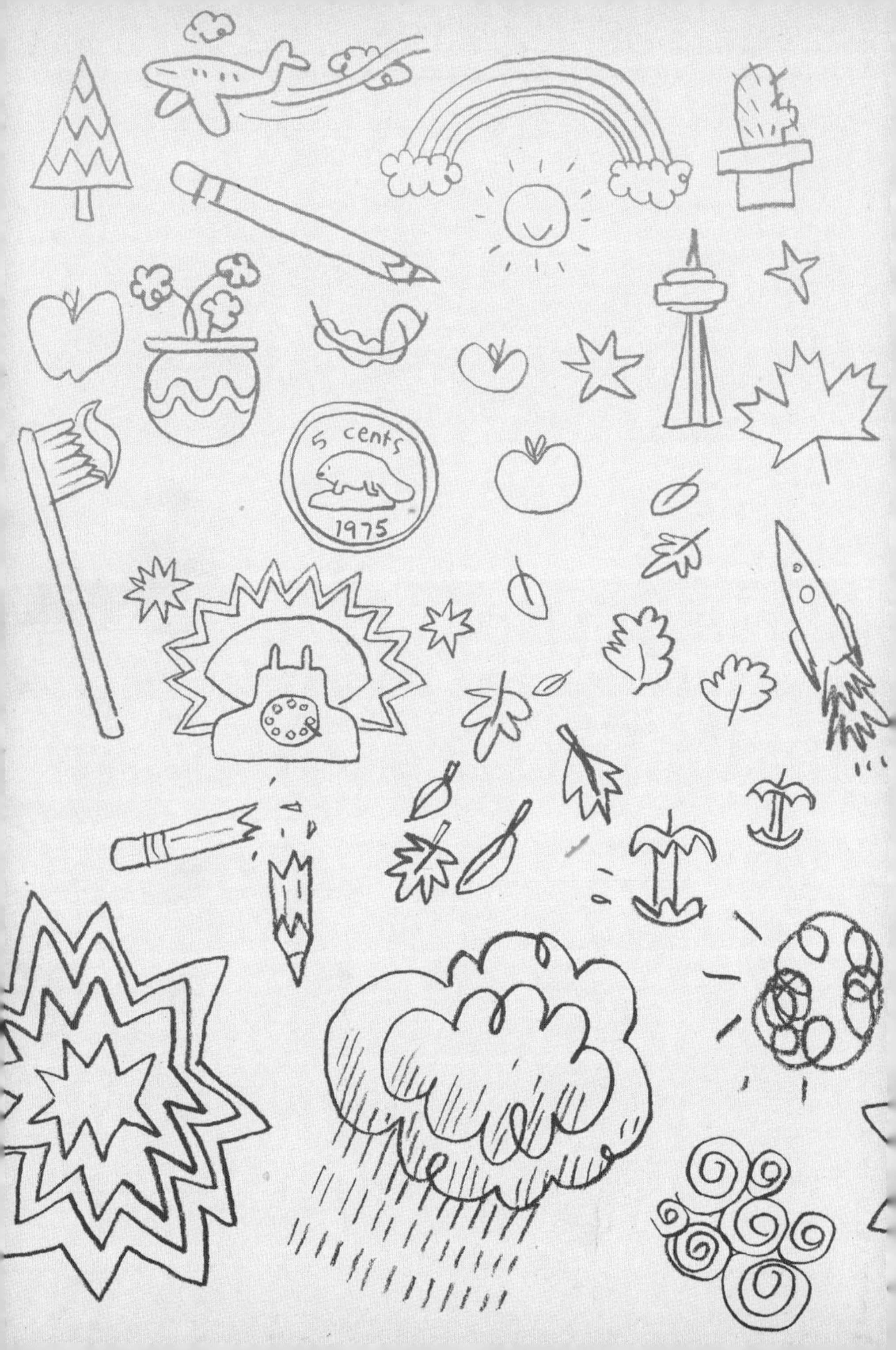
5 cents
1975